# Diversity and Eq
# Early Childhood:
# An Irish Perspective

St Aelrm
Sandove Rd

# Diversity and Equality in Early Childhood:
# An Irish Perspective

Colette Murray and Mathias Urban

*Gill & Macmillan*

Gill & Macmillan
Hume Avenue
Park West
Dublin 12
with associated companies throughout the world
www.gillmacmillan.ie

© Colette Murray, Mathias Urban and the individual contributors, 2012

978 07171 4994 0

Index compiled by Kate Murphy
Print origination by Carole Lynch
Printed by GraphyCems, Spain

Front cover photographs: Derek Speirs, IRE; Anissa Thompson, CA, USA; Luiz Baltar, RJ, Brazil;
Benjamin Earwicker, ID, USA; Lucy Colleary, Dublin, IRE; Horton Group, TE, USA; Anton
Malan, GT, South Africa; Jody Angell, CT, USA; Julia Freeman, NH, USA.

*The paper used in this book comes from the wood pulp of managed forests. For every tree felled, at least one tree is planted, thereby renewing natural resources.*

A CIP catalogue record is available for this book from the British Library

# Contents

# Acknowledgements

It takes a village to raise a child, according to an overused but nevertheless true African saying about the importance of the community for children and families. It took a 'village', too, to write this book. Our 'village' is a professional community committed to making a difference for children, families and communities. Many individuals and organisations have contributed to this Irish perspective on Diversity and Equality in early childhood – some through their immediate contributions to this book, others through their support and encouragement over the years. In particular, we would like to thank:

Louise Derman-Sparks for her inspiration, for setting an example and for her tireless work that shows that it is necessary and possible to stand up against discrimination in our work with young children, and especially for her friendship and support;

The Bernard van Leer Foundation, The Hague, for supporting and funding the work of the '*éist*' project in Ireland and in Europe;

Pavee Point Travellers' Centre, Dublin, for believing in the importance of equality for *all* children and for providing a home for this work for many years;

Our friends and colleagues in the European DECET network for being a critical but always constructive and supportive learning community from the very beginning;

The members and supporters of EDENN, the Irish Equality and Diversity Early Childhood National Network, for sharing their expertise;

Nóirín Hayes, DIT, for speaking out for children's rights in Ireland, and for her encouragement over the years;

Karen McCarthy, County Clare Childcare Committee, and Kathryn O'Riordan, Cork City Childcare Committee, for never stopping to spread the word, for keeping us grounded, and for bringing this work into all corners of this island through the Preschool Initiative for Children from Minority Groups;

The fabulous women who attended the first national Diversity and Equality Training of Trainers in 2008 and who are now delivering the Anti-Bias Diversity and Equality Training to practitioners, students and services all over Ireland: Patsy Baissangourov, Máire Uí Bhroin, Deirdre Curtain, Martina Mc Govern, Anne Halligan, Brid Hickey, Liesl Marcroft, Geralyn Molan, Marian Quinn, Siobhan Walsh. Thank you for taking up the baton!

Joanie Barron (Wallaroo Playschool, Cork); Kathryn O'Riordan (Cork City Childcare Committee); Ann Halligan (Curious Minds Preschool, Castlebar); Patsy Baissangourov (Donegal); Martina McGovern (Cavan); and Orla Fitzpatrick (Ruan Children's Centre,

Co. Clare) for sharing their expertise and experience and providing strong voices from the sector.

We are grateful to practitioners and facilitators from all services that participated in the Family Wall project: Inagh Ark Community Centre, Ennis; Childcare Services, Liscannor; Community Centre, Athy; Tír na nÓg, Athy; The Haven, Ballina; Traveller Preschool, Castlebar; Little Acorns Children's' Centre, Claremorris; An Doras Buí, Dublin; Wallaroo Playschool, Cork; Ashbourne House Accommodation Centre, Cork.

Thanks to Emma Byrne for the 'disability' scenario; Marion Quinn, Joanie Barron and Kathryn O'Riordan and other colleagues for reading and discussing our drafts with a critical eye. Sincere thanks also goes to Caroline Rogers, Andrej Pacherova and a west of Ireland practitioner, all of whom tell their stories on the *Diversity and Equality* page on the Gill & Macmillan website: www.gillmacmillan.ie.

Many practitioners, students and trainers gave us permission to share their stories, journals, examples and quotes that give this book a truly Irish perspective. Without your contributions and support, this book would not have been possible.

A particular acknowledgment goes to the Gill & Macmillan team, especially Marion O'Brien and Catherine Gough for their invaluable support through all stages of the realisation of this book.

Many thanks must go to family and friends who have lived patiently with this work.

Last but not least we would like to acknowledge all children, their families and communities whose everyday experiences in Irish society have made this book necessary and who, through the diversity and richness of their individual and collective contributions make Ireland who she is in the twenty-first century.

# About the Authors and Contributors

**Colette Murray, MSc,** has more than 20 years' experience in the early childhood education and care sector in both national and international contexts. She has worked as a practitioner, trainer, lecturer, advocate and researcher. As the initiator and coordinator of the '*éist*' project and the Equality and Diversity Early Childhood National Network (EDENN), Colette has introduced Anti-Bias work to Irish ECEC, and fought for a comprehensive Diversity and Equality approach in practice, training and policy. She is a founding member of the European Diversity in Early Childhood Education and Training (DECET) network. Colette currently coordinates the National Pre-School Education Initiative for Children from Minority Groups, which is implementing the work developed in '*éist*'.

**Dr Mathias Urban,** Reader in Education (Associate Professor), works for the Cass School of Education and Communities, University of East London. His research interests unfold around questions of professionalism, quality and diversity and equality in working with young children, families and communities in diverse socio-cultural contexts. His recent work includes a pan-European study on Competence Requirements in Early Childhood Education and Care (CoRe), and international studies on change processes in early childhood systems (Strategies for Change) and on professional epistemologies and habitus (*A Day in the Life of an Early Years Practitioner*). Mathias is convenor of an international special interest group on professionalism in early childhood. He is a member of DECET and of the American Educational Research Association (AERA) special interest group on critical perspectives on early childhood education.

**Patsy Baissangourov** has 19 years' experience working in early childhood, youth and family support provision. She has been tutoring since 2008 and delivering childcare modules at FETAC Levels 5 and 6. Patsy previously owned and managed a Montessori preschool and has worked as a Development Officer in the Donegal County Childcare Committee.

**Joanie Barron** has been a childcare practitioner for 30 years. She trained in a Humanistic Education Approach at Play Mountain Place Los Angeles where she also worked as a Head Teacher for two years. Joanie is a founding member of Wallaroo Playschool, the Cork Early Years Anti-Bias Network and EDENN.

**Orla Fitzpatrick** has worked in Ruan Children's Centre in north Clare since 2007. Orla has a degree in Social Studies (Social Care) from IT Sligo and has completed the FETAC Level 5 Certificate in Diversity and Equality in Early Childhood Education and Care.

**Ann Halligan** has been working in early childhood care and education since 1995 as a practitioner manager and trainer. In 2004, Ann attended the '*éist*' Training of Trainers accredited programme in Pavee Point, supported by Mayo County Childcare Committee. She is currently delivering that module at FETAC Level 5 as part of the Pre-school Education Initiative for children from minority groups.

**Martina McGovern** has a BA in Early Childhood Studies and has worked in early childhood education and care for over 20 years. She has experience in the HIV/AIDS field in both domiciliary care and group care and has worked as an Early Years Childcare Inspector in London. She has tutored on both FETAC Level 5 and 6 Childcare awards and currently delivers equality and diversity training as part of the National Preschool Education Initiative for Children from Minority Groups.

**Kathryn O'Riordan** is the Childcare Co-ordinator for Cork City. She has many years' experience of working as a childcare worker and is a trained play therapist. Kathryn is a founding member of the Association of Childcare Professionals, the professional body of the early childhood sector in Ireland.

# Diversity and Equality in Early Childhood: an Irish Perspective

## Why this book – and why now?

It doesn't take much to see that Ireland in 2012 is a hugely diverse society. A stroll down your street, a look at the paper, a trip on a bus are enough to realise that we are with people from all walks of life, all the time. As Ireland continues to change as part of a changing world, there is no denying that diversity is a reality in our society. 'So what?', you might say. 'People are not the same, what's new about that?' You would be right, there is absolutely nothing new about people not being the same. We all are unique and special, as individuals and members of our families and communities. However, as your own experience will no doubt tell you, diversity in Irish (or any other) society quite often means that people experience being different in negative ways. Most modern societies are unequal and twenty-first-century Ireland is one of the most unequal societies in Europe (Wilkinson and Pickett, 2009). Inequality often goes hand in hand with people being identified as different from or inferior to the majority population. Stereotypes, prejudice, discrimination, sexism, homophobia and racism are the ugly side of the diverse society we live in.

Recent research by the Immigrant Council of Ireland (2011) confirms that experiencing racist harassment and bullying is an 'everyday fact of life' for migrants into Ireland:

> […] these experiences have also created a perception that there is an underlying racism within Irish society, a society that condones and fails to challenge racist speech. Several respondents who had lived in other European countries remarked that racist speech in Ireland was especially coarse.
>
> (p. 30)

Ireland today is diverse and unequal in many respects. Many ethnic and cultural differences are easily visible – and so are the prejudices and the discrimination that are based on them. There are, however, many other diversities we seem to fail to respect on a regular basis: gender, class, disability, religion, sexual orientation, economic status, language and age – to name some of the differences that are frequently targets of discrimination, disrespect and bias. Discrimination and inequality, it seems, are deeply rooted in Irish society; they 'continually and profoundly affect the lives of children and their families' (Murray and O'Doherty, 2001, p. 18).

> However, against this the Irish have shown themselves as capable of standing up against the negative forces of prejudice and discrimination: inequalities in Irish society have been created and perpetuated by Irish people and can only be changed by Irish people. All children are entitled to equality of access, partici-pation and quality outcomes, which includes the opportunity to learn in an inclusive, stimulating, culturally appropriate and non-discriminatory environment.
>
> (Murray and O'Doherty, 2001, p. 19)

The passage above is from the '*éist*' report, published following a long and thorough consultation with the Irish ECEC sector in 2001. It is as valid today as it was then – this is what this book is about.

## Who this book is for
This book is about the effects of diversity and (in)equality on young children – and about professional early childhood practices that engage proactively with those effects to ensure more just and equitable experiences for *all* children in early childhood settings.

The book is for those who work (or are studying to work) with young children in the Early Childhood Care and Education (ECEC) sector in Ireland:

▸ Childcare students at FETAC level 5 and 6
▸ Those studying early childhood education at degree level in Institutes of Technology and universities
▸ Montessori courses
▸ Primary teacher education courses
▸ Social Care courses

The book can – and should – be used at different levels, whether you are a beginner or an advanced learner. The chapters of this book offer content of various complexity, allowing for different 'entry points' at different levels: some chapters focus on giving necessary background information, while others ask you to critically engage with theories and concepts. A whole section of the book offers insights into innovative early childhood practice, collected and written together with Irish practitioners. Therefore, we would invite you to take an open, fluid approach to this book. You can use it according to your needs – starting from where you are at the moment and returning to themes and chapters with new questions and insights as your knowledge base, reflection and confidence develops over the course of your studies.

Children experience and notice difference from a very young age; it is an important part of their making sense of the world and developing their identity in relation to this world. Whether we work directly with young children in ECEC settings, study to become an early childhood professional, or support practitioners and students in a role as lecturer or trainer, we have a responsibility to proactively address children's experiences and work towards more just and equitable experiences and outcomes for *all* children in ECEC.

How children learn about diversity and equality issues is closely bound up with the acquisition of their identities and attitudes within a broader set of social relationships and contexts in which they live. Within their sphere, children learn and come to internalise the types of relations and attitudes to difference from their immediate environment and local communities. What children learn about diversity and difference varies from one context to another. However, children all learn attitudes both positive and negative associated with difference (Connolly, 1998; Mac Naughton, 2003; Van Ausdale and Feagin, 2001).

Diversity and Equality issues have long been absent from the mainstream of training, professional preparation and professional development in early childhood – not only in Ireland. An official communication from the European Commission, published in February 2011, states that while working with 'children at risk' is part of initial training in many countries, 'many other aspects of diversity are not sufficiently covered' (European Commission, 2011, p. 6).

But as early as 1998 a conference in Dublin Castle, hosted by Pavee Point Travellers' Centre, stressed the need to address these critical issues in the Irish ECEC sector: *Education without prejudice: a challenge for early years educators in Ireland*. From this starting point, the *'éist'* project has advocated a comprehensive approach to Diversity and Equality in Irish ECEC.

Change has been slow but steady since then, and today the value of diversity and the benefits of engaging with it in systematic and proactive ways are widely recognised in the sector.

At European level, policy documents and reports at European emphasise the central role played by early childhood education and care in countering social inequalities and exclusion (Eurydice, 2009). This is supported by findings of a European research project on 'competence requirements in early childhood education and care' (CoRe). This is the conclusion of the CoRe research project from data gathered in 15 European countries. Thorough knowledge of 'cultural diversity and anti-discriminatory practices' as well as knowledge of 'comprehensive strategies for tackling poverty and socio-cultural inequalities' are key components of competent early childhood systems (Urban, Vandenbroeck, Van Laere, Lazzari and Peeters, 2011, p. 44).

In Ireland, key documents to guide practices and policies embrace respect for diversity as the foundation of important tasks for the ECEC sector, such as supporting each child's identity and belonging. Síolta, the National Quality Framework for Early Childhood Education (Centre for Early Childhood Development and Education, 2006) and Aistear, the Early Childhood Curriculum Framework (National Council for Curriculum and Assessment, 2009) are important achievements for Irish ECEC; both documents require practitioners and providers to focus on diversity and equality in their practices and policies.

*This book supports the implementation of Síolta and Aistear, and the Diversity and Equality Guidelines for Childcare Providers. It directly addresses the learning outcomes of the FETAC module 'Diversity and Equality in Early Childhood Education and Care' at levels 5 and 6, and supports the delivery of this module.*

## Equality and Diversity Principles

### Aistear
Nurturing equality and diversity is important in early childhood. Promoting equality is about creating a fairer society in which everyone can participate equally with the opportunity to fulfil his/her potential. Diversity is about welcoming and valuing individual and group differences, and understanding and celebrating difference as part of life.

### Síolta
Equality is an essential characteristic of quality ECEC. Quality early childhood services acknowledge that all children and families should have their individual, personal, cultural and linguistic identity validated.

Qualification requirements for ECEC practitioners are changing, too. As a concrete step towards a comprehensive Diversity and Equality approach, practitioners now have the option to choose a module titled 'Diversity and Equality in Early Childhood Education and Care' at FETAC levels 5 and 6. This is also part of the degree-level courses (e.g. at DIT).

## Why do we need an 'Irish perspective' on Diversity and Equality?

A lot has been written about the need to address human diversity, and to counter discrimination and exclusion from an early age. There has been, and continues to be, a lively international debate about these issues in a wider context of social justice. Most important for a critical understanding – and practice – of working with young children in the context of diversity and equality is the work of Louise Derman-Sparks who has developed and championed the Anti-Bias Curriculum in the United States (Derman-Sparks, 1989). Much of the work in Ireland that has lead to the inclusion of diversity and equality issues in Irish ECEC policy and practice has been inspired by her work. Glenda Mac Naughton, together with her team at the Melbourne-based Centre for Equity and Innovation in Early Childhood (CEIEC) in Australia, has also hugely contributed to our critical understanding of how children learn about difference from an early age. Her work demonstrates how critical early childhood practitioners can make a difference for children and families.

The Diversity in Early Childhood Education and Training (DECET) network has actively promoted diversity and equality in early childhood in many European countries. It has developed a range of resources and materials for early childhood practitioners and trainers, including 'Diversity and social inclusion. Exploring competences for professional practice in early childhood education and care' (DECET, 2011). The *'éist'* project represents Ireland within this network; Colette Murray is a founding member and current board member of DECET. Together with colleagues from Belgium, France, The Netherlands, Scotland, Serbia and the US, Colette Murray and Mathias Urban are co-authors of 'Diversity and Social Inclusion'.

If so much has been written about Diversity and Equality in Early Childhood – and many examples of excellent practice are available – why do we need this book? The short answer is that the vast majority of publications, practice examples and resources that are out there have been developed in professional ECEC contexts outside Ireland. They build on experiences and practices from the US, Australia, the UK and other countries. Considering the rapid changes in Irish society and in the Irish ECEC sector, there is a need for an Irish perspective on Diversity and Equality in Early Childhood – a resource for students, practitioners and lecturers that is grounded in the Irish ECEC sector, and that builds on the experiences of Irish practitioners, learners and trainers in working with children and families in this country.

There is another, particularly Irish angle to this book. The work that forms the basis for this book has its roots in the support for Traveller children as driven by Pavee Point Travellers' Centre. John O'Connell, founding director of Pavee Point was convinced that working towards equality for Traveller children had to be embedded in a much broader and much more comprehensive approach including *all* children. He supported the vision of *'éist'* from the very beginning.

The *'éist'* project, and since 2006, the Equality and Diversity in Early Childhood National Network (EDENN, http://pavee.ie/edenn/) have advocated for the introduction of a comprehensive Diversity and Equality approach in ECEC in Ireland. The project has held conferences and seminars (e.g. 'We make the road by walking', 2010), developed resources for practitioners and trainers (Murray, 2010, 2001; Murray and O'Doherty, 2001) and has informed framework documents for the Irish ECEC sector, e.g. Síolta (Centre for Early Childhood Development and Education, 2006), Aistear (National Council for Curriculum and Assessment, 2009) and wrote the Diversity and Equality Guidelines for

Childcare Providers (Office of the Minister for Children, 2006). But perhaps most importantly, *'éist'* has worked with trainers, practitioners and students in many ECEC settings, colleges and trainings across the country. It has spread ideas, encouraged and supported innovative practice, and collected and documented the experiences of practitioners and learners over many years – all of which have informed this book.

### *An Irish perspective? Not one, but many!*

D.W. Winnicott, paediatrician and psychoanalyst, once famously wrote 'there is no such thing as a baby, there is a baby and someone'. What he wanted to point out was that a child can only be fully understood in her or his relationships – with the immediate carer, the family and the community. Just like this child, this book is the result of collaborations and relationships of many people over many years. We, the authors, have worked together for many years, and are both passionate about more just early childhood experiences for *all* children. However, we have come to this work from different backgrounds and different personal and professional histories. We share our perspectives in this book; at the same time we each maintain our own voice in writing the different parts of it. We have invited many other contributors (practitioners and trainers) to share their experiences, stories and examples. Each one of them brings their own voice and perspective to this book. Many quotes and stories from practitioners and learners add to the picture. Therefore, this book is a book of many voices and many perspectives. They all come together out of a shared conviction that a comprehensive Diversity and Equality approach in early childhood education and care is necessary – and possible.

## What is in the package?

We have divided this book into four sections, each one focusing on a broad thematic area, and divided into several chapters concentrating on more specific topics.
The four main sections are:

1.  Diversity is real – and so is exclusion
2.  (Re)thinking early childhood education
3.  Walking the walk: voices from the sector
4.  Roadmap to Equality: conclusions and recommendations for policy, professional development and practice in the Irish ECEC sector

**Diversity is real – and so is exclusion** presents a framework for what adults (early childhood practitioners and students) need to know to address diversity and equality proactively. The section has four chapters: it begins with a historical perspective on diversity in Irish society; defines the key concepts used throughout this book; explores acceptable and unacceptable language and terms you will encounter in a context of diversity; and finally, introduces you to important legislative frameworks and documents that orient non-discriminatory practice in ECEC and beyond.

As an ECEC practitioner or learner you might ask why you need to know all about the broader Irish context and history. What is the benefit of having knowledge and understanding of concepts like discrimination and oppression? Does using the right terms when talking about diversity really make such a difference? You might ask why you have to know about national and international legislative frameworks that go far beyond ECEC policy and legislation. It matters because as an ECEC professional you will have to consider how to best provide early childhood services to children, families, communities and our society on the whole. Therefore you need to understand what makes us what we are – how we became who we are and what shapes and influences the broader developments of this society. It matters, too, because it will give you a more solid foundation for implementing Síolta Standards, Aistear Themes, and the Diversity and Equality Guidelines for Childcare Providers in a critically reflective and comprehensive manner.

**Diversity is real – and so is exclusion.** The first chapter in this section takes you back into the history of this island. It is important to understand that diversity has always been a reality in this country – it has made us who we are. Just like the Traveller community, and new communities arriving in this country today, Irish people themselves have experienced emigration and have met prejudice and exclusion. In our history there have always been individuals and movements that have challenged injustice and championed human rights.

Whenever we talk about diversity and equality in ECEC, we use specific concepts and terms that relate to people's experiences in daily life and in society in general. As ECEC practitioners you need to have a sound understanding of these terms and the meanings behind those concepts. The second chapter in this section therefore explores key concepts and their meanings: what exactly do we mean by 'diversity'? Does 'equality' mean that all children should be treated the same? How is a stereotype different from a prejudice, and how do they relate in the bigger picture of exclusion, discrimination and racism? The chapter helps you define these key terms and it encourages you to think critically about their meaning for children's life experiences.

While you might have a sound understanding of the more abstract concepts that frame your work in diversity and equality, you might still be nervous or insecure about how to engage with people from diverse backgrounds without 'getting it wrong'. What language we use to identify and describe members of minority groups in society makes a huge difference. The third chapter of this section explores diversity terms and their meanings. It helps to clarify myths and encourages you make the effort to use acceptable language.

The last chapter in this section introduces you to legislative documents and frameworks that are key to realising equality in ECEC and beyond. The chapter begins with a short discussion of Irish legislation affecting children and families and how they are influenced, and often initiated by, international legislative frameworks and conventions. We then ask the obvious question: 'I'm working in an early childhood setting – why do I need to know about all this?' Children, in ECEC and in society, have rights, which are spelled out in an international document: the United Nations Convention on the Rights of the Child (UNCRC). Children's rights are widely embraced in the ECEC sector. However, besides the UNCRC there are many other legal documents that shape and influence children's and families lives in positive or negative ways. Making children's rights real and not aspirational is what counts.

**(Re)thinking early childhood education**, the second section of this book, focuses on how we interact with the social realities from a professional perspective. The three chapters in this section help you explore how we think and reflect critically about our professional practice with children, families and communities, how we can understand our professional knowledge about children and how this affects our practice and the approaches we can take to ensure more equal and just experiences for all children.

The first chapter in this section explores a concept that inevitably will come up in your studies: the reflective practitioner. There is an expectation, reinforced by recent policy documents, e.g. Aistear, for you to become a reflective practitioner. But what exactly does that entail? What is there to reflect upon – and how does it make a difference to how we engage with children and families in the setting? In this chapter, we suggest that reflection per se is not enough. Reflecting upon our practice needs to go hand in hand with asking critical questions about the conditions for our practice, and about the social realities that shape children's and families' lives.

Becoming critically reflective, and asking critical questions, is closely linked to the topic of the second chapter in this section: how do we know what we know about early childhood? We all agree that professional practice, with young children or otherwise, builds on a professional body of knowledge. But what shapes our knowledge and our understandings of the child? These questions are part of a more fundamental exploration we encourage you to undertake in this chapter: what do we mean by knowledge? What is the role of theory when it comes to our professional practice with young children? What is our own role in bringing about new professional knowledge? This chapter supports you to explore these (admittedly challenging) questions and it encourages you to take a critical stance on ideas we take for granted too often.

The third and final chapter in this section asks what practical and conceptual approaches are there to engage with diversity and equality in early childhood settings. The chapter helps you to understand concepts such as multiculturalism and interculturalism and their implications for early childhood practice. We then explore in more detail an approach based on the Anti-Bias Curriculum and the diversity and equality practice as developed by the '*éist*' project in Ireland. The Anti-Bias approach informs key documents for the Irish ECEC sector, including Síolta, Aistear and the Diversity and Equality Guidelines for Childcare Providers.

**Walking the walk: voices from the sector.** This third section of the book takes you right into experiences and examples from the sector. We have invited practitioners, trainers and learners to share their experiences in working with the Anti-Bias approach in ECEC in settings and across Ireland. Building on the conceptual framework we have laid out in the first two sections of the book, these examples illustrate how services are engaging with diversity issues in practice. They all share a common understanding of the importance of a proactive approach to dealing with diversity and working towards equality.

The chapters in this section have been provided by different authors (listed below); we – Colette Murray and Mathias Urban – have edited them to bring them into the overall structure of this book. In doing so, we have tried to interfere as little as possible with the authentic 'voice' of each contributor.

Joanie Barron, from Wallaroo Playschool, Cork, explores how gender differences impact on children's lives both now and in their future. In her chapter she asks how we can get an understanding of the experiences of children, and how they might be changed by intervention.

The Family Wall is a creative way of engaging with children and families through photos. Stories and experiences from a project with ten services across Ireland show that introducing a Family Wall, informed by the Anti-Bias Approach, supports children's identity and belonging – two key themes in Aistear.

Kathryn O'Riordan from Cork City Childcare Committee explores common difficult situations in ECEC settings. In her chapter, she shows how working in partnership with parents can help to find constructive ways forward.

Working with Persona Dolls in an Anti-Bias framework is a powerful way to help children develop empathy and respect for people who are different to them and also discover the ways in which they are similar. Ann Halligan, trainer from County Mayo and practitioner of Curious Minds introduces working with Persona Dolls and shares her experience of how they can be used to reflect children's individual and group identity and introduce children to social and cultural diversity in an Irish Context.

How can we embrace the richness of many languages in our service, and how can we best support children whose first language is not English? Patsy Baissangourov and Martina Mc Govern illustrate the advantages for bilingual children, their peers and adults in the childcare setting.

Orla Fitzpatrick, practitioner from Co. Clare, shares with us her personal journey as a learner and practitioner beginning to engage with Anti-Bias Approach. Her reflections show how the knowledge she gained through the Anti-Bias training informs both her practice and her thinking.

When did you last take a critical look at the environment in your setting? Have you ever tried to see it through a child's eyes? Colette Murray explores the issue of proofing the physical environment for diversity in the ECEC setting. Her chapter looks at why it is important to represent each child for their well-being and in particular to support their identity and sense of belonging.

Travellers and Roma are the most marginalised communities in Ireland and Europe. Colette Murray (EDENN, Pavee Point) outlines the background of Travellers and Roma exploring their relationship with the settled or majority community.

Where can we go from here? Building on the questions, suggestions and experiences we have explored in this book, the final section takes a look at possible ways forward. What are the necessary steps towards a comprehensive Diversity and Equality approach in Irish early childhood education and care, in practice, professional preparation and policy? Is there a **Roadmap to Equality**? The concluding chapter gives our preliminary answers.

Throughout this book you will occasionally find various types of boxes. They contain examples, questions, and quotes from practitioners and students related to the topic of the chapter. Sometimes they provide short explanations and definitions of terms and concepts discussed in the main text; we call them Jargon Busters. Here are two examples:

## Jargon Buster: Transformative Practice

Transformative practice, in this book, refers to seeing the day-to-day work with children (teaching, caring) as inseparable from issues of equality and social justice, and how they are addressed in your setting. Transformative practitioners aim to change (transform) themselves, and how they understand their role – and at transforming their way of working with children, families and communities in order to actively address diversity and inequality.

Transformative practice involves:

- being strategic and reflective – using your knowledge as basis for action and questioning your knowledge and how it affects children
- working with others to build a critical community: with colleagues, other professionals, parents and carers and members of the community. Each person's history, knowledge, experience and who they are (their social and cultural identities) are valued.
- socially just teaching, learning and caring. This includes developing your own awareness of who is advantaged and disadvantaged by the way your setting and your day is organised, and working towards change for social justice.

### Practitioners' voices:

I always understood that equality is about the same access. I have never actually thought about the same opportunity or outcomes for people. I think it's a basic mistake in the childcare services – there might be pictures of children of different ethnicities sticking on the wall, but no one ever does anything with them. This is my experience.

(Practitioner, 2010)

With this book, we aim to give you all the information you need to come to a better understanding of diversity and equality issues in early childhood education and care. However, there is only so much information that you can pack between the covers of a book. Therefore we have set up a page on the Gill & Macmillan website for additional resources – more detailed information, stories, vignettes, etc. Simply go to www.gillmacmillan.ie, search for *Diversity and Equality* and click on the link in the right-hand column.

Enjoy the journey!

# SECTION ONE

# Diversity is Real and So is Exclusion

This island has been inhabited for more than five thousand years. It has been shaped by pre-Celtic wanderers, Celts, Vikings, Normans, Huguenots, Scottish and English settlers. Whatever the rights or wrongs of history, all those people marked this island: down to the small detail of the distinctive ship-building of the Vikings, the linen-making of the Huguenots, the words of Planter balladeers. How could we remove any one of these things from what we call our Irishness? Far from wanting to do so, we need to recover them so as to deepen our understanding.

(President of Ireland Mary Robinson, 'Cherishing the Irish Diaspora', 1995, Irish Oireachtas)

## Overview

As ECEC professionals we want all children to benefit from, and be secure, included and happy in our services. An implicit part of our professional preparation is the exploration of our value base, which informs our thinking, perceptions and understandings (see Section 2: Critical Reflection). Our beliefs and attitudes are also central to our understanding and engagement with diversity and equality in ECEC. Experiences from teacher education (e.g. Lenskietal, 2005; Haritos, 2004) suggest that learners' beliefs are well established prior to their participation on training programmes. Research also indicates that many learners enter education training programmes with a thin base of knowledge relative to their own and other cultural histories and value systems (Cockrell et al, 1999, Dufrene, 1991, in Clarke and Drudy, 2006).

Our beliefs, attitudes and disposition are tightly interwoven with our knowledge, skills and behaviours, and so it is for those working with children. How we look at the world, or the 'lens' we look through, how we see ourselves and others, is influenced by our education, our family, the society around us.

Working with diversity and equality is more than focusing on approaches and methodologies for the setting. It is about being aware of your own values and attitudes, building a knowledge base and gaining skills for implementation. Our individual beliefs are strongly influenced by the prevailing beliefs, values and attitudes of our society. Working towards a more just society and equality of provision means continually examining the local and national context around us, continually rethinking what we do, what we say and how the influences on our lives as individuals and professionals have determined our attitudes and our behaviour.

Diversity is a reality in Irish society – it can be considered an asset, but this is not always the case. Where there is diversity you will generally find a 'shadow side', which can cause inequality, hurt and insecurity. This shadow side manifests in stigma, stereotyping, prejudice, discrimination, oppression, racism, sexism, homophobia, ableism, etc. In reality it is not the diversity that causes the problem, but how we respond to it individually and institutionally. As individuals we sometimes just don't know what to do and may struggle with the language of diversity. That's OK because addressing equality and diversity issues in ECEC is relatively new and we are all on a learning curve.

Hopefully, getting some direction will help to build your knowledge base, support your reflection and make the journey of addressing equality and diversity in ECEC less daunting.

To begin, it is our contention that ECEC professionals engaging in diversity and equality work do need to investigate and build on their current knowledge around the social and historical, political context. It has informed who we are and our relationship with diversity and equality in Irish society. Knowing about legislation beyond ECEC that can support equality or be a source of conflict for individuals or groups is also beneficial. Our historical context and the implicit values of our society contribute to our beliefs, attitudes and our social prejudice, which in turn affects the behaviour of individuals and institutions on issues of diversity. ECEC professionals are not immune to the values and social prejudices of the broader society, hence linking the historical context to our understanding of how discrimination works and to the legislative context opens up a space for building understanding, knowledge and empathy.

Also crucial to our engagement with Diversity and Equality is our capacity to engage in dialogue on these issues. Having a good understanding of diversity and equality terminology will enable this engagement. Along with your understanding and recognition of inequalities, it encourages other ways of thinking and being.

This Section is divided into four chapters. Here we take the focus away from the child and concentrate on the ECEC professional as a social actor: an individual who comes from a particular social, political, economic and cultural climate, Irish or otherwise. This is a space where you can make the connections between the broader society and what that means for your ECEC practice. You can also explore concepts and meanings that may be unfamiliar and begin to make a link between ECEC work and its influence within society and in particular with families.

# SECTION ONE

SECTION ONE

## CHAPTER 1

# Historical Context

Within an understanding of history as possibility, tomorrow is problematic. In order for it to come, it is necessary that we build it through transforming today. Different tomorrows are possible. The struggle is no longer reduced to either delaying what is to come or ensuring its arrival; it is necessary to reinvent the future. Education is indispensable for this reinvention. By accepting ourselves as active subjects and objects of history, we become beings who make division. It makes us ethical beings.

(Freire, 1997)

## Overview

Ireland has always been diverse. The myth that Ireland has been culturally homogenous (the same) prior to recent immigration is inaccurate. Unfortunately, Irish politicians have naively contributed to this belief. In 1991 an Irish MEP in the European Parliament Committee of Inquiry into Racism and Xenophobia stated:

Ireland is a racially homogeneous country with **no** ethnic minority groups. As a consequence there are no racial problems of the kind experienced in countries with such groups. Neither is there a large presence of foreigners ... the position could alter if the influx became sustained ... there is, however, a minority group of travelling people giving rise to some of the problems associated with racism. (Our emphasis.)

The problem with this statement is that it insinuates that prejudice, discrimination and racism surface only on the arrival of newcomers. This is worrying because it effectively blames the immigrant for Ireland's uncomfortable response to difference. Mac Gréil (2011) in his revealing book *Pluralism and Diversity in Ireland* shows that while Ireland's attitude to diversity has improved and we are fairly open and tolerant, social prejudice with regard to many diversities including culture remains a matter for urgent address. Mac Gréil's call for action is backed up by a recent study on racism in the Dublin area by the Immigrant Council for Ireland (ICI), which illustrates the need for political leadership in tackling racism in our communities.

In this chapter we aim to dispel the illusion that Ireland has been historically homogeneous and also identify the challenges for the Irish who have had to emigrate. The recognition and exploration of our history can help us identify what makes us who we are today in twenty-first-century Ireland. By drawing attention to, and asking you to reflect upon our past, we hope to open up a discussion and create a climate of empathy for addressing diversity in ECEC and Irish society today. Equality is a partner of diversity and the struggle to achieve equality is ongoing. Ireland's history of resistance and struggle has produced champions who have worked to nurture equality and respect for human diversity, and to counter social prejudice both individual and institutional. We also give attention to some of them here.

You might ask why we are addressing the historical context of diversity and looking at human rights champions in a book about ECEC. Up to relatively recently a diversity and equality focus was absent in ECEC policy and curricular documents. This has changed, and its inclusion is welcome. Finding out what that means and what it encompasses is what this book is about. Similar changes have occurred as our view of childhood has altered. A sociological lens (sociology of childhood) looks beyond the individual child and its individual development (developmental psychology). The focus has moved to recognizing the multiple layers and influences in a child's life: ideas of childhood are 'socially constructed' and children are 'social actors'. How we live our lives and interact with children is informed by history.

For those who wish to address diversity and equality issues holistically, it is crucial to confront the history of our past addressing both the positive and negative aspects of our development as a society. Haritos (2004, p. 376) maintains that our prior beliefs represent the 'interpretive lenses' through which learners and practitioners attempt to 'focus on, visualise, perceive, characterise, understand and ultimately resolve their [teaching] concerns' in practice. The societal and cultural context (our Irishness) is part of that interpretive lens. Our awareness needs to go beyond understanding children as individuals alone to understanding our societal context and how our history has influenced how we see difference and respond to it. Our awareness can also contribute to our future history through the choices we make regarding our relationship with equality and social justice, and in particular in the work we do with children.

The report *Taking Racism Seriously in the Dublin Area* (ICI, 2011) concludes, following a description of racial abuse from a young children, that 'It is inconceivable that Ireland should be a place where we tolerate a young child [6 years] racially insulting a neighbour without taking meaningful action to address the glaring issues this raises.' (ICI, 2011, p. 16)

## After reading this chapter you should be able to:

▶ recognise that diversity has always been a feature of Irish society
▶ recognise that racism, sexism and homophobia are not new to Ireland
▶ understand that taking action can create positive change for individuals and groups
▶ understand that awareness and knowledge of the historical context will enhance your capability for working towards diversity and equality, with positive implications for all children in the setting.

## Introduction: Demographic change in Ireland

There is a tendency to think that Ireland has become demographically and culturally diverse only recently, particularly in the last 15 years. This perception is directly linked to the Celtic Tiger economic boom in the late 1990s and early 2000s and Ireland's extraordinary increase in inward migration. There is more visible and linguistic diversity on our streets and in service provision including ECEC. Between 1996 and 2002 Ireland saw a 26% increase of inward migration; much of that migration, believe it or not, consisted of returned Irish. The 2006 census illustrates that the Irish population remains predominately white (94.8%) and of Irish ethnic background (88.9%) including the Traveller community (0.5%). Other white backgrounds constitute 7.1%, and only 3.5% of the population are non-white (CSO, 2006).

Ethnic diversity, which includes linguistic diversity, has been broadly welcomed in Ireland and Mac Gréil's study maintains that in general Ireland has managed to integrate the increase in numbers of foreign-born people in a relatively short period of time (ten years). This has occurred primarily because of the dissemination of new communities throughout the country, which has 'prevented the large ghettoes and it enabled Irish people and migrants to get to know each other better' (Mac Gréil, 2011, p. 19). The arrival of immigrants, however, has not been without its challenges at individual and institutional levels. Negative responses to the visible change on our streets come in the form of the following statements and questions:

> With all this diversity, will we lose our Irishness – our own culture?
>
> (Student, female, 19 years)

> Racism and discrimination have only come to Ireland since black and other minorities have arrived.
>
> (Male, 26 years)

> Why should we accommodate people who come to scrounge off our social welfare system when they have not contributed anything to this country?
>
> (Service provider, male, 40 years)

These concerns must be addressed, but what is it that prompts and influences these questions? What is the thinking that supports individuals or communities to say such things, which are commonly tinged with resentment? Ireland has experienced oppression at home and abroad. Some may question the disparity between the Irish experience of oppression and the not-so-welcoming 'Ireland of the welcomes' for newcomers to Ireland. How does our experience of oppression affect our empathy for immigrants to Ireland? Or does it affect it at all? Being oppressed doesn't mean that you automatically have empathy for others who are oppressed. The ICI (2011) report on racism in the Dublin area illustrates that we have some distance to go. Investigating and understanding certain strands of our history will support a greater awareness of the need to address diversity and equality issues in ECEC.

## Discrimination and racism

> Social prejudice is a universal phenomenon which has played a most destructive role throughout the history of humanity.
>
> (Mac Gréil, 2001, p. 4)

Many deny that racism was a problem in Ireland until recent migration, and it is common to perpetrate the myth that no one experienced racism in Ireland until the changes in the demographics; 'The proposition that Ireland did not have a "problem" of racism because no black people lived there denies that fact that a perceived lack of racialised people in a given society does not mean an absence of racism.' (McVeigh, 1992)

Another view is that if groups did experience racism, it was generally their own fault, arising out of some form of deficiency on their part, or the failure of such groups, especially Travellers, to allow themselves to be subsumed into Irish society (Farrell, F. and Watt, P., 2001, UCD, 2011).

As the discussion above suggests, new communities are not immune to discrimination and racism. 24% of immigrants feel they have been discriminated against. This is over twice the rate for Irish nationals in 2002–2007. The increased likelihood of reported discrimination among immigrants is most particularly pronounced in employment and then in the following domains: housing, shops/pubs/restaurants, financial services and transport (Equality Authority, 2009). A review of existing surveys in Ireland on attitudes to minority ethnic groups indicates an increase in hostility towards groups such as black people, Roma, Travellers, refugees and asylum seekers (FRA, 2009). Various surveys have documented alarming levels of racism in Irish society. Anecdotal evidence also suggests that there has been an increase in incidences of racism since the beginning of the economic crisis.

The European Union Agency for Fundamental Rights (FRA, 2009) reported that 73% of black Africans surveyed in Ireland believed that discrimination based on ethnicity or immigration status was prevalent in the country. The EU–Midis report found that 76% of black respondents did not report their experiences of discrimination to the Irish authorities. This is backed up by a finding in the ESRI (2005) study where 18.7% of black Africans described being treated badly or not receiving an adequate healthcare service on at least one occasion (compared to 9.2% of Asian respondents). Of those who described substandard treatment, most (82.5%) did not make a formal complaint. Underreporting of racist incidents in Ireland would appear to be widespread (ICI, 2011), as illustrated by the table below.

## Reported Racially Motivated Incidents

| Year | 2003 | 2004 | 2005 | 2006 | 2007 | 2008 | 2009 |
|------|------|------|------|------|------|------|------|
| Incidents | 64 | 68 | 100 | 173 | 214 | 172 | 126 |

Source: Central Statistics Office (19 February 2010). It is generally accepted that there is under-reporting of racially motivated incidents. (NCCRI, 2011)

These findings provide the backdrop for the daily life of children and families from minority ethnic and Traveller backgrounds attending ECEC services.

## Media engagement

The media portrayal of immigration has often been unhelpful in its representation of new communities. Negative representation exposes xenophobic attitudes (see Chapter 3) within Irish society and can contribute to discrimination of newcomers. Misinformation also contributes to the stigmatising of individuals and groups and can lead to segregation. Lynch (2007) in Mac Gréil (2011, p. 25) maintains that:

> The media can play a positive and negative role in the struggle against racism. In fact, the media is a key mechanism in bringing our attention to racist incidents and crime. It is also a powerful mechanism for the promotion of positive images of ethnic minority groups. [...] However, it can also play a negative role. In the Irish context this negative role has included scapegoating and inciting hatred against ethnic minority groups through scaremongering biased and inaccurate reporting.

The question is what other influences, besides the media, are at play in our relationship with diversity?

## Diversity is not confined to culture

Cultural diversity is the essence of a multicultural society, and it contributes to society in a myriad of ways. The impact of cultural diversity on society is greater than other forms of diversity (i.e., gender or disability). What is it about cultural diversity that 'gets us', when in reality culture is only one element of identity, one element of diversity? 'Identity flows from a range of sources' (Crowley, 2006, p. 4), which include gender, nationality, disability, ethnicity, skin colour, age, sexual identity, religion, language, geographical context, family background and economic status. Hence diversity is not confined to culture. Diversity in all its form can illicit many levels of prejudice and discrimination. However, it is mostly cultural diversity which has been driving national policy to respond and produce anti-discriminatory and anti-racist policies. Representative organisations continue to lobby for more robust implementation of these policies. There is concern that they do not adequately protect minority communities, nor do they tackle perpetrators of discrimination. Mac Gréil (2011), in *Pluralism and Diversity in Ireland*, writes about the 'urgency in addressing racism and discrimination in Irish and other societies'.

## A timeline of migration and struggle for equality

For the rest of this chapter we will take you on a journey through the history of migration into and from Ireland, and through the struggle for equality and human rights that has always been part of Irish history.

The timeline in this book can only give a brief overview; more detailed information can be found by searching for *Diversity and Equality* on www.gillmacmillan.ie and clicking on the link in the right-hand column. The timeline below is divided into three parts:

▶　Part 1: Cultural migration into Ireland
▶　Part 2: Irish emigration
▶　Part 3: Struggles for equality in a diverse Irish society and the voices of champions of equality and social justice.

We begin by briefly highlighting historical and contemporary cultural influences, along with evidence of some problems associated with diversity and cultural identity for new communities. We find that Ireland today mirrors Ireland at various times in her past. If we look more closely we see that many aspects of diversity including gender, disability and sexual orientation consistently emerge in the struggle for equality (see Chapter 2). Since the arrival of the first people in Ireland in 8000 BC, Ireland's demographic landscape has shifted and changed to make what is today a dynamic population.

We find that Ireland has for centuries embraced new immigrants (at times unwillingly and not without difficulties) along with their ideas and beliefs. In order to understand our relationship with and responses to cultural diversity, it is useful to look at our own historical context and how it has contributed to who we are and how we have responded to cultural diversity. Looking at our own cultural context is the first step in working towards diversity and equality and in building respect for human diversity and empathy in our ECEC work.

# Part 1: Timeline of cultural immigration

Below, we outline the arrival of a variety of people to our shores, showing the complexity of immigration for the immigrant and its impact on the indigenous community from 400 AD to the present day. This timeline is a snapshot, and although you may be familiar with some of the arrivals, you may not have associated them with the building of a diverse Irish society. *Reading these vignettes will not be enough;* discussion with other learners is necessary and follow-up exploration essential. See suggestions throughout this chapter for further exploration and reading to enhance your knowledge and understanding.

## 8000 BC: Arrival of the First People in Ireland
Mesolithic people arrived around 8000 BC (the Stone Age). Sometime around 4500 BC, in the Neolithic period, people arrived with agricultural skills. They were responsible for major Neolithic sites such as Newgrange and contributed to agricultural development in Ireland.

## 100 BC: Arrival of Gaels
The Gaels or the Celts came to Ireland between 800 BC and 100 BC. They established five kingdoms. The geography and tribes of the country were recorded by the Roman geographer Ptolemy during this time.

## 432 AD: Christianity Introduced to Ireland by St Patrick
This time was a period of creativity and joining of Celtic and Christian traditions. The Ardagh Chalice, the Book of Durrow and the Book of Kells were produced during the seventh and eighth centuries AD.

## 795: Vikings Arrive
The Vikings had a huge influence on Ireland. They developed towns such as Dublin, Limerick, Cork and Waterford and gave the country the one thing it came to love more that all else – 'money' (O'Toole, 2011).

## 1079: Reference to First Jews in Ireland
Ireland has a long-standing Jewish community. Jews first immigrated to this country in 1079, and came from Spain and Portugal in the 1400s. The 2002 census revealed that there were 1,790 Jews living in Ireland; in the 2006 census, figures had increased to 1,930.

## 1100s: Earliest Documentation of Traveller Craftspeople, Tinkers or Tin-smiths

Travellers played an important role in Irish society by carrying information and providing entertainment and they also supported the Irish economy through farm labour and tin-smithing.

## 1170: Arrival of the Normans

Strongbow led the Norman invasion of Ireland in 1149 on invitation from the King of Leinster – the beginning of colonisation.

## 1608: The Plantations of Ulster

The Plantations of Ulster were one of the most successful and destructive immigration projects in Ireland. The plantations had major negative consequences for Irish society, and their impact has continued into present-day Northern Ireland.

## 1709: Palatines Arrive in Ireland

The Palatines, Lutheran Protestants from Germany, contributed significantly to the development of Irish farming (www.irishpalatines.org).

## 1845–48: The Irish Famine

The Great Famine (Irish: *An Gorta Mór* or *An Drochshaol*, 'the Bad Life') was a period of starvation, disease and mass emigration between 1845 and 1852 during which the population of Ireland was reduced by 20 to 25 per cent (See 'Emigration' for more detail).

## 1904: Anti-Semitic Boycott in Limerick:

There are dark spots in Irish history with regards to the Jewish community.

> By 1904, there were roughly 35 Jewish families in Limerick, a total of 150 people. Media reporting fuelled violent attacks on the community, supported by a sermon from Father Creagh:
> … Twenty years ago and less Jews were known only by name and evil repute in Limerick. They were sucking the blood of other nations, but those nations rose up and turned them out. And they came to our land to fasten themselves on us like leeches and to draw our blood…
> (From the sermon of Father Creagh, cited on http://politico.ie)

This was the worst ever recorded anti-Semitic violence in Irish history, which culminated in a general boycott of the Jewish community in Limerick. (www.irishcentral.com/news).

## 1950s: Muslims begin arriving in Ireland

The Muslim community began to settle in Ireland in the 1950s. In the 2006 census, 32,500 people stated their religion to be Islam. After the attack in New York on 9/11, the community suffered from anti-Muslim incidences and verbal abuse (NCCRI).

## United Nations Refugee Programme

Over many years, many groups of people came to Ireland under a UN agreement, and they were known as 'Convention Refugees' (see Chapter 4). Convention Refugees have the right to work and are entitled to training and support.

> My first memories of Ireland are from my playschool. It was here that I noticed I was a bit different from the other children. [...] I was brought up in two cultures, the Vietnamese culture and the Irish culture. We spoke Vietnamese in the home and English at school. But I feel completely Irish because I have lived here for so long. At times, though, I do feel there is a conflict inside me over my identity.
> – Nguyen Mai, who was two when her parents fled Vietnam in 1979.

(*Irish Times Magazine*, 18 June 2011, UN Refugee Agency exhibition: 60 years – Stories of Survival and Safe Haven.)

## Asylum Seekers

> When I landed in Dublin I couldn't believe the cold. I thought I would never warm up. At first it was quite amazing, all the strange white faces, but once I found recognisable faces, I felt more at ease.
> – Emika, Nigerian asylum seeker (NCCRI, no date, p. 33).

In 2001, there were 10,325 applications from asylum seekers from 103 different countries. Contrary to the experience of the refugees settled here through programmes in the 1960s, there was little empathy for the new arrivals. Racial hostility and attacks became commonplace (Cullen, 2000, Harris and Byrne 2001).

The recent ICI report *Taking Racism Seriously: Migrants' Experiences of Violence, Harassment and Anti-social Behaviour in the Dublin Area* (2011) confirms the continued harassment of new communities in Ireland. The comments of an ECEC practitioner in a Diversity and Equality workshop (2010) also confirm the need to address these challenges in ECEC training and practice: 'Why do we have to make changes and pussyfoot around everyone so that we don't insult them? It's their choice to be here. They can go home if they don't like it. Do you think that they would change if we went to their country? They would in my foot. I'm sick of it.'

## Immigration

In 2006 there were 420,000 newcomers living in Ireland from 188 different countries. While the vast majority of these people were from a small number of countries – 82% from just ten countries – there was a remarkable diversity in the total range of nationalities (See www.cso.ie/census). Between 2000 and 2004 there were also 39,882 work permits and 5000 work visas granted to new communities as economic migrants.

(www.integrationcentre.ie, Press Release, 4 May 2011)

Migrants to Ireland have experienced exploitation and abuse in employment. This has led to migrants becoming undocumented. Migrants and their families are very vulnerable both economically and socially. Like the undocumented Irish working in the US, they cannot travel home. Exploitation is also a risk factor. While many undocumented migrants work, pay taxes and PRSI, they are not in the position to access social services and benefits. It is virtually impossible for undocumented migrants to access their rights under national or international legislation.

Migrants have been coming to Ireland for centuries. As you can see, they have brought a wealth of experience and knowledge which has benefited Ireland. New communities have also suffered exclusion and social prejudice. The Irish have also experienced hardship from colonialism and forced emigration. Below we examine the Irish experience of emigration.

> ### 1.2 Discuss
>
> * Were you surprised by any of the information outlined in the historical timeline?
> * Do you think new arrivals to Ireland in recent years have made a contribution to Irish society?
> * Do you think our colonial past has affected how we respond to new arrivals in our country?
> * How can knowing about the historical and demographic changes in Ireland support your work with diversity and equality in ECEC?
> * Take one of the areas above and research the effects of inward migration at that time. Discuss with your learning group.

# Part 2: Timeline of Irish emigration

While people have always been arriving and seeking refuge for centuries in Ireland there has also been a parallel story of emigration. The Irish are among the ten top nationalities to emigrate for work, and Ireland has the second-highest proportion of its population living in other countries of the EU (Migrant Rights Centre, 2010).

It is common to hear Irish people proclaim Irish popularity abroad; they also love to hear that musicians, actors, dignitaries from abroad love to come to Ireland. However, the Irish emigrant story has not always been so welcoming or so easy.

There are about 70 million people worldwide who can claim Irish descent. The largest number of people of Irish descent live in the United States – about ten times the population of Ireland itself. There are an estimated 800,000 Irish-born people living abroad today (www.irishtimes.com/timeseye/whoweare/p8topa.htm).

The Celtic Tiger trend of immigration has stalled, and there is a shift again to emigration as a result of the economic downturn. Irish people have settled all over the world, but mostly in English-speaking countries. The Irish have been very successful abroad, but the challenge of settling into new communities has not been easy, as seen in the examples below from the 19th and 20th centuries.

## The Great Famine

Between 1845 and 1852 the population of Ireland was reduced by 20 to 25 per cent by starvation, disease and mass emigration. Approximately one million people died and a million more emigrated from Ireland's shores despite massive quantities of food being exported from Ireland.

During the famine period, emigration was largely to America and Canada on 'famine ships'. Many people were also deported by the British to Australia for petty and more serious crimes. A further wave of emigration, mainly to England and America, took place between the 1930s and 1960s escaping poor economic conditions following the establishment of the Irish Free State (Cowley, 2001).

Emigration numbers have begun to increase again as Ireland experiences recession post the Celtic Tiger years (1995–2007). New challenges meet the Irish émigré in 2011. Australia, the US, Canada and the UK continue to be the main destinations for the emigrating Irish, although immigration laws in these countries have become more stringent. There are many undocumented Irish in the US and a strong Irish lobby is working for their recognition. The examples below include the voices of emigrants and their experiences.

## Survival in a harsh landscape: Challenges for the Irish émigré through the centuries

### United States

Conditions were very hard for Irish immigrants in the eighteenth and nineteenth century US. The Irish along with the black community suffered the scorn of those better situated in American society. Colour was important in determining a person's social position. The Irish were frequently referred to as 'niggers turned inside out' and Irish characters on the stage were depicted as drunken and foolish. Over time, the Irish learned that to distance themselves from black people would support their social capital. The Democratic Party (eager for the Irish vote) lobbied the Irish labourers and organised the exclusion of black people from their trades and professions. As such they forced black people out of numerous trades and occupations. It was when Irish policemen appeared on the streets that it was clear the Irish had begun to climb the social ladder, and the Irish had 'become white' (Ignatiev, 1995).

> Perhaps no class of our fellow citizens has carried this prejudice against colour to a point more extreme and dangerous than have our Catholic Irish fellow-citizens, and yet no people on the face of the earth have been more relentlessly persecuted and oppressed on account of race and religion than have this same Irish people.
>
> (Frederick Douglass cited in Rolston and Shannon, 2002, p. 44)

### Britain

The relationship between England and Ireland has been fraught with difficulties and contradictions over the centuries. For over 200 years the Irish have immigrated to Britain. As many as six million British are estimated to have at least one Irish grandparent.

The Irish have contributed to Britain at many levels, but in particular to the construction industry. In the 20th century, living in England for many was a struggle. The Irish were stigmatised and stereotyped, and exploited in employment (Cowley, 2001). The stigmatisation of the Irish goes back a long way. Caricatures of Irish people as ape-like or monstrous beings occasionally appeared in satirical magazines like *Punch*. The Northern Ireland troubles contributed to media outrage and maintained and contributed to Irish hiding their identity in the UK (www.movinghere.org.uk).

*Voices of those who experienced scapegoating and stereotyping, prejudice, discrimination, disadvantage and exploitation can be found by searching for Diversity and Equality on www.gillmacmillan.ie and clicking on the link provided.*

### Australia

Forced immigration (deportation) and the stigma of criminal ancestry played a part in Irish Australians playing down their ethnic roots until relatively recently. A public anti-Irish campaign was prompted in the 1980s following a surge of Irish jokes which stereotyped and stigmatised the Irish. The Australian population is made up of 30 to 40% of people claiming Irish roots; this is more than double the percentage of Americans who claim Irish ancestry (www.thewildgeese.com/pages/aus_kel.html, 2011).

*Anti-Irish Jokes*

Anti-Irish jokes have been widespread throughout the centuries in America, Australia and Britain. The most prevalent portrayals of Irish people in jokes are as stupid, drunken and brainless and Irish accents are ridiculed. A survey in 1994–1995 on discrimination and the Irish community in Britain initiated by the Commission for Racial Equality and written by Mary Hickman and Bronwen Walter (1997) found that 70% surveyed thought anti-Irish jokes offensive and only 30% accepted them as 'harmless fun'. *The Sun* newspaper ridiculed the announcement of the report describing it as 'a load of codswallop', and it greeted the news with a page of Irish jokes 'to give the researchers a flying start' (*The Sun*, 22 January 1994, p. 9).

How communities are stigmatised and stereotyped can lead to prejudice, discrimination, racism (see Chapter 3) and oppression. Irish people abroad have been afraid of asserting their identity for fear of reprisals or exclusion and so over the years have 'kept their heads down'. The Irish have been reluctant to protest at racist treatment partly for fear of being identified, but also for shame arising from a partial acceptance of guilt by association (e.g. ancestral criminality in Australia, association with the IRA in Britain). Attacks and intimidation of the Irish abroad have not always been reported to the police largely due to the perceived lack of justice for complainants with Irish accents based on the immediate association with Irish stereotypes and the Northern Irish political context. Above, we outlined similar experiences of newcomers to Ireland not reporting discrimination or poor service.

## 1.3 Discuss

- Can you see any similarities in how the Irish behaved in Britain in the face of media misrepresentation, stigmatisation and discrimination, and how new communities respond to similar behaviour in Ireland?
- How do you think emigration has affected the self-esteem of the Irish?
- Do you think we treat new communities in the same way Irish people were treated abroad?

# Part 3: Struggles for equality in a diverse society

There are always individuals and groups who lead the way in the search for equality and rights for all citizens. As part of our colonial, tribal and religious history over centuries, struggles for justice for all have been attempted. Champions for social justice in all societies have a common experience of resistance as they generally cause discomfort to vested interests. Without champions of social justice to promote change for those who experience discrimination, Irish society would be all the poorer. Champions of social justice generally work with allies in human rights groups or non-governmental organisations (NGOs).

Change generally comes slowly, but it can and does happen. There are many reasons that champions for social justice causes are driven to act, but the key elements in their drive for change is their vision for an egalitarian society. This vision often includes eliminating discrimination, respecting diverse identities and ensuring that the recognition and acknowledgement of the experiences and situations of different groups and individuals be respected and valued in society. We can all be champions for social justice, for equal respect and recognition of all citizens, even as we work in an ECEC setting. Irish citizens over the centuries have championed for equality and justice at international and nationals levels. Below, we outline some critical changes that emerged in the struggle for rights and justice linked to a primary champion for social justice and their support groups. These people can also be celebrated for their contributions to human rights in Ireland in teaching exercises with young children. We have presented some people of influence under racial, ethnic and religious oppression, gay rights, women's rights and children's rights. See the *Diversity and Equality* page on www.gillmacmillan.ie for further details of champions for social justice.

## Racial, ethnic and religious oppression
### *Daniel O'Connell: The Liberator (1775-1847)*

Daniel O'Connell was committed to humanitarianism. 'He supported the emancipation of Jews, was at the forefront of the anti-slavery movement, denounced colonialism and its victims where it existed, preached the brotherhood of man with conviction and denounced sectarianism'. (Lydon, 1998, p. 284). The Catholic Association which he founded became the first mass political party in history. The party collected small dues every week in Catholic churches throughout the country. Daniel O'Connell, the first modern agitator, held mass meetings and is credited with developing the method of grass roots organising. Under British rule Catholics were prohibited from holding office. He led the campaign for Catholic Emancipation (Lydon, 1998) and won. He also was a key figure for the 1833 Anti-Slavery and Abolitionist Movement.

Daniel O'Connell denounced slavery, criticising American hypocrisy despite the Irish in America objecting to his calls for freedom for black slaves:

> Let American in the fullness of her pride wave on high her banner of freedom and its blazing stare ... In the midst of their laughter and their pride, I point them to the negro children screaming for their mother from whose bosom they have been tore... Let them hoist the flag of liberty, with the whip and rack on one side, and the star of freedom upon the other.
>
> (Ignatiev, 1995, pp. 9–10)

### Mary Manning and Karen Gearon (1980s)

We won... We didn't start the movement, the movement was there before us, but we certainly brought a new life to it, and we raised its profile. Before this strike there were about six divisions of the Apartheid movement in Ireland. By the time we finished there was an anti-apartheid division in every single county, and some had three or four.

– Karen Gearon, Dunnes Stores worker

Mary Manning refused to handle South African fruit as a cashier in Dunnes Stores in 1984. Her decision was based on a directive of the Irish Distributive and Administrative Trade Union regarding apartheid in South Africa. Eleven young workers took a stand against apartheid and become global symbols of resistance. Their actions caused two and a half years of upheaval for Dunnes Stores. The workers suffered considerably both economically and socially. They experienced abuse, were spat on and were called 'nigger lovers' and told to 'look after their own instead'. Bishop Desmond Tutu from South Africa supported the strikers which gave them an international profile (Sweeney, 2010). Finally the government relented and banned the importation of South African goods in 1986. Through their commitment to human rights they demonstrated what 'ordinary' people can do to fight injustice at a global level (Sweeney, 2010).

### John O'Connell (1949–99)

In his short life, John O'Connell always took the road less travelled in supporting the rights of poor and oppressed people. He began his work in the Philippines and continued this path in Ireland championing Travellers' rights. He worked tirelessly to support the empowerment of Travellers through education programmes and community initiatives. He founded Pavee Point, the national Travellers' centre, to work in partnership with the Traveller community. A firm believer in the need to act locally and think globally, he pioneered the development of European and international links for and with Travellers and other Irish marginalised groups. He advocated for Travellers' recognition as a minority ethnic group and the rights associated with such a status. His vision may yet come to fruition following the indications given at Ireland's Universal Periodic Review of Human Rights hearing in Geneva in October 2011 that consideration is being given by the Irish government to the recognition of Travellers as a minority ethnic group.

His legacy lives on in his writing, initiatives and especially in the people he inspired to take action for change on their own behalf.

## Women's Rights (1970s)

Countess Markievicz and Hannah Sheehy-Skeffington worked tirelessly to secure the right of women to vote. They succeeded, though in 1922 woman were required to own property and be over 30 to vote. In 1922 all Irish women over 21 were given the right to vote (Ward, 1997).

### The Women's Liberation Movement

In 1970 the Irish Women's Liberation Movement was founded. Their message was disseminated by members working in the media. The publication *Chains or Change*, in 1971, demanded: equal pay for women; equality before the law; equality in education; availability of contraception; justice for deserted wives, single mothers and widows; and a house for every family. This publication influenced the Commission on the Status of Women Report.

**At that time:**
▸ a married woman was still regarded as the chattel of her husband
▸ there was still a marriage bar for women in the Civil Service
▸ Irish women workers earned only 55% of men's wages
▸ 'chivalry' and 'respect' applied only to manners,
▸ contraception was illegal
▸ after a lifetime in the home, many widows ended their days in degrading poverty
▸ the plight of unwed mothers, deserted wives and those with broken marriages demanded attention.

In their determination to secure legal contraception, members of women's liberation groups protested against Archbishop McQuaid's letter to the public, in which he said, '*contraception is evil; there cannot be, on the part of any person, a right to what is evil*' by walking out of Mass and protesting at the Archbishop's Palace in Drumcondra. They journeyed to Belfast on the '*condom train*' and publicly displayed illegally imported contraceptives at Connolly Station in Dublin. They held large meetings and organised pickets, marches and demonstrations. These women raised awareness among Irish women and challenged them to demand change. They also raised political awareness of the rights and needs of women (Sweeney, 2010, p. 21).

*Mary McGee: Contraception and the High Court (1973)*
*Mary Robinson: Cherish, Josie Airey and Equal Pay (1973–6)*
*Removal of the Ban on Married Women Working (1973)*
*Anti-Discrimination (Pay) Act (1974)*
(see the *Diversity and Equality* page on www.gillmacmillan.ie for details)

## Gay Rights (1970s)
### David Norris
In the 1970s homosexuality was illegal in Ireland. In 1973–1974 homosexual men were sentenced in court for acts of gross indecency and for being practicing homosexuals. In 1970s David Norris began campaigning for gay rights and gave his first interview as an openly gay man. He and law students at Trinity College set up the Campaign for Homosexual Law Reform. It wasn't until 1988 that the National Gay Federation took the legal route to challenge the legal ban on homosexuality on the ground that it was an unconstitutional infringement of personal privacy. David Norris took the case. The judge ruled against Norris, and stated 'it is reasonably clear that current Christian morality in this country does not approve of buggery, or of any sexual activity between persons of the same sex' (*Irish Times*, 11 October 1980). They took this 'long and arduous struggle through' (Mac Gréil, 2011, p. 48) the Supreme Court and then finally to the European Court of Human Rights. In the European Court, Ireland was found to be in breach of the European Convention on Human Rights on the grounds of privacy, and on 30 June 1993, the Irish Parliament passed a law to decriminalise sex between men (Murray et al, 2010).

## Right to marry for Same-sex Couples
### Katherine Zappone and Ann Louise Gilligan (2006–)
*For more information, see the Diversity and Equality page on www.gillmacmillan.ie.*

## Children's Rights
### Nóirín Hayes (1992–)
Children's rights have been slow to come onto the agenda in Ireland. Nóirín Hayes (DIT, CSER) has continually championed both children's rights and the importance of ECEC provision for young children. As chair of OMEP Ireland (world organisation for early childhood education), she endeavoured to get greater and wider attention in Ireland focussed on the ratification of the UN Convention of the Rights of the Child in 1992. The reaction of the government was limited. The OMEP committee decided to bring together NGOs, trade unions and education institutions to attend a meeting in May 1993. While this meeting was well attended it was limited in terms of political engagement. Hayes continued to pursue the issue and in September 1993 held a further meeting: 11 people representing nine organisations attended. One of the organisations, Barnardos, had access to a small grant from the Calouste Gulbenkian Foundation. This grant was used to move things forward on the topic of children's rights. The core group was mobilised into what eventually became the Children's Rights Alliance (see www.childrensrights.ie). Hayes continued her involvement in the CRA as a board member and Chair, and continues to keep the issue of children's right on the agenda through her research. In the late 1990s, she

took the opportunity provided by the EU NOW funding programme to initiate the OMNA project, which brought the sector together again. This was important in developing a shared sense of purpose for ECEC provision for young children. The idea to bring the sector together was borrowed by the National Childcare Strategy in the Department of Justice, Equality and Law Reform. This initiative subsequently led to the development of the Síolta Quality Framework (2006) and the Aistear Curriculum Framework (2010).

## 1.4 Activity

- Find out who has championed children's rights in Ireland. What were the issues and barriers that confronted them?
- Champions of human rights are generally – but not always – activists. What qualities do you think are needed to make a champion or activist?
- Why do you think it takes so long for the state to allocate rights to its citizens?
- Source and explore stories from new communities, asylum seekers, refugees and Travellers or Irish immigrants. Investigate:
  - what type of welcome they have had in their host country.
  - what kind of struggles they had or continue to have.
  - how attitudes towards them personally or towards their group have affected their lives.
- Learn about an individual or organisation that has been successful in changing policy for a particular group i.e., women, people with disabilities, the Traveller community, newcomers, etc.

## Summary

At a glance, this timeline gives a sample of the way that the development of diversity in Ireland has contributed to the richness of our heritage and current society. It also highlights some of the challenges associated with the inclusion of cultural diversity for indigenous and new communities, and Irish emigrants' experiences as newcomers in other states. Historically, cultural and broader diversity within the population has not always been valued nor have differences been equally cherished. As a result, Ireland has not always shown due regard for the diverse needs of all people. The struggle for equality and protection against discrimination in all its forms continues to pose challenges for Irish society, a society in which children learn in a system that can continue to reinforce those challenges.

Diversity in all its forms, and how we have embraced or rejected it over the centuries has influenced how we as a nation embrace cultural diversity and difference today. Our history of colonialism, immigration and the negative treatment of Irish immigrants abroad also contributed to the collective possessiveness about 'Irishness' and nationalism. Our perceived homogeneity comes largely from the notion of having to create a unique Irishness in the wake of our becoming an independent nation in 1922. As part of that

Irishness, we have created a self-image of 'Ireland of the welcomes', which has been severely challenged in the past ten years. Ironically, the colonisation and oppression of a nation does not make its people empathetic to those who are immigrating or experiencing disadvantage. Yet this is juxtaposed with a history of respect for the oppressed as seen in such key figures as Daniel O'Connell, Mary Robinson, John O'Connell, the Dunnes Stores workers, John O'Connell, Katherine Zappone, Anne Louise Gilligan and Nóirín Hayes to name a few.

As an example of our continued negative relationship with colonialism, in the late 1990s and early 2000s, many Irish immigrants to Britain returned to settle into their original communities. Reports from some schools in the south west of Ireland indicated that the most significant bullying issues centred on the English accents of children of returned Irish parents.

The demographics of Ireland have shifted in terms of a visible racial and cultural diversity in the past 15 years, but diversity is in fact much broader than what we can see. Diversity encapsulates social class, gender, the returned Irish, family status, people with disabilities, gay and lesbian people in families, ethnic minorities, the Traveller community, economic migrants, refugees, asylum seekers, Irish-language speakers, religious minorities, the multiracial Irish, the majority population and many others. The changes in our demographics have raised many issues for our society, and in particular in the way we develop and provide services for communities.

So why is it important to be aware of Ireland's historic diversity, its challenges and how equality change has come about in Ireland as an ECEC learner or provider? Because it helps to remind us that we are who we are *because* of our mixed heritage, background, abilities, etc. It gives us perspective, and it may help to show a level of empathy for those who are new and not so new, able and not so able, privileged and not so privileged in our communities. It also draws our attention to the inequalities in society, and helps to dispel some myths that surround diversity and equality issues.

By gaining knowledge about history we can begin to critically reflect on diversity and equality issues in contemporary society, which in turn will enhance our work with children and support the implementation of Síolta (2006) and Aistear (2010). Children will encounter diversity and inequality in life and addressing these issues with young children will benefit them in fulfilling their own potential and in their active engagement as citizens.

## CHAPTER 2

# Understanding Terminology: Concepts and meanings explored

I'm beginning to understand how oppressive behaviour towards a group can result in behaviour which I find unacceptable.

(Learner, 2011)

## Overview

It is not possible to talk about diversity and equality in ECEC without using specific words that relate to how diversity manifests itself in daily life and in society more generally. It can also be difficult to identify what is going on for particular children, families and groups in society if we don't have an awareness and understanding of the meaning of diversity-related concepts and terms, as there are many forms of inequality in society based on both individual and group identity. Inequality is closely connected to the economic, political and cultural structures of our society, and to the (often taken for granted) ways we talk about 'difference'. It is our contention that it is not enough to read terms to truly understand their meaning. We have to analyse these concepts and their implications for the work we do with children. Policy developments now recognise the need for a diversity- and equality-driven focus in work with children, i.e. Síolta (2006), Aistear (2009), Diversity and Equality Guidelines for Childcare Providers (2006), Preschool Regulations (2006) and the recognition of the importance of implementing the UN Convention on the Rights of the Child (UNCRC). We know from the previous chapter that issues of prejudice and discrimination, racism, sexism, homophobia, etc., have been and continue to be at issue in Ireland, in the Irish diaspora and across the world. Most people would like the world to be an equal place where each person can reach their full potential, but the reality is that we are not all equal. Privileges that are taken for granted by some are impossibilities or mere dreams for others. For example: middle-class children may take it for granted that they will go to college, while children from disadvantaged areas don't have a college education in their sights. There are many factors that influence children's reality including expectations at school, home and the student's own expectations, economic issues such as poverty, opportunities and status in society. The reality is that **we are not all equal**. My son most likely doesn't recognise his privileged position and may assume that people without a university degree have made a choice not to enter third-level education, that they didn't work in school, or are simply too lazy. Because we don't always see the advantages given to us by our economic class, they are known as 'internalised privileges'.

Our concern is young children and their future life chances. Equality does not exist as of yet and for this reason it is important that ECEC professionals equip themselves against discrimination in early education. In this way you can act against inequality and support children to have better chances in life. We are role models for children and families, and how we use language in respect of individuals and groups matters. In this chapter we will outline key diversity and equality terms, highlighted throughout with real examples of how these issues manifest in reality for individuals and groups. We also encourage you to continue your investigation though the discussion points and activities supplied at the end of the chapter.

## After reading this chapter you should be able to:

▸ define stereotype, prejudice, discrimination, racism, sexism, ableism, etc., and give concrete examples of how they manifest themselves in society.

▸ understand that the way of seeing the world through our different social, political lenses can lead to ways of thinking that undermine ourselves and others.

▸ explain the importance of knowing and understanding terms associated with diversity and equality work.

▸ use specific language and refer to particular concepts in discussing diversity and equality issues respectfully, and think critically about the work we do with children and parents.

### 2.1 Jargon Buster

#### What do we mean by diversity and equality?

Concepts such as diversity and equality are complex, and their meanings vary depending on the social conditions and academic or political understanding at a given time. At the same time, our beliefs about diversity and equality are important because they inform our understanding of families and communities and our approach to working with them. The perspectives on equality and diversity outlined below reflect some of the views of those advocating for social and economic justice in Ireland.

#### Diversity

Diversity describes the kaleidoscopic nature of a society. Diversity is about all the ways in which people differ and how they live their lives as individuals, within groups and as part of a wider social group. For example, a person can be classified or classify themselves by their social class, gender, disability, family structure, sexuality or family status. They can be seen – or see themselves – as part of a minority group, a minority ethnic group, or part of the majority/dominant group.

Differences are a natural part of life. No two people are the same, and this means that many different elements make up the communities you belong to, work, learn and live in. Diversity is something that should be recognised, accepted and respected and many elements can be celebrated. There is a dark side to diversity that includes stereotyping, prejudice, discrimination and racism, sexism and classism, and for that reason, diversity has a partner: equality.

*Everybody seemed to have a different opinion as to what diversity meant. We all gave our opinion on what diversity was and by the end we had filled up a whole page of different things.*

(Learner on D&E training, 2009)

### Equality

Equality is closely linked to recognising, accepting and respecting diversity and to supporting individual and group needs. Inequalities can be instigated by an individual or through policies at an institutional level. Equality is about equal opportunities, which means ensuring equal access, participation or outcomes for all children and their families. Equality of participation is particularly relevant when working with children and parents. This means the practitioner actively acknowledges and respects the child in the ECEC setting and also works in solidarity with the family.

*In our setting we treat every child the same.*

(ECEC practitioner, 2010)

This is a very common statement by learners and practitioners when asked what goals we should have in terms of equality in an ECEC environment. In fact, equality is <u>not</u> about treating people the same, but rather that different people's needs are being met in different ways. Equality is also not about political correctness, but is value-based, making sure that people are not discriminated against and that power relations are addressed.

## Equality of Condition

Baker et al (2004) believe that we are all entitled to 'equality of condition', which is broader in its scope than the idea of equal opportunities – the idea that we all should have equal chances to compete for social advantages (p. 25). The problem with this take on equal opportunities is that it is based on the assumption that 'many major inequalities are inevitable and that our task is to make them fair' (p. 33). It focuses on the individual, rather than examining disparities between groups. The main problem with equal opportunities is that it can co-exist with significant levels of inequality.

Equality of condition, Baker et al argue, has a much more ambitious agenda: it recognises that inequality is rooted in oppression, and in social structures that can be changed (p. 33). 'Those who espouse equality of condition seek to focus on root causes and to identify how inequalities are generated and passed on from generation to generation by structures and systems. They promote the need to review the structures in society ... so that people can realise a sense of belonging and ownership in society.'

Equality of condition is about 'enabling and empowering people to make real choices among real options' (Baker et al, 2004, in Crowley, 2006, p. 17).

It focuses on five key dimensions,

**Equality of:**
▸   respect and recognition
▸   resources
▸   love, care and solidarity
▸   power
▸   working and learning.

Equality of love, care and solidarity are important components of equality and are basic human needs. Equality of care means that each person can feel a basic sense of value, importance and belonging – of being appreciated and cared for. 'Equality is an expression of the value placed on human worth by society' (Crowley, 2006, p. 4). In terms of equality, the European Union is concerned with social cohesion and equality of opportunity. In Ireland we have equality legislation, which makes discrimination unlawful on nine grounds (see Chapter 3). In Chapter 4 we will explore in more detail how equality legislation is relevant to ECEC settings.

Learners often talk about equal opportunities, but when pressed, they are not really sure what that means. Equal opportunities are broken down into three components: access, participation and outcomes. One learner describes this well in the quote below:

I always understood that equality is just about having the same access. I have never actually thought about the same opportunity or outcomes for people. I think this is a basic mistake made in the childcare services. For example, lots of the crèches in their policies emphasise that they allow access for every child but they never talk about participation and then outcomes. They do not explain how they are going to work with children from minority groups. It is a similar situation with childcare workers; they might have children from minorities in the group, and what's more they are proud of the fact that they are equally open to every child. But they do not know how to work with these children; they do not have proper equipment, ideas, preparation. There might be pictures of children of different ethnicities sticking on the wall, but no one does anything with them. This is my experience.

(Practitioner, 2009)

---

### 2.2 Discuss

- What might equality of
  - access
  - participation
  - outcome
    mean to a child from a Traveller family going to school?
- Access to school can be problematic for Traveller families. Why?
- How would you ensure that Traveller children participate in the school system?
- Do you need to consider imagery, curriculum, resources, bullying policies, etc.? If so, why?
- Traveller children don't always have the same outcomes as other children. Why might this be?
- If Travellers do not have a sense of belonging and if their identity is not recognised and supported, how might that affect their outcomes in school?
- Look at the five dimensions of Equality of Condition. What might Travellers' experience of equality be in relation to the five dimensions?

(See Chapters 3, 4 and 15)

---

## Introduction: Links between societal structures and Diversity and Equality

The larger social and cultural field in which children find themselves is not of their own making ... they must cope in and learn their meaning and negotiations.

(van Ausdale and Feagin, 2001, p. 42.)

The values and ideology of a society inform the actions and decisions of a society and its governance. There are political, economic, cultural and affective (care) systems that either sustain inequality or promote equality. Beliefs and assumption about these systems influence, among others, government decisions that affect all levels of society. The ECEC system is just one example of how government decisions impinge on the lives of young children their families and communities. For example:

### Politically:

Governments make decisions on how to provide services for children. Prioritising ECEC services for children is within the gift of the government.

## Economically:

Providing quality services for children and families is linked to the allocation of funding. Political decisions are closely linked to funding priorities. Funding allocated to ECEC still remains low compared to that allocated to other areas of education, although it has improved in recent years. This piecemeal approach to ECEC has serious ramifications for the quality of service provision.

### 2.3 Discuss

- Do you think ECEC is a priority at government level? Discuss.
- Do you think ECEC funding is the poor relation to education. If so, why? Discuss.

## Culturally:

Who is recognised, respected, valued and made visible in ECEC training programmes and curriculum development at state level? This is linked directly to participation for all children. If some children's backgrounds are absent from the imagery or content of curricula, their participation and belonging can be affected.

### 2.4 Discuss

- Do you think all children are represented in the curriculum and materials in ECEC?

## The Affective (Care) System in society:

Being human means we have 'both a need and a capacity for intimacy, attachment and caring relationships' (Baker et al, 2004, p. 37) and this is what the idea of the 'affective system' in society is about. How do we honour, recognise and value carers and care in society? If you compare the conditions of ECEC workers and educators you will find huge discrepancies, yet children are learning from birth, and children in school have to be cared for. The care and education divide is a false divide, one which it supports and maintains inequality for ECEC workers.

### 2.5 Discuss

- How do you think the care and education divide maintains inequality? Discuss.

This is a very short glance at a complex area that attempts to show how the systems are interlinked. Having an awareness of the effects of societal structures and systems that also affect the daily lives of families will give you an insight into the challenges they face. This knowledge also helps to build empathy, solidarity and mindfulness regarding the needs of both minority and majority children. The needs of families are also directly linked to 'equality of condition' and the five elements of equality.

Mac Gréil (2011, p. xv) maintains that there is need for 'a greater understanding of the social situation, unbiased rearing of the young, strict control on incitement to hatred, and conditions conducive to favourable interpersonal and intergroup contact are among the most effective conditions of greater social tolerance in society'. ECEC practitioners can contribute to a more just society through their work with children.

## Why discuss terminology and concepts?

> Children do not notice difference. They do not notice difference. They don't say anything or comment.
>
> (Practitioner, Learner, 2010)

### Young children and responses to diversity: Prejudice and discrimination

The simple truth is that children *do* notice difference from the day they are born. Me, mammy, the world outside – we're not the same. This is how learning works. What is more interesting is *what* children learn about difference/diversity and how they respond to that difference. As professionals, we are role models for children. They learn from us in a multitude of ways: through our interaction with them, our interactions with others, our responses to situations, the media, etc. Similarly, they learn from their own interaction with peers and adults. Children learn positive and negative attitudes and sometimes muddled ideas about difference, which they begin to learn from birth, engage with more actively as they get older (2 years +) and begin to voice or act on at 3 years (Milner 1983, van Ausdale and Feagin, 2001; Connolly et al, 2002). See www.gillmacmillan.ie for information on research.

### What children say

> A white boy (3) won't sit beside a black girl. He says he doesn't like her because she is chocolate.
>
> (Practitioner, 2009)

> During 'Circle' we were complementing each other. One white boy was sitting beside a black girl, and when it came to his turn he said 'I have nothing to say'. I gave a complement to the girl, and the boy interrupted and said, '*No! She is not from Ireland, she is from Africa.*' The black child happened to be 'black Irish'.
>
> (Practitioner, 2007)

Traveller children aged 5 to 11 years were interviewed in 2006 about their primary school experience, and were asked if there was one thing the Minister for Education could do to support them in school. Without exception, they answered along the same theme: 'Stop the name calling', 'Stop the hurt', 'Stop the slagging'.

## What adults say

We don't have any Travellers or foreign children here, so equality and diversity doesn't apply to us.

(Practitioner, 2009)

I'm not sure how to deal with staff who have very ignorant opinions toward parents of children who are not Irish [new community children]; they are very negative towards black families.

(Practitioner, 2008)

Just tell me, if you hadn't been working with Travellers for so long, do you think you would actually like them?

(Learner, 2011)

— I hate the Polish.
— My next door neighbour is Polish and she is lovely.
— Yeah, I know some lovely ones too, but I hate the Polish.

(Learner, 2010)

*Learner journal entry, week one:*
In our service I haven't seen the need to address the bigger issues of racism or inequality because for the two years I have been working these issues have never been raised by the children.

*Learner journal entry, week three:*
Well, well, work was very interesting today: I have noticed children talking about difference. In my previous entry I said I hadn't seen children this young noticing their differences and I didn't believe it, but I have been proven wrong. Now I am listening more to the children as they are chatting and I am becoming more aware of the need to say something.

(Learner journal comments during Anti-Bias training)

## Does diversity training work?

> I have been trying to figure out how prejudiced I am. Do I stereotype? What do I think about other ways of life, cultures, etc.?
>
> (Learner, 2011)

As professionals, we want children to learn about difference in a positive way. This means intervention at an early stage to counter negative prejudices and to work on attitudinal issues. The quotations on page 27 tell us that children do react to difference and that adults are sometimes unaware or even in denial about difference and children's learning about it. It is imperative to have an understanding of concepts and terms in order to grapple with the phenomena of prejudice in society and how it operates. This understanding includes addressing attitudes to others, notions of culture and recognising that we all have multiple identities (woman, mother, shopkeeper, dancer, teacher, lawyer). It also means working analytically from within a critical education or Anti-Bias Approach in ECEC sector; an educational approach that questions practice instead of just accepting the status quo. Sometimes people think this is too complicated for working with children. Goldstein (2002, p. 179) maintains that in her teaching, children who came from families who were struggling to survive economically, culturally and socially could benefit from 'teaching practices that are rooted in critical theory [Anti-Bias] because these children already have an awareness that all is not just in the world'. Exploring the concepts involved is a starting point, and training on these issues as been shown to have an effect in adult thinking and practice with regards to children.

## How discrimination works

The section below looks at how stereotyping, prejudice, discrimination, racism, sexism, etc., operate in society. In the next chapter we will examine notions of 'acceptable language' and 'political correctness' along with the 'fear of saying the wrong thing'. Our experience in working with learners shows that the training has an impact. Research indicates that teacher training programmes with a high diversity, social justice and global awareness content show that students are more positively orientated to diversity (Clarke and Drudy, 2006).

### Social prejudices

> I have a lot to learn regarding my thoughts and stereotyping.
>
> (Learner, 2008)

To begin, we are going to take a snapshot of the effects of social prejudice on attitudinal development and behaviour. The matrix below provides an overview of the link between key diversity and equality concepts and how they build on each other. There are five stages in the process, each stage increasingly negative in terms of its impact on the perpetrator and the victim. Participation in these behaviours is fundamentally unhealthy for perpetrators, and still more damaging for the victim. The matrix from p. 30 begins with the definition of the term in question, then an example of how the concept works, and finally suggestions are given to counter the attitude or behaviour linked to ECEC practice. We invite you to take each term and analyse it with your peers, using the matrix for support in your discussion.

## How diversity concepts build on one another

Our behaviour toward others is always influenced by our prejudices and our social preference, hence the importance of raising awareness of attitudes which are prejudiced and the injustice of discrimination.

(Mac Gréil, 2011, p. 29)

### 2.6 Concept Stages

Stage One: Stereotyping
Stage Two: Prejudice
Stage Three: Discrimination
Stage Four: Racism or Sexism or Homophobia or Ableism, etc.
Stage Five: Extermination

(Adapted from Allport, 1954)

## Stage One

I try to get people who are ranting and raving to think about what they are saying, and I regularly ask them to think of the other person (a bit like walking in other's shoes). I have learnt that it is important to dismiss myths and engage in discussions in which people are being stereotyped.

(Practitioner, 2010)

### 2.7 Stage One: Stereotyping (Assumption)

An over-simplified **generalisation** about a particular group, 'race' or sex, based on widely-held assumptions, and that offers a **rigid view** that can be difficult to change (OMC, 2006).

## 2.8 Stage One: Stereotyping

### How it works

Anyone can stereotype.

**Assumptions** are made about a whole group. Stereotypes can be positive or negative. It is a form of generalised **labelling** and is often accompanied by a simplistic remark such as:

- 'Blondes are dumb'
- 'Men are better drivers'
- 'Irish are drunks'
- 'Travellers are dirty'
- 'Catholics are hypocrites'
- 'Blind people love dogs'
- 'Working class people don't care about education'
- 'Gays are all paedophiles'

*Remember* that all groups are made up of different individuals.

- You are not the same as the others in your group, and the same is true for everyone, regardless of what minority they belong to.
- We are all individuals, and we differ in our opinions, ways of being and living our lives.

### What you can do

Intervention is crucial at this stage. We all must be careful to counter sweeping statements about groups of people, comments along the lines of, 'Ah sure, they are all like that'. This is often the stage at which a challenge to this type of stereotypical comment leads to accusations of 'political correctness' to undermine the challenge, such as: 'Ah it was only a joke, you're too serious'.

People should be very careful about making generalised remarks about individuals or groups.

'Generalisations about negative behaviour and traits are often "given legs" by careless talk.'
(Mac Gréil, 2011, p. 26)

### What you can do in ECEC

'Be alert to what you don't know about a particular group.'
(Mac Naughton, Hughes, 2011, p. 198)

- Question your own awareness of assumptions and stereotypes. Ponder the inaccuracy of your own assumptions.
- Note the comments made by other staff members or parents. Counter these generalisations. (See Anti-Bias Goals for Adults, Chapter 3).
- Provide accurate information for children through images and discussion activities.
- Use accurate and appropriate language with children.
- Never show contempt for the background or culture of any family.
- Counter stereotypical gender roles for women and men with non-stereotypical images (See Family Wall, Chapter 9).

# Stage Two

## 2.9 Stage Two Concept Definition: Prejudice (Opinion)

Prejudice involves pre-judgment and the formation of opinion without regard for evidence or reason. Prejudice is a negative belief about or attitude towards a person who belongs to a group simply because she/he belongs to that group, and is therefore presumed to have the objectionable characteristics ascribed to the group.

(Platform Against Racism: Glossary of Terms)

## 2.10 Stage Two: Prejudice

### How it works

Anyone can be prejudiced. A prejudice is a formed opinion about a group, e.g.:

- I don't like Travellers because they are rough.
- I don't like Nigerians because they tell lies.
- I don't like rich people because they are snobs.

Prejudice has negative consequences for members of minority groups. It is fuelled by stereotypes.

Prejudice can lead to **scapegoating** in which the whole of a minority group can become the object of misplaced aggression, e.g. the scapegoating of Jews in times of economic and other crises (see Chapter 1).

### What you can do

Favourable contact between members of the dominant group and those of minority groups seem to be the most effective way of 'replacing' negative attitudes and prejudice with positive or tolerant dispositions.

(Mac Gréil, 2011, p. 513

New communities and Travellers are often criticised for sticking to their own. This is because they are comfortable with what is familiar to them, where they feel secure. Remaining with others of their own minority is sometimes necessary for support and self-determination (supporting one another and maintaining their self-esteem) and as a response to attempts at forced **assimilation** (see Chapter 3).

### What you can do in ECEC

- Openness to all is key to inclusion, respect and recognition: policies, curricula and open-day activities should be inclusive, with no individual or group left out.
- Openness does not mean treating all people the same; it is being aware of their needs and accommodating them.
- Understanding prejudice will support you in your observation of children. Listen to what they say.
- Always address children's negative statements regarding diversity: don't ignore them. Support both the child who makes the statement and child who is hurt by the statement.

# Stage Three

## 2.11 Stage Three Concept Definition: Discrimination (Behaviour)

Policies, practices or behaviours that lead to unfair treatment of individuals or groups on the basis of their identity or perceived identity. Discrimination can be intentional or unintentional and may be direct or indirect, personal or institutional.

## 2.12 Stage Three: Discrimination

### How it works

A selective **negative behaviour** towards members of a minority group because of their membership of such a group or category. Discrimination is *active*.

### Examples of conscious/ intentional behaviour:

- Traveller children are refused access to schools.
- Children are called derogatory names based on their colour, ethnicity, etc.
- Gay people jeered at and intimidated.

### Examples of unconscious/ unintentional behaviour:

- People with foreign names on their CVs are less likely to be called for a job interview in Ireland (ESRI, 2009).
- Sending all Travellers their hospital appointment through the post, thinking that everyone has access to regular postal deliveries. The problems with this are:
  - Post may not be delivered to the intended person and all post for a whole halting site may be delivered to one person from the site, so the final delivery can be delayed.
  - There may be more than one individual with the same name on that site.

### What you can do

The effects of doing nothing to counter the first two stages results in discrimination.

Equality Legislation in Ireland deals with discrimination on nine grounds.
- gender
- civil status
- family status
- age
- race
- religion
- disability
- sexual orientation
- membership of the Traveller community

Class is notably absent from Equality Legislation.
(See Equality Authority: www. equality.ie)

UN Conventions also support non-discrimination (see Chapter 2).

### What you can do in ECEC

Equality Legislation is there for the protection of individuals or groups who are targets of discrimination. Find out about Equality Legislation and UN Conventions and their relevance to your work. Ensure that the policies in your service reflect the Legislation and the Conventions.

**How it works** *contd.*

- There may be very poor literacy on a particular site.

Those who experience discrimination can feel unsafe and unsure in work situations and in situations that are unfamiliar to them. It may result in them trying to hide their identity or in their being 'silenced'. In other words, they fear expressing themselves openly lest there be negative repercussions because they are seen as different, or they may simply feel that they are unseen and unheard.

**What you can do** *contd.*

- The mission statement of your centre should reflect your ethos regarding diversity and equality.
- Settings should have anti-discrimination policies which are monitored and updated.
- Rules should include:
  - exclusion and name-calling are not acceptable
  - immediate intervention in alter-cations between children and working with both children to support each child and to resolve the situation.
- Assume that each individual or group has valuable ideas to offer. Be alert to the silencing of particular children. Actively seek out the ideas and views of minority parents as appropriate.
- See Diversity and Equality Guidelines for Childcare Providers for ideas and www.pavee.ie/edenn under 'Resources'.

## Stage Four

### 2.13 Stage Four Concept Definition: Racism (Belief)

Any theory which involves the claim that racial or ethnic groups are inherently superior or inferior, thus implying that some would be entitled to dominate or eliminate others, presumed to be inferior, or which bases value judgments on racial differentiation, has no scientific foundation and is contrary to the moral and ethical principles of humanity.

(UNESCO, 1978: Declaration on Race and Racial Prejudice)

Ethnocentrism and xenophobia are closely linked to racism. See Jargon Buster at bottom of matrix.

## 2.14 Stage Four: Racism

### How it works

Racism can manifest itself in an active denial of someone's human rights because of their ethnicity, race, culture or religion, or in an active, physical attack.

**Racism is about power**: one group perceives that they are better than another, and attempt to 'keep them in their place'.

### Examples of intentional racism

- Black people were denied use of the same facilities as whites in the US and South Africa.
- When a Traveller family attempted to move into a local authority house, the neighbours glued shut the front door lock and an intimidating group with placards that read 'Travellers out' appeared (Ireland, 2008).
- African women are often targets of racial abuse in Dublin city centre:

  'Mutale's husband recounts: Last year Mutale was subjected to horrible abuse from a woman she was trying to help in Henry Street' (Dublin, 2008).

  'Mutale spotted that the woman's purse was hanging out of her bag. She alerted the woman.

  Instead of thanking Mutale said to her: 'Mind your business, you black bitch, and fuck off to your own country.' Mutale's husband is always concerned when she is in the inner city and keeps in close contact.
  (www.guardian.co.uk/world/2008/may/04
  /ireland.immigration)

### Unintentional racial prejudice

When a black woman had her baby in an Irish hospital, the nurse congratulating her said, 'Ah there, she looks just like a little monkey!' (Ireland, 2009)

### What you can do

The state must intervene to prevent racism. This usually means mean providing Equality Legislation covering hate crimes and the ratification of UN Conventions. However, failure to implement and monitor legislation is an abdication of the state's duty to protect human rights and its citizens. The laws must work effectively and racist incidents should be reported. Unfortunately, sometimes a lack of action on the part of the state leads to underreporting.

Recognition and prevention of racism is essential to tackling this highly destructive behaviour.

### What you can do in ECEC

- If you are racially prejudiced against another ethnic group it will inevitably affect the way you relate to and deal with individuals from that group, both personally and in the context of any situation, including ECEC.
- Racism affects all children, and therefore having effective policies that are monitored is essential for all ECEC settings.
- If possible, staff should be representative of the children attending the setting. Regardless of the mix in the setting it is good to have staff from a variety of backgrounds.
- 'Equality-proof' your policies and curriculum. (See Jargon Buster p. 38.)
- Parents from all backgrounds need to be involved in consultations and decision-making as appropriate.
- Resources should be representative of all children in setting.
- Positive images of Ireland as a multi-cultural society should be displayed at the child's level and discussed.

**How it works** *contd.*

**Institutional racism** is in general the result of biased decision-making. Decisions are made by those in power without being conscious of the needs and rights of those in the minority. Institutional racism can be intentional and unintentional.

**Intentional examples** include apartheid in South Africa, slavery in the US and the treatment of Irish in Britain.

**Unintentional examples:**

Traveller children are taken out of Irish class for resource teaching, the assumption being that Traveller children won't need Irish as they won't become teachers or go to university.

**What you can do** *contd.*

- Even if all the children in the classroom are white, racism in society is still an issue.
- Children from all communities learn prejudicial ideas and discriminate, so it is vital to address these issues, even if the children have no direct contact with minority groups.
- Remembering to check your own assumptions in any situation.
- Recognise that there are more ways to raise a child than the one with which you are most familiar.

Racism makes and keeps peoples different, separate and unequal.

(Lentin and Mac Veigh, 2002).

## 2.15 Stage Four Concept Definition: Sexism (Belief)

A superior attitude, action or institutional practice that oppresses or undermines people because of their gender.

(OMC, 2006, p. 47)

## 2.16 Stage Four: Sexism

**How it works**

**Examples of intentional sexism**

- Making derogatory comments about ability based on gender.
- The man in a heterosexual relationship controlling the money in the home.
- Violence against women so that they can be 'kept in their place'.

**Unintentional sexism**

Few would admit openly to being sexist, but many people may still make assumptions based on gender, such as providing certain kinds of activities (sport, creative, athletic, etc.) for one gender, and not for another.

**What you can do**

- Assume that difference between people is normal.
- Be alert to any silencing or exclusion or of behaviour that hurts, harms or offends people.

**What you can do in ECEC**

- Ensure policies are gender-proofed.
- Give girls and boys the same opportunities to play with all equipment.
- Images should promote non-stereotypical male and female roles.
- Take note of and discuss with staff how you interact with boys and girls, what type of play is provided for all children. Does it differ between the sexes?

## Stage Four: Concept Definition: Homophobia (Belief)

A negative attitude towards people deemed to be homosexual; an irrational fear of or aversion to homosexuals; prejudice that can result in discrimination against LGBT people.

## 2.18 Stage Four: Homophobia

**How it works**
**Intentional homophobia**
Gay-bashing: physical attacks on LGBT people.
**Examples**
- Lesbian couple intimidated into leaving their home by local youths throwing rocks through their window and eggs at them as they left the house.
- During the Holocaust, LGBT people were identified in the concentration camps by a pink triangle.
- No parenting rights for non-biological lesbian or gay parents in Ireland.

**Unintentional homophobia**
LGBT people being treated as if they were heterosexual in a medical or counselling situation, in which questions asked presuppose heterosexuality, i.e. 'are you on birth control?'

**What you can do**
- Assume that difference between people is normal.
- Be alert to any 'silencing' or exclusion or of behaviour that hurts, harms or offends people.
- Ensure you policies are equality proofed.
- Ensure all families are depicted in the setting.
- Discuss different types of families in the setting.
- Support your work with the Family Wall.

## Stage Five: Concept Definition: Extermination

**Extermination** is killing, but usually in the context of racial, ethnic or religious grounds. Ethnic cleansing and genocide are now recognised as crimes against humanity, and have occurred throughout history.

## 2.19 Stage Five: Extermination

### How it works
### Examples:

- USA: Native Americans
- Germany: Jews, Gypsies and LGBT people were all targets of the Holocaust.
- Balkan states: Bosnian War
- Iraq: Kurds
- Ireland: Cromwellian Act of settlement in 1654: expulsion of Irish from the land.
- Ireland: Although contested, some commentators have likened the Irish Famine to genocide.

Hate Crime Legislation should be implemented and monitored by the state.

(Sources: Lane, 2008; Mac Gréil, 2011; Murray, Cooke and O'Doherty, 2004; Mac Naughton and Hughes, 2011)

There is no compromise when people are being attacked physically for who they are. The legitimacy of the State itself is at stake if it allows physical attacks on minorities. The sad fact is that physical attack on a minority member and on their domestic property ... is quite universal where dominant–minority relations are not equitably resolved.

(Mac Gréil, 2011, p. 30)

### What you can do

When stage five is reached, all the above interventions have failed.

After the the Holocaust in 1939–1945, the world believed that no such atrocity could occur again in civilised society. However in 1992–1995, the Balkan states engaged in a war of expulsion and genocide, among many other examples.

**N.B.:** remember that there are only four prior stages to this process.

Looking at terms is challenging! There are lots of personal views to be argued out!

(Practitioner/Learner, 2010)

## 2.20 Jargon Buster: Ethnocentrism and Xenophobia

**Ethnocentrism:** The belief or conviction that one nationality, culture or way of life is superior to all others. 'Ethnic prejudices consist of rigid, negative, hostile attitudes towards people who are defined as members of groups or categories that are perceived to differ from one's own group or category in matters of culture and nationality. It is basically a belief of the superiority of the members of one's own ethnic groups or categories' (Mac Gréil, 1977, p. 263).

**Xenophobia:** Describes an extreme feeling of fear or hostility towards people perceived as outsiders, expressed through attitudes, views or action in response to individual or groups from a different national, ethnic, religious or cultural backgrounds.

## 2.21 Jargon Buster: Equality-proofing

Screening of policies, procedures, information and materials as well as the physical environment and curriculum activities to ensure that every child can participate on equal terms, eliminating bias, stereotyping and discrimination, and giving priority to equality considerations.

Equality-proofing involves incorporating an equality perspective in all aspects of policy development (NESF, 1996). The ultimate objective and potential of equality-proofing is to promote the development of a more equal society. Equality-proofing is about recognising diversity and acting to ensure fair treatment and non discrimination. It is about providing appropriate services to workers and end users. It is about meeting real needs (CWU, 2008).

## Oppression and internalised oppression

People who experience oppression (stereotyping, prejudice, discrimination, etc.) because of their gender, ability, sexuality, marital status, ethnicity, etc.) can believe that the negative messages that they are receiving are true. This is called *internalised oppression* and it is a learned behaviour that can be formed very early with ideas like: Travellers are useless in school, Black people are untrustworthy, poor children are not academic, etc. Internalised oppression leads to mixed feelings about who you are and can curtail your ability to form a strong sense of your own identity (Derman-Sparks and Olsen Edwards 2010). It can mean that you believe the stereotypes about yourself or your community, or that you adopt the majority culture's standards, or believe that those in the majority are superior. This internalisation can lead to underachievement and low self-esteem. If the negative attitudes of the dominant/majority group were to improve, so too would the services towards minority groups and, as a consequence, minorities experiencing oppression would respond to those positive attitudes. (Mac Gréil, 2011).

Some time ago I (Colette Murray) had the following experience: a Traveller woman had completed her ECEC training and began her work within a segregated pre-school for Travellers. At that time there were no other Travellers qualified as ECEC workers. The Traveller parents were a bit unsure of this new situation – a Traveller working as a teacher in pre-school? One parent came to the woman's co-worker and asked that her child only work with her, and she explicitly asked that her child not work with the new Traveller ECEC worker. This encounter is an example of internalised oppression, for the parent didn't believe that a Traveller was capable of working as a professional with the children. She felt her child could only benefit from working with an 'educated' settled person. The situation resolved itself and the Traveller parents soon realised that their children we well cared for by their fellow Traveller. Having Traveller workers or other minority workers working with minority children enables them to see positive role models from their community and helps break down the cycle of internalised oppression.

## 2.22 Anti-discrimination case

Anhalt, 37, who grew up in Gdansk, Poland, the birthplace of the Solidarity movement, revealed that he is dealing with ten cases connected to Irish employers banning the use of Polish at work. 'I have cases lodged with the Irish Equality Authority of workers being penalised or threatened with the sack simply because they were speaking Polish in the work canteen,' he says (http://www.guardian.co.uk/world/2008/may/04/ireland.immigration).

A similar situation was reported by a learner in an early childhood setting in 2009.

- Why do you think the Polish men were banned from speaking Polish?
- What do you think the problem is? How is the problem connected to the concepts you have been studying?
- What would you do in this situation?

### Internalised privilege

We touched on internalised privilege before. Sometimes we are not aware of the position we hold in society and how it gives us an advantage, be it socially, economically, culturally or politically. This can lead to some people thinking that everyone is in the same position as them, and that effort is all that is required to achieve in life. They may not recognise that there is inequality of access, participation and outcome for people less privileged than they in society. For example, in terms of participation, it is worth considering that Travellers might feel uncomfortable in a group of settled people when they go to school or college. The consequence of not feeling a sense of belonging may result in Travellers leaving education.

## Racism, discrimination and ethnocentrism affects many people

As we have already seen, some white people experience hostility, prejudice and discrimination in some of the same ways that people of other ethnicities do, including Jewish people, Travellers and people who have migrated here from recent accession countries to the EU like Poland and Romania. 'The basic premise of unjustifiable differential treatment on grounds of who you are is the same for all forms of racism, and all racism must be taken seriously' (Jane Lane, 2008, p. 53). There are usually historical reasons for hostility towards different groups; in Ireland, for example, our history with the UK continues to influence our hostility towards the English.

> Also of course the fact of our own history, what one was taught and what one read in school was dinned into one's head the catastrophic story of what had happened to our country.
>
> (O'Brien p. 39 in Quinn, *The Curious Mind*, 2009)

One would be forgiven for thinking that our 'catastrophic' history would lead us to be more open, positive and empathetic to newcomers. It has in fact provided for our generosity in the developing world and in particular times of crisis around the globe, as with the tsunami in Indonesia and the nuclear disaster in Chernobyl. We are very generous when it comes to supporting good causes abroad, but on our doorstep, it is somehow different. Just because a country or a group has experienced or experience oppression doesn't mean we will behave emphatically to others. In fact it can allow us to reproduce the oppression we have learned. Following their introduction to Irish history, Irish children often have very negative feelings about the English. We have to find another way of deconstructing our past, expressing our history and breaking a cycle of hatred. In recent years returned Irish have resettled in areas of the country they left because of unemployment. Their children have English accents and as a consequence they have been vilified and ostracised by their peers (Discussions with various practitioners, teachers and parents 2007/2009). This is despite the children having Irish heritage.

## Homophobia

> I can't remember much about the years of physical and emotional abuse my brother Eamon suffered. I was very small. The thing I do remember though, quite literally, his blood on his school shirt when he came home in the afternoon. The beatings and taunting were very frequent for him and a constant part of his school years. I didn't understand at that time the concept of 'difference'. Back then, as now, he was just my big brother.
>
> (Colin Farrell, April 2010, press release from www.belongto.org)

In Ireland, many people fear being fired from teaching positions because of their sexuality. If members of the LGBT community are teaching in a Catholic school, this can be particularly problematic. The lack of recognition of different sexual orientations in school reflects a wider social isolation and rejection of those who are not heterosexual (Moane, 1995). Children are also growing up in a school system that doesn't openly recognise the historical contribution of LGBT people to Irish society. At the same time, Mac Gréil (2011) in his study *Pluralism and Diversity in Ireland* found that between 1998 and 2008, the greatest positive change in Irish attitudes to difference has come in the category 'Gay People' (p. 535). This is a welcome development, but there remains much to be done which also requires leadership from our public representatives. In the recent presidential debate one candidate suggested that he accepted civil partnership, but that wasn't sure about adoption by gay couples. He said he didn't know enough about it, or whether having gay parents would be damaging to the child.

In a study carried out by Lodge, Gowran and O'Shea (2008) in post-primary schools, homophobic bullying and name-calling were major concerns. The schools were able to give detailed examples of targeted incidents, both verbal and physical, on lesbian and gay students or those perceived to be LGBT. Students also identified the general use of the term 'gay' as an insult. The Gay and Lesbian Equality Network (GLEN) has developed guidelines for including lesbian, gay and bisexual students in school policies (see www.glen.ie). This is a step in the right direction in addressing homophobia in schools and society. Recognition of families with same-sex parents can begin in ECEC.

## Changing attitudes

A prejudice exposed is a prejudice undermined, and Christa Preissing (2004) explains that the term 'tolerance' always implies a hierarchy and as existing hierarchies cannot be denied, they should be recognised explicitly. She outlines how to be without prejudice is an important goal, but that in reality it is impossible to achieve. 'To become conscious of prejudice is a feasible and exciting way forward, in which everybody may discover more about themselves and their fellow travellers,' (p. 78) *Therefore, to be 'prejudice-aware' means that you go through a process of becoming aware which moves beyond tolerance and assumes a participatory engagement in moving towards changing attitudes and looking at issues from a different and perhaps more open perspective.*

Mac Gréil (2011) also emphasises that it is impossible to remove negative attitudes once they exist without removing the focus of that attitude (your own negative experience). All we can do is to replace our attitudes. He explains that if a person has negative attitudes towards Travellers, it is impossible to eradicate the attitude completely as if the Traveller no longer existed for that person, but rather, 'the only way to change the situation is to replace the negative attitude with a positive one or one less negative'

(Mac Gréil, 2011, p. 40). In other words, an attitudinal vacuum is impossible to correct as long as the focus remains relevant to the person.

Mac Gréil (2011) discusses the need for communities to interact and go beyond the boundaries between them to get to know one another. Similarly, Cantle sited in Gaine (2005) suggests that meaningful contact between communities is necessary to avoid ignorance growing into suspicion, fear or worse.

Breaking down barriers is paramount to building a socially just society, and stretching your knowledge and understanding of diversity issues as is relevant to families will support your engagement with children and their parents. Your ability to observe children in an ECEC setting will be enhanced by your knowledge of words and concepts discussed here and the diversity and equality lens you look through. It will help to shift possible assumptions and support you in planning an inclusive setting for all children.

## 2.23 Internalised oppression made visible

We have one black woman on our staff and she came to me concerning child ratios in her room. She has always refused to be left alone with the children even if she is within her ratio while tea breaks are going on. Staff felt that she was only causing trouble and couldn't see why she wouldn't stay on her own for 15 minutes. We knew it was OK for one staff to stay according to Health Board regulations but she said she is not comfortable doing this. When I pressed her, she said it was because she was a black woman and if any children said anything negative about her, who would believe her? She said she had to cover her own back because she is a black woman and needed to have protection against any accusations. This took a lot out of her to say openly. I felt sad and angry to think she was feeling this way and she had never said anything. The black woman knew I was doing this course and I'm sure she felt that because of it she could come talk to me. I felt as if a huge wall has come down for her and I said if I could help in any way I would.

I have brought it up with the manager and the manager said she fully understands where she is coming from. The girl has since told me the manager has come and apologised to her for not seeing the problem sooner.

(Extract from Learner Journal, 2009)

- What is happening for the black woman in this situation?
- What has the black woman internalised?
- The manager said she fully understood. What do you think she understood?
- Do you think the word 'problem' is relevant to this situation?
- Do you think that the manager should have apologised for not seeing the 'problem'?
- How would you address this situation if it were revealed to you?

## 2.24 Discuss

- Have you heard friends, family, teachers stereotype people?
- Give examples and discuss the implications for the groups involved.
- Have you witnessed instances of discrimination, i.e. comments, hurtful remarks, the exclusion of individuals or groups in shops or services, media coverage? Discuss the various scenarios you identify with your peers.

## 2.25 How '–isms' work

Prevailing biases deny people's access to equality. This applies equally to any form of diversity where people experience discrimination based on their perceived difference, 'undesirability' or 'abnormal' status. On the website we outline how racism works in more detail – but *the word 'racism' can equally be replaced with sexism, ableism, homophobia, etc.*

# Summary

This chapter builds your knowledge base of diversity and equality concepts. Understanding and analysing these complex concepts will support and increase your ability to recognise stereotyping, prejudice, racism and other forms of discrimination at societal level and in your work with children and families. Recognising that children are not disconnected from the broader society, but begin to notice difference and form opinions about difference at an early age will help you to engage social justice ideas in ECEC. The voices in this chapter show how understanding these concepts help us to recognise and work with diversity issues with young children and in our broader personal relationships. The matrix gives a clear overview of how these concepts work in society and how you can begin to tackle them in ECEC. Continued discussion and exploration of these concepts is necessary for clarity and engagement with diversity and equality issues. Coming to terms with the affects of injustice and inequality is also tackled with an emphasis on the challenge of addressing attitudinal change. Breaking down barriers is vital to transforming our society, and we have a role to play in ECEC.

## CHAPTER 3

# Terminology: Getting it right as language evolves and changes

No one should be lambasted for getting language wrong, particularly if there is no intent. On the other hand there is increasingly less excuse for using inappropriate language no matter what the circumstances.

(Philip Watt, 2006)

## Overview

In Chapter 2 we explored our understanding of diversity and equality concepts, and traced how stereotypes, prejudice, discrimination and racism, sexism, etc., build on one another with damaging results for children, families and communities. In this chapter we build on the concepts by addressing the use of **identity terminology**; acceptable and unacceptable terms. People are often fearful of using the 'incorrect' term, and as a consequence say nothing. In this chapter, we attempt to put you at ease with key diversity terms. We also challenge the use of derogatory words including the telling of inappropriate jokes, which can enhance negative stereotyping and prejudice. Finally, we ask you to connect your position on such issues with your work with children.

### After reading this chapter you should be able to

▸ use diversity terminology and recognise negative or inappropriate diversity terms.
▸ use key terms regarding social diversity while understanding that terminology is continually changing.
▸ explain the importance of knowing and understanding terms associated with diversity and equality work.
▸ question and discuss some of the stubborn myths around use of language regarding diversity.
▸ refer to specific language and concepts to support your discussion on diversity and equality issues respectfully.
▸ reflect critically on the work you do with children and parents.

# Introduction: Acceptable language, myths and political correctness

Sometimes people are nervous about using diversity terms to describe others for fear of 'getting it wrong'. ECEC practitioners and students are all learning about this area, we all make mistakes and that is OK. Making the effort is what counts. Just as it is important to understand diversity concepts and how they build on each other, it is important to understand diversity-related language in order to engage effectively in discussion on these issues with colleagues and families. Hence we need to take the time – preferably together – to discuss the terminology, and in doing so make the unfamiliar familiar. Misunderstandings can lead to inaccuracy and even stereotyping of individuals or groups. In saying all that, just to make it more confusing, terminology changes over time. A given term can shift from being harmless to being insulting, or it can change to offer a more positive outlook on a challenge, e.g. using 'English as an additional language' instead of 'English as a second language'.

Language is not static, but many basic terms such as 'racism' are defined by reputable EU organisations and NGOs. Using their definition is usually the best way to ensure you are as accurate and up to date as possible.

It goes without saying that people would rather be described in terms that they find acceptable. Sometimes, people use pejorative language that they do not deem offensive to a group. When challenged they suggest that 'people are being too sensitive or PC' (politically correct). It might be no harm to reflect on this and put yourself in the position of a minority here (i.e., a gay person, person with a disability, black person, Traveller, etc.) if you are not from a minority yourself.

## 3.1 Learning point

The use of the terms 'majority' and 'minority' is not necessarily a reflection of numerical strength. There are more women than men, for instance, but women had and to a great extent still have minority status in relation to institutions of power (Máirín Kenny, 2010, p. 34).

To turn the circumstances around; put the shoe on the other foot, so to speak, and consider what it might feel like to be at the receiving end of negative name-calling or 'slagging' (as used in the Irish context for 'teasing'). Maybe you have been labelled because of your hair colour, wearing glasses or for being overweight. Language can be used to insult and hurt, but when challenged for using hurtful or pejorative language, we often excuse our actions by saying it was 'only slagging', which seems to be a way of letting us off the hook and putting the blame for being 'over-sensitive' on the person experiencing the hurt.

Having a term imposed on you or your group is different than choosing how you identify yourself. Who coined the term and imposed it is also significant, e.g. How the word 'black' is used by a South African will have different connotations to its use by people in Ireland. In Ireland you might call your friend a Paddy, but if it was used by an English person it would have much more negative connotations stemming from the history of the word and how it was used in England. Words are often about constructing important social meanings including hierarchies.

| | |
|---|---|
| **Irish in Britain:** | Irish have had the name 'Paddy' imposed upon them when they declare themselves to be or are identified (generally by accent) as Irish in Britain. This term is not acceptable to most Irish people because of its history and how it was used, though it may be used among Irish people. |
| **'Black' in South Africa:** | The term 'black' in South Africa has connotations with the apartheid era that it does not, for example, in Ireland. |
| **Traveller:** | Preferred term of the Traveller community. Travellers for many years were called 'itinerant' a name imposed on Travellers by the state. |

How words are used and who they are used by is what counts. Lane (2008) is direct about this in her excellent book *Young Children and Racial Justice*, in which she says 'it is always important to try to use terms that acknowledge, value and respect people and everyone should be explicit about wanting to do this'. Some people who are not wholeheartedly concerned about such matters often retort to people trying to be respectful that they are just victims of political correctness gone crazy.

## Slagging and jokes

I know you don't like sexist jokes, but this is a really funny one.

Humour is very important for all of us, but particular types of jokes can be seen as demeaning to many individuals or groups, and are unacceptable to many. What constitutes funny differs from person to person, and some people think you are being politically correct or humourless if you object to some types of jokes.

Humour is a very complicated area, but basically, the context and the purpose of the joke is relevant to its appropriateness. In the end, only the person or people involved know how the joke affects them, but it is a question of awareness, and the recognition and respect of others. Consider this: would you tell a joke if you knew a member of the group it referred to were present? Does that mean it is alright to tell it?

What I am really pleased about is that people no longer tell hurtful jokes around me. For a long time I stayed silent where racist, sexist, etc., jokes were being told. I usually pretended to laugh, but I find this kind of humour offensive. The Anti-bias Goal 4: Standing up for yourself and others really influenced me and made me think about what I was doing. So I asked people to stop telling these jokes and to stop sending me offensive email, and it has worked! I am delighted with myself. I may not be able to change their views but I can protect myself from hearing them. I do not try to force my opinion down their throats but I will give my opinion where appropriate even if it goes against the general consensus.

(Practitioner and Trainer, 2010)

Humour is important, but do we want it to be at the expense of others?

## Labelling

Language can be 'co-opted to promote a hierarchy of difference and it can also diminish the human complexity and status of a given group'.

Kenny (2010, p. 35) outlines a number of things to be aware of:

▸ Avoid lumping people together under homogenising labels: the old, the poor, the disabled, the blacks…

▸ Gender language: As collective terms, use 'humankind' or 'people' instead of 'mankind' or 'man'. when referring to a person of unspecified gender, alternate between 'he' or 'she' and 'her' 'him', or use 'she/he', or 's/he'. Alternatively, use the plural. Avoid the exclusive use of 'he' and 'him'.

▸ Nationalities, for example 'Nigerian' or 'Bosnian', do not reflect an often marked ethnic diversity within those nations. Irish society is astonishingly simple in terms of its ethnic fabric compared to many immigrants' countries of origin.

In a recent discussion of terms with students from around Ireland, they proceeded to list the names they were called since they came to study in Dublin, including 'bogger' and 'culchie'. The use of such language aims to create dividing lines, but in a way that is hierarchical (involving some being better or lesser than others) rather than diversity-based.

Kenny (2010, p. 9) maintains that 'the us/them language contributes to maintaining and even building the boundary walls that makes attention to terminology so necessary'.

---

### 3.3 Consider this

We carried out a project in which pictures of people engaged in non-traditional roles were sourced and displayed. Captions were included giving gender-neutral job titles, e.g. fire fighter, postal worker, Garda, sports person, home-maker. A week later, one of the older children came in to the centre and said that she had been in trouble in school. She had told her teacher that she shouldn't say 'mankind'. When the teacher asked her what she meant, the child said 'mankind doesn't sound like it includes, so you should use "people kind" or something like that'. The teacher told the child to sit down and not to be so silly.

I think adults need to be brave enough to accept challenges from children and engage in constructive discussions with them. These children should be encouraged in their endeavours.

(Practitioner and Trainer, 2010)

---

### Identity terms

> I think it is wrong to say you can't talk about the word black. I think it's wrong because you're ignoring me. If you can't say I am black, what are you saying about ME? It is better to raise differences than sweep them under the carpet. (Black practitioner, and a black learner in training made a similar comment which included 'I'm proud to be black' in video celebrating diversity, Team Video Productions, no date.)

Identity terms change and shift in time for many reasons. Sometimes it is because a term gradually becomes offensive or a term of abuse to a certain group. In some cases, derogatory terms have been reclaimed by groups or individuals in a given group, and this can cause confusion, e.g. the use of the word 'nigger' by black rap artists. A derogatory term may be used internally by the group to which it refers, but its use by others would not be acceptable, e.g. Irish people calling each other 'Paddy'. Offensive terms that are intended to hurt are unacceptable and include 'nigger', 'knacker', 'paki', 'retard' and 'gay', the latter depending on how it is used; these are explored on p. 54. Sometimes a nickname can have a upsetting effect on individuals especially if given and not accepted by the individual.

Lack of certainty about terms can lead people to avoid using any term for fear of being rude or offensive. The best route is to ask people what they use or prefer. If you are unsure, ask, as people are often happy to be asked their view. Having some knowledge base is also useful (see References). The terms discussed below will give you some relevant information, but you need to maintain an awareness of the continually shifting nature of diversity-related language. Individual people from within the same minority group may differ in their knowledge, understandings and preference. Building your knowledge base and becoming confident about the issue will support your practice.

> It is not about 'being all the same underneath the skin. While it is the same physically and physiologically, it is not the same experientially.... So notions of being black or white being only skin deep are untrue – they are the accumulation of what racism means at a personal level and how they affect feelings.
>
> (Lane, p. 77)

### Black:

A term chosen by people from or descended of people from Africa to describe and themselves. The term 'Black' is not just a colour in terms of race; it is a political term and it is a signifier of history (Gaine, 2005). It is a reclaimed word that once had negative connotations. Many Black people see the word Black as unifying, one which signifies their survival of oppression, and particularly their oppression and slavery in the US Black children living in Ireland sometime ask their parents are they 'black or brown'. Many Black parents explain to their children that it isn't about the lightness of skin, it is a unifying recognition of their collective group.

Many practitioners/educators say 'I see all the children as individuals and I treat them all the same'.

This is usually coming from a well-meaning positions but its effect can result the invisibility of that child's identity in the setting. This is called being 'colour blind', it also applied to other diversities i.e. 'Traveller blind', 'gender blind'. It is not useful to deny what is very important to individuals and their group or community background.

### Asian:

A term used to describe people from or descended of people from Asia, be it East Asia (China, Japan, Korea, etc.), South Asia (India, Pakistan, Sri Lanka, etc.) or Southeast Asia (Vietnam, Laos, Malaysia, etc.). South Asians are often incorrectly referred to as 'black'. In Ireland, the use of the term 'Asian' is mainly to describe those from the Indian sub-continent (Gaine, 2005).

*People of colour:*

A phrase used in the US to refer to non-white or mixed heritage people. It encompasses all those who may experience discrimination and racism on the basis of skin colour. This term is not much used in the UK or Ireland, but it has the advantage of including the Chinese and Vietnamese, for example.

*Coloured:*

An outdated term that should be avoided as it is generally viewed as offensive to many Black people. The terms Black or Mixed Heritage, where appropriate, are preferred. Sometimes people use this term as they feel it might be rude to use Black.

*Black Irish:*

A Black person who was born in Ireland and/or has Irish citizenship.

Black children growing up in Ireland with Irish citizenship may consider themselves to be black Irish of Nigerian or Somali decent, for example. Black children with an Irish parent and Nigerian parent may consider themselves to be simply Black Irish. This is personal choice. It is better not to assume that a Black child is either African or Black Irish, as they may not have any connection with a particular country in Africa, or they may be newly arrived in Ireland.

- Coming from Dublin where I would have been practically the only Black chick, with all the insecurities that comes with that.... to arrive in a place (New York) where not only did I not stand out, but I actually looked completely average – it was obviously really different.
- Have you been unhappy in Ireland?
- Not unhappy, just...well, imagine if you grew up in Africa – you spoke like a local, you acted like a local, but you were always a white guy with red hair and freckles. Wouldn't it be nice to go somewhere where you looked the same as other people? It was nice to explore that other part and have that kind of connection with people.'

Interview with Laura Izibor, R&B singer-songwriter currently living in New York, talking about growing up black in Dublin with Eoin Butler:
(*Irish Times Magazine,* 16 May 2009)

*Asian Irish:*

An Asian person who was born in Ireland and/or has Irish citizenship. Asian Irish children may experience issues relating to identity similar to those of Black Irish children.

## Traveller:

In the Equal Status legislation (See Chapter 2) the Traveller community as is defined as

> The community of people that are commonly called Travellers and who are identified (both by themselves and others) as people with a shared history, culture and traditions including historically a nomadic way of life in the island of Ireland.

'Pavee' means Traveller in Travellers' language, Cant (or Gammon). Travellers have had names superimposed on them by the state and by non-travellers including tinker, gypsy and itinerant. Some of these have been used by Travellers themselves, particularly 'tinker', a term associated with the trade of making pots, buckets, etc. Travellers have also suffered from their association with horses by being called the pejorative word 'knacker', which causes much hurt for the Traveller community and in particular for Traveller children within the school system and in broader society.

The term 'settled Traveller' has come into use in more recent years as Traveller nomadism has been curtailed through legislation. This term is problematic, because Travellers remain Travellers even if they are not nomadic, as they maintain their values and beliefs, which are the determinants of culture. To turn it on its head, if settled people moved into a caravan, would they become Travellers? No, as they would not be a part of Traveller culture, they would simply be settled people living in a caravan. Conversely, Travellers living in a house are just that, and not 'settled Travellers', a term that offends many Travellers.

## Migrant:

People migrate for many reasons: some to escape persecution, some to make a better life, some for work, some for adventure. In Chapter 1 we opened with some negative comments made regarding perceptions of new communities living in Ireland, and we saw that if misinformed, we can make assumptions about a whole group of people. This can lead to prejudice, discrimination and much worse. The terms below address the status of asylum seekers, refugees and immigrants.

> I was shocked to learn that not everyone knows or understands the differences between asylum seeker and refugee. Having said that what I did learn tonight was that I felt more empathy for asylum seekers and refugees than I did before tonight.
>
> (Learner on D&E training, 2009)

During training programmes it never ceases to amaze me that virtually no one knows the difference between the terms 'asylum seeker' and 'refugee'. The terms are often used together in a sentence or interchangeably in a conversation. It is startling because the assumptions connected to the terms are generally negative, i.e. people 'sponging' off of the welfare system, somehow getting more than Irish people or lying and cheating to get into the country (see the *Diversity and Equality* page on www.gillmacmillan.ie).

### Refugee:

An immigrant, who, on the basis of personal circumstances including fear of persecution, has attained the legal status refugee as stipulated in the 1951 Geneva Convention. A refugee has many of the same rights as an Irish citizen; they can work, study, travel into and out of Ireland, etc. Refugees are in the country legally.

### Asylum Seeker:

An immigrant who has applied for refugee status on the grounds that they fear persecution in their country of origin or because their life and liberty is threatened by armed conflict or violence. Asylum seeker status is temporary while a claim for refugee status is put through a very strict process. Asylum seekers are in the country legally.

An **asylum seeker** (often fleeing persecution or some may be economic migrants: people seeking a better life for themselves and their families) has to go through a very strict regimen to attain refugee status. They are not illegal but they have limited rights and have very limited resources. Their accommodation and food is provided including €19.10 per adult and €9.60 per child disposable income per week. Chris Gaine (2005, p. 97) suggests that the 'phrase "people seeking asylum" may serve to remind us that these are after all people like us'.

### Immigrant:

A person who enters and lives in a country other than their country of origin on a temporary or long-term basis.

### Economic migrant:

A person who voluntarily leaves his or her habitual place of residence in order to take up a job or seek a better standard of living in another country. Many Irish have migrated to other countries like Australia, the US or the UK as economic migrants.

### Illegal immigrant:

The Illegal Immigrants (Trafficking) Act, 2000, defines a person who enters, seeks to enter or has entered the State unlawfully as an 'illegal immigrant'. The Immigrant Council of Ireland believes that no person is 'illegal', and thus prefers the term 'irregular' or 'undocumented' to refer to this category of immigrant (ICI, 2005).

*Irregular Immigrant:*

A person who enters a country without the correct legal documents, technically speaking, enters illegally. S/he may be in possession of false identification or no documentation at all. A person is also an irregular immigrant if s/he resides in a country without formal permission. It is common for people seeking asylum to travel with false or no documentation. This is because they are frequently not in a position to seek the necessary documents from their own government or an embassy. Article 31 of the Refugee Convention [Geneva Convention relating to the Status of Refugees, 1951] acknowledges this difficulty and obliges states not to impose penalties on asylum seekers who arrive illegally in their state (ICI, 2005).

## 3.4 Learning point

There is no such thing as a 'non-national'. We all have a nationality. 'Foreign national' is the preferred term for people who aren't from Ireland, but remember that you can't tell what passport someone holds just by looking at them.

## 3.5 Want to know more?

Visit www.immigrantcouncil.ie.

*LGBT:*

LGBT (or GLBT) is a term used since the 1990s as a self-designation by what was formerly known as the 'gay community'. It refers collectively to 'lesbian, gay, bisexual, and transgender' people. The term LGBT is intended to emphasize a diversity of 'sexuality- and gender-identity-based cultures' and is sometimes used to refer to anyone who is non-heterosexual instead of exclusively to people who are homosexual, bisexual, or transgender (See www.glen.ie).

*Disability*

Within the Disability community some people prefer to use the phrase 'people with disabilities', and some prefer the phrase 'disabled people'. This is to do with how people wish to be defined, and whether they want to be defined by their ability/disability or as an individual first. People tend to have a strong individual preference: some are comfortable to use the two terms interchangeably, while others strongly prefer one over the other. If you are unsure, ask the individual or parents for guidance.

## Unacceptable terms

It would be my preference not to put most of the following words on paper. Unfortunately, it is continually necessary to address these terms to remind people of the distress they can cause. To be fair, some people find it challenging to unravel which words are offensive and which are not, which can cause frustration and resentment. The aim of this section is to support understanding of what terms are accurate *at this time*. Take the time to discuss the use of these words, because the goal is not to ban words, but to choose words that are not offensive to people. It is to this end that they are discussed below.

### *Nigger:*

Nigger is a slur against black people. The word originated as a term used in a neutral context to refer to black people, as a variation of the Spanish/Portuguese noun *negro*, a descendant of the Latin adjective *niger*, meaning the colour black. Black people find this word offensive and its use is unacceptable other than by part of the black community who have reclaimed it for use amongst Black people. It might seem strange to even talk about this word, 'the N word' as it is often referred to, because of the recognised offence it causes to the black community. This word is an example of the complexity of language and its association with social meaning in particular social contexts. An example of this is the relatively recent reclaimed use of 'nigger' by black rap musicians to remove the power and the put-down associated with the word. White people don't always understand the relevance of this, and some Black people are concerned that this lack of understanding will give licence to white people to use the word inappropriately. Overall, Black people find this word offensive and its use unacceptable.

---

### 3.6 'Does Black mean nothing to some people'?

Toyosi Shitta Bey (15), from Mount Eustace in Tyrrellstown, Dublin, originally from Nigeria, was fatally stabbed in the heart as he walked through his estate towards home with a group of friends in 2010. His mother said, 'They killed my son because he was Black. God has taken him from me but in my dreams I can see my son. My life is finished in Ireland. I regret ever coming here.'

Before the stabbing, the two men accused of the murder racially abused Toyosi and his friends about the colour of their skin, and called them 'niggers' several times, according to a local source.

(*Sunday Tribune*, April 2010)

---

### *Knacker:*

The word 'knacker' comes from the association with the 'knacker's yard' as a place where old horses were slaughtered. Many people use the phrase 'I am knackered', which means

I am very tired. The word 'knacker' is used as a slur against the Traveller community. Travellers have a long association of working with horses, buying and selling them in markets and fairs throughout the country. This association has led to the labelling of Traveller as 'knacker' meaning beyond use.

More recently it has shifted in its social meaning and has come to refer to people living in disadvantaged areas or perceived to be from a lower class, people who are not Travellers. The word is now used to describe people who are perceived to be unacceptable socially (as Travellers are stereotypically viewed in Irish society). The characteristics associated with 'knacker' include lower-class accent, style of dress, anti-social behaviour, petty crime, living in public housing and attaining low levels of education.

### Retard:

Retard has come into use more recently as a derogatory term to put someone down as developmentally delayed, slow or stupid. This word is totally unacceptable as it is offensive to people with intellectual disabilities.

### Half-cast:

This term is widely disliked. 'Mixed race' is often preferred, as it is seen to include the social and cultural aspects of race. 'Other terms that will not be perceived as offensive are "mixed heritage" or "dual heritage"' (Gaine, 2005, p. 98). Some people of mixed parentage choose to call themselves 'black' or 'Asian'; this may depend on how they are treated in society.

### Gay (as insult):

'Gay' is the most-used offensive term used to describe all things that are 'not ok', as in, 'That's so gay'. The predominance and persistent use of this expression has caused much grief for young gay people within the school system. It also has some prevalence among middle-class adults who, like children, don't necessarily mean it as a term of offence to gay people. Being gay is considered by some to be unacceptable, so the word is used as a put-down because of its association with gay people. All derogatory terms associated with undermining minority groups are offensive, and if used beyond the minority group they maintain their offense. Some people, especially young children, may not understand the pejorative meanings behind the use of the word 'knacker' or 'gay'. They need to be informed.

In my own case, my son came home from school (age 6) using the word 'knacker'. I had then worked with Travellers for more than ten years and I was concerned about his use of this word. I explained the significance of the word for Travellers through discussion and explanation. He never used the word again. He is now 17, and over the years, other terms emerged, including 'gay', which was more of a struggle to shift.

*Race (a problematic term)*

A socio-political concept which categorised people into biologically distinct, superior or inferior species or 'races' and has been used to justify cruelty, exploitation and discrimination, but in fact has no scientific basis. There is only one human race.

(Murray et al, 2004, 2011)

In many ways it would be better to use 'ethnicity' as a descriptive term rather than 'race'. The concept of race was falsely developed to maintain the superiority of one group over others and to justify colonialism. It does not have the biological meaning many people think it has. It is also problematic as it focuses social prejudice primarily on skin colour, and while skin colour is a prime area of discrimination, it narrows and distracts from an *ethnocentric* problem of superiority against many groups that goes beyond colour (Mac Gréil, 2011; Lane, 2008; Murray, 2002; Gain, 2005).

## Ethnicity

Please note that we all have an ethnicity whether we are conscious of it or not. Some of us happen to be in the minority ethnic group population others of us happen to be in the minority ethnic group situation.

(Crickley, 1998, p. 10)

In discussions about diversity and inclusion with learners and practitioners, black children and families are generally discussed as a single group, i.e., 'families from Africa'. When I ask where in Africa the families come from, I am often faced with blank expressions. There is a view that Africa is a homogenous continent of Black people. If you have several families from Africa in your service and their nationality is Somali, they may come from different ethnic groups within the country of Somalia. As a consequence, traditions, values, language and many areas associated with the culture of their ethnicity will vary.

### 3.7 Jargon Buster: Values

Values are qualities that an individual believes to be important and worthwhile for themselves and for others. Values guide your goals, choices and how you live and work. Values are personal, you acquire your values growing up within your home culture, and they will be different depending on that culture.

(Murray et al, 2004, 2011)

Anthropology considers ethnicity to designate groups which

▸   are largely biologically self-perpetuating;
▸   share fundamental cultural values;
▸   make up a field of communication and interaction;
▸   have a membership which identifies itself and is identified by others as constituting a category

(Fredrik Barth in Crowley, 2006).

So for example, when a couple from Somalia comes to Ireland, their ethnic origin will never be lost. They may maintain many culture-based customs from their ethnic group while being Somali in Ireland. Their children born in Ireland will be Irish nationals and will acquire black Irish culture. The role that their ethnic background plays will depend on the family in question and their own preference. Hence there is a fluid nature to ethnicity that is closely linked to culture (Lane, 2008). Many people choose to simply state their nationality when identifying themselves, usually so as not to confuse things.

It is important to be accurate about a child's ethnicity. It is also vital to ask how people identify themselves rather than ascribe a group to them. People come from different geographical regions across Africa, Asia and elsewhere, and have different nationalities and ethnicities. Travellers, for example, are recognised as an ethnic group in Britain, but their ethnicity is contested in Ireland.

***Ethnic status:***
Ethnicity is not about colour as Crickley (1998) points out when she says 'we all have an ethnicity'. In ECEC each child should be recognised and accurately represented in the setting. Don't assume that dolls or books depicting black, Chinese, majority or Traveller children and families are representative of an individual child in the setting (see Chapter 14).

## Being clear about where you stand

Anti-Bias work is connected to fairness and action (see Chapter 7). In order for you to operate from an anti-bias educational perspective, you will need to build your knowledge base and be clear on where you stand regarding social justice issues. Part of being clear, having empathy and engaging with diversity and equality issues is standing up for what you believe in. So when you hear a belittling joke or when you hear someone saying 'Asylum seekers are spongers' or 'they are all knackers', what are you going to do? Having good information on diversity-related terms and a clear understanding of what offensive terms mean and how they diminish, undermine or hurt people will help you engage more constructively with this work. It will also help you implement the rights of the child in your setting and in the broader community. So if you stand up against the poor treatment of someone, you are supporting that person or group. When you stand up for yourself or your group, you are empowering people as you are resisting what is happening for yourself or your group.

---

### 3.8 Discuss

- Do we all have bad habits?
- Can we change them?
- What is your worst fear about what might happen if you stood up against something?
- How would you feel if you did nothing?
- If you did speak up, what is your best hope of what might happen?

(Adapted from Derman-Sparks and Olsen Edwards, 2010)

This work is relevant to Anti-Bias Goals for Adults (see Chapter 3).

### Aistear Theme: Identity and Belonging

By embracing difference, exploring their own attitudes in relation to equality and diversity, and by realising that their attitudes and values influence children, adults can develop the insight, self-awareness and skills that are needed to help children develop a strong sense of identity and belonging. This helps to ensure that all children are respected and valued and that they can recognise and deal with discrimination and prejudice (NCCA, 2009, p. 25).

---

## Summary

Terminology is never cast in stone; it is always evolving. Chosen terms can change over time or across different cultures (e.g. 'coloured'). The terms discussed in this chapter are words that describe people all of whom require sensitivity and respect (e.g. refugee, black, Traveller). It is important to remember that words and jokes can convey prejudice, stereotypical thinking and disrespect, or our choice of words can convey respect and empathy. Practitioners can ask families about their chosen terms for describing themselves or their children, e.g. deaf or hearing impaired, a disabled child or a child with a disability. You can also consult with representative organisations for guidance. Accurate information on the term 'race' also helps in dispelling the myths of inferiority and superiority, and ethnicity might in fact be a more useful term to describe people. Language is forever changing; the important thing is to be continuously aware of and sensitive to diversity- and equality-related words. It is essential to be in tune with how people use language and also how they react to our use of language. Using the anti-bias goals for adults to explore your own values, attitudes and empathy will support your engagement with diversity and equality in your social and ECEC interactions.

## 3.9 Links

- *Diversity and Equality Guidelines for Childcare Providers* (Murray et al: OMC, 2006) at www.pavee.ie/edenn
- Chris Gain (2005) *We're all white, thanks: The persisting myth about 'white' schools*. Trentham Books.
- Immigrant Council of Ireland at www.immigrantcouncil.ie.

## CHAPTER 4

# European Law and Irish Legislation

It is interesting to note the links between discriminatory acts and the development of legislation and also how long it takes legislation to come into effect after it is passed. The fact that equality legislation is so recent gives rise to the notion that equality has not been a priority in this country and one could even question whether it still is. In times of recession support for minority groups is one of the first things to go. There is also much talk of 'looking after our own people' and 'getting foreigners to go home to their own country as we can only support our own'. The reality is we haven't ever supported our own, just look at the Traveller community and child poverty in Ireland.

(Practitioner, 2009)

## Overview

Legislation and policy affect the development of services provision and civil rights for all citizens in society. If issues of consequence are absent from legislation or policy documents then it is extremely difficult for individuals or groups to assert their rights in a state. In Chapter 1 we looked at some champions of human rights who have worked to ensure that regardless of their individual status or difference (i.e. gay, disability, women) people could assert their rights as citizens in Ireland. In this chapter we will look at legal instruments at European and national levels that support children's rights with particular reference to ECEC provision and including a focus on equality and anti-discrimination legislation and UN Conventions.

The chapter begins with a short discussion of Irish legislation affecting children and families and how it is influenced by, and how it is often initiated by, international legislative frameworks and conventions. Children, in ECEC and in society, have rights, which are spelled out in an international document: the United Nations Convention on the Rights of the Child (UNCRC). Children's rights are widely embraced in the ECEC sector but beyond the UNCRC, there are many other legal documents that shape and influence children's and families' lives in both positive or negative ways. This chapter gives you an opportunity to familiarise yourself with these documents.

We begin our overview with a look at international and EU documents and conventions including the UNCRC and the Convention on the Elimination of All Forms of Racial Discrimination (CERD) and some of the international instruments and institutions that support human rights and democratic principles. We then move on to Irish legislation. In a last step, we take a look at the Childcare and Preschool Regulations – a document with which every ECEC practitioner needs to be familiar.

Like Chapter 1, this chapter is very much about giving you the information you need in order to develop a critical understanding of the wider context and the preconditions for your work with young children, families and communities. You don't have to become a lawyer or an historian to understand this wider legal context. The Anti-Bias approach, which will be discussed in detail in Chapter 7, is about becoming conscious of it and confident in engaging with issues of diversity and equality, and having empathy, and about countering discrimination proactively. Knowing the legal context of your work in ECEC will help you to realise the Goals of the Anti-Bias approach.

## After reading this chapter you should

▸ have a better awareness of national and international legislative frameworks, including the Convention on the Rights of the Child and the '7th Comment'.
▸ better understand how legal frameworks impact upon the lives of children and families.
▸ be able to use the knowledge of these frameworks to examine ECEC practices, including your own.
▸ be aware of some of the shortcomings of conventions and legal frameworks.
▸ be able to link articles of the UN Conventions on the Right of the Child (UNCRC) with the Anti-bias Goals for children and adults.

# Introduction: ECEC legislation

ECEC in Ireland is regulated by specific legislation that builds on wider national legislation and policy frameworks, e.g. equality legislation. Many of these wider legislative documents are themselves grounded in international agreements, conventions and directives that Ireland is obliged to translate into national Irish legislation. ECEC professionals will find it valuable to understand the context of their practice beyond immediate ECEC legislation. In the previous sections we discussed how children growing up are influenced by their family circumstances and the broader society, and how social, cultural, economic and political factors help to shape the well-being of the children and families that attend the ECEC service. Historically, 'the richness of diversity among the population has not always been valued, nor have differences been equally cherished. As a result Ireland has not always shown due regard for the diverse needs of all people with equal concern' (OMC, 2006, p. 8).

When we look at the developments of legislation in Ireland for children and equality issues more generally, we find that the European Union has played a valuable role in stimulating and shaping legislation in Ireland. In the case of equality, Irish legislation and policy development has largely been motivated by directives from the European Union. Senator David Norris' case at the European Court of Human Rights in 1988 (see Chapter 1) is a case in point, in that the findings lead directly to the Irish Parliament passing a law to decriminalise sex between men.

A report entitled *For a Europe of civic and social rights 1996* and a report from an expert committee on Fundamental Rights laid the foundations for a European Charter of Fundamental Rights in 2000. This charter has now been incorporated into the Lisbon Treaty 2006, for which Ireland voted in 2008. The Treaty specifically references children. The Charter of Fundamental Rights applies to EU countries when they implement EU law. In 2007 the European Commission requested that the Fundamental Rights Agency (FRA) develop indicators to measure how children's rights are implemented, protected, respected and promoted across the EU in line with the UNCRC. These indicators are not a mechanism to monitor the compliance of individual countries with the UNCRC, but can provide a good example for EU Member States to consider applying (FRA, 2010).

## Why do I need to know all of this?

You might still be asking why you need to know all of this for your work in ECEC. You don't need to know all the ins and outs of EU Directives, UN Conventions or Irish legislation, but it is useful to have some general information and be aware of how the EU is responding to early childhood, children's rights and anti-discrimination issues. To keep up to date, visit 'Start Strong' at www.startstrong.ie and sign up for their newsletter, which will keep you posted on EU developments for ECEC. This information is useful for your professional development and the advancement of the ECEC profession. It's good to be aware of the bigger picture.

Having some detailed information on these issues will also support your practice with children. For example, I have asked students many times what they know about the UNCRC. The response varies, but generally their knowledge is very limited. Finding out more about what is important about the UNCRC and other conventions is good for practice, so consider the discussion questions below:

▸ What do you think the rights of young children are in ECEC?
▸ Should children have specific rights for and within their own group (of children)?
▸ What vision of the UNCRC do you think that Ireland has signed up to implementing?
▸ How do we incorporate into our everyday practice a focus on the rights of children?

We know that children are social beings, active agents in their own development, but they are also part of families and communities. Hence the need for ECEC to recognise the implications of inequality and discrimination for a family or community, regardless of which communities the parent(s) or child may be part of – gay, lone parents, Traveller, black, etc. In other words, children do not live their lives in isolation from their family or community. Legislation that affects a child's social context and daily life, be it positively, negatively or insufficiently, has implications for the well-being of the child. To implement the Childcare Regulations 2006, for example, it is necessary to have a holistic picture of the child and family, the social context matters.

## 4.1 Consider this:

Alison Murphy is a four-and-a-half-year-old girl with a diagnosis of ASD (Autism Spectrum Disorder) who has been attending a pre-school within a specialised disability service, for a year. Alison's parents are committed to her accessing mainstream education and they are hopeful that she will enter her local school in Junior Infants. However, they feel that she may not be ready to do so for another year. In the meantime, they would like to access a place for Alison in a playgroup close to where they live. The disability service has told the family that if they leave the pre-school, supports that Alison currently uses, such as Occupational and Speech Therapy, may no longer be available.

In spite of the legislative and policy trend towards inclusive education in recent years in Ireland, many families still face very real disincentives to accessing mainstream provision for their children. Interventions that benefit children are often unavailable outside specialised settings; assistance and support to create continuity for children is not comprehensively put in place. This can create major barriers to facilitating the key transition for children from specialised to inclusive settings.

When parents of disabled children contact ECEC services to seek a place for their child, the attitude of the person they speak to is a central factor. Managers and practitioners in settings sometimes make the assumption that if a child has a diagnosis, then they will automatically require additional or specialised support. Staff may then feel discouraged or fearful about catering for children with specific requirements and parents are refused a place on this basis over the phone. In contrast, ECEC staff (with their professional knowledge and experience) can play a vital role in advocating on behalf of the child and accessing available supports within community settings to underpin their inclusion.

Parents of disabled children may appear to be either overly apologetic or unusually combative. It is important to understand that these attitudes may have been directly influenced by the experience of the family both prior to and since their child was given a specific diagnosis.

There is a range of legislative and policy provisions that can impact on children like Alison and her family, both positively and negatively.

**Legislation**

- **United Nations Convention on the Rights of the Child (UNCRC) (1989):** Article 23 of the UNCRC states that children who have any kind of disability should have special care and support, so that they can lead full and independent lives.
- **Child Care Regulations (1996–2006):** The Regulations require that every pre-school service provider ensure that every pre-school child attending the service have suitable means of expression and development through the use of books, toys, games and other play materials, having regard to his or her age and development. In planning activities to support each child's development that reflect the philosophy and ethos of the service, each child's individual needs, interests and abilities should be considered. The provider should be pro-active in ensuring that appropriate action be taken to address each child's needs in co-operation with his/her parents and following consultation, where appropriate, with other relevant services.
- **Equal Status Act (2000–2004):** Disability is one of nine grounds on which people may not be discriminated against in this Act, and the term 'disability' is broadly defined. It covers a wide range of impairments and illnesses. It covers all physical, sensory and intellectual disabilities. 'Discrimination' includes a refusal or failure by the provider of a service to do all that is reasonable to accommodate the needs of a person with a disability by providing special treatment or facilities. Therefore, *if a childcare provider refuses to accept a child on the grounds of disability, this can be seen as discrimination.* Childcare services must attempt to reasonably accommodate a 'child with a disability', unless it places a disproportionate burden on the service to do so.
- **Ombudsman for Children Act (2002):** The Office of the Ombudsman promotes the rights and welfare of children and directly investigates complaints by or on behalf of children against public bodies.
- **Education for Persons with Special Educational Needs (EPSEN) Act (2004):** The EPSEN Act lays down specific processes and responsibilities for schools and local primary care teams to plan for and review the educational needs of disabled children. *The process of having a child's needs assessed can now be initiated by parents, the HSE, a school principal or the National Council for Special Education* (NCSE), which was set up under the 2004 Act.
- **Disability Act (2005):** With effect from 1 June 2007, children with disabilities in the 0–5 age group are entitled to receive an *Assessment of Need.* The roll-out of this provision has been somewhat erratic and there remains a significant cohort of children who were just over age 5 at the commencement of the Act who may not have received formal assessment.
- **United Nations Convention on the Rights of Persons with a Disability (UNCRPD) (2006):** The UNCRPD does not view persons with disabilities as objects of charity, medical treatment and social protection, but rather as subjects with rights, who are capable of claiming those rights and making decisions about their lives based on their free and informed consent as well as being active members of society.

**Policy**
- **Free Pre-School year in Early Childhood Care and Education (ECCE) Scheme:** ECCE makes a number of provisions to facilitate children with disabilities and special needs. The upper age limit is waived where children have been assessed as being developmentally delayed or where they have a physical, sensory or mental condition which will result in them starting school at a later age.
- **Síolta, The National Quality Framework for Early Childhood Education**: Equality is a fundamental characteristic of quality provision, in which the child's individuality, strengths, rights and needs are central to the provision of quality early childhood experiences.
- **Aistear, the Early Childhood Curriculum Framework:** Children should be supported to develop a positive sense of who they are, and feel that they are valued and respected as part of a family and community.
- **Diversity and Equality Guidelines (2006):** The Guidelines are important for recognising different individual needs and ensuring equity in terms of access, participation and benefits for all children and their families (Emma Byrne, 2011).

# UN Conventions, EU Directives and other international legal and policy documents

The values of society are condensed into EU Directives, United Nations Conventions, and national legislation and policy, some of which make explicit reference to early childhood. There are other international and national legal documents that address specific issues such as anti-discrimination or human rights, which have equal relevance to children within their social, cultural, economic and political contexts.

## 4.2 Jargon Buster: Directive

EU Directives lay down certain end results that must be achieved in every Member State. National authorities have to adapt their laws to meet these goals, but are free to decide how to do so. Directives may concern one or more Member States, or all of them. Each directive specifies the date by which the national laws must be adapted – giving national authorities the room for manoeuvre within the deadlines necessary to take account of differing national situations. Directives are used to bring different national laws into line with each other, and are particularly common in matters affecting the operation of the single market (e.g. product safety standards).

(http://ec.europa.eu/eu_law/introduction/what_directive_en.htm)

'Directives' are European acts of legislation that require member states to achieve a particular result without stipulating the means of achieving that result.

## 4.3 Jargon Buster: UN Conventions

A UN convention is a formal multilateral treaty with a broad number of parties. Conventions are normally open for participation by the international community as a whole, or by a large number of states (e.g. Convention on Biological Diversity of 1992, United Nations Convention on the Law of the Sea of 1982). The same holds true for instruments adopted by an organ of an international organization (e.g. the 1951 ILO Convention concerning Equal Remuneration for Men and Women Workers for Work of Equal Value, adopted by the International Labour Conference or the 1989 Convention on the Rights of the Child, adopted by the General Assembly of the UN).

(http://treaties.un.org/)

In the case of EU Directives, member states are required by law to ensure that particular EU Directives be implemented by law. In other words, national legislation is developed to support a particular Directive in the member states. Once in national law, Directives must be enforced and monitored. UN Conventions require ratification by a state and the country then has to adhere to criteria for implementation, monitoring and reporting.

## UN Convention on the Rights of the Child

The UN Convention on the Rights of the Child was ratified in Ireland in 1992. By ratifying the UNCRC, **the Irish State committed itself to promote, protect and fulfil the rights of children** as outlined in the Articles of the UNCRC. Eight years after ratification, the state produced a ten-year Children's Strategy. Implementation has been limited, but some critical progress has been made, which includes the establishment of an Office for Children and Youth Affairs with a dedicated Minister for Children, the establishment of an Office of the Ombudsman for Children, and the development of mechanisms for hearing the voices of children nationwide, the Dáil na nÓg.

Nineteen years on, children' rights are as yet not fully realised in Ireland. The NGO sector has been calling for a referendum to amend the Constitution in favour of children's rights for many years. Until amended, the rights of Irish children cannot be fully realised in policy development. In October 2011, Ireland was examined for the first time by other United Nations (UN) countries on our human rights record. This process is called the Universal Periodic Review or UPR. It is a new mechanism and is the first time that UN states directly examine each other on their human rights record. The objective of the review is to highlight Ireland's gaps in human rights protections. A broad range of human rights are given consideration at the review including the right to health, liberty, the rights of children, older people and people from minority groups. Each country is examined on its obligations under the following:

▸   Charter of the United Nations (UN)
▸   Universal Declaration on Human Rights
▸   Human rights agreements ratified by Ireland
▸   Voluntary pledges or commitments by Ireland
▸   International humanitarian law

(See the Irish UPR website: www.rightsnow.ie)

Ireland has been criticised in the past at a number of levels and under various conventions for being slow to improve human rights for all its citizens and in particular for children. There is sustained pressure on the State from the NGO sector, including the Children's Rights Alliance, the Irish Council for Civil Liberties and Pavee Point, to name a few, to fulfil its commitments to ratified conventions.

Minister Alan Shatter confirmed under that review that a referendum on children's rights would be held in early 2012 in order to bring Ireland into line with the UN Convention on the Rights of the Child. This concrete action must be implemented, as the next appointment with the UPR review process is March 2012.

The UNCRC has changed the policy landscape dramatically, with advocacy for early childhood increasingly based on recognition of young children's universal rights. As Woodhead (2007) reminds us 'realising the rights of every child is not just about more comprehensive service; it also entails a more fundamental shift in the image of the child within society.' Framing early childhood policy in terms of children's rights is a significant departure from the usual. Children as ECEC participants need the commitment of the State and providers so that they can realise their rights in practice.

## General Comment 7: Implementing children's rights in early childhood

To enhance a rights focus on the young child in early childhood the UN published General Comment No.7 in 2005. This was a result of reviewing State parties' reports on their implementation of the UNCRC and identifying the lack of focus on young children. The UNCRC is the the first legally binding international instrument to incorporate the full range of human, civil, cultural, economic, political and social rights.

General Comment 7 (Paragraph 3) confirms that:

> young children are holders of all the rights enshrined in the Convention … [and] that the Convention on the Rights of the Child is to be applied holistically in early childhood, taking account of the principles of the universality, indivisibility and interdependence of all human rights.

The comment goes on to review the implications of the UNCRC for policy development in early childhood education and care, covering general principles, assistance to parents and families, development of comprehensive services, young children in need of special protection and resources and capacity building.

The recognition that children have human rights beyond those of adults prompted the development of the UNCRC. Making use of other UN Conventions on human rights puts pressure on the state. The recent Universal Periodic Review supports this view.

## UN Convention on the Elimination of all Forms of Racial Discrimination

The UN Convention on the Elimination of all Forms of Racial Discrimination (CERD) 1969 was ratified by Ireland in 2000 after 41 years. Children's and families' right to a life without discrimination has direct relevance to Early Childhood Education and Care but CERD is rarely cited in ECEC documents. By ratifying CERD, the Irish State **committed itself** to take action for the achievement of one of the purposes of the United Nations which is to promote and encourage universal respect for and observance of human rights and fundamental freedoms for all, without distinction as to race, sex, language or religion.

(www2.ohchr.org/english/bodies/cerd/)

Compliance of countries that have ratified the CERD is monitored by an international body, the United Nations International Committee on the Elimination of Racial Discrimination (UNICERD). Its legal powers enable the Committee to check whether states are meeting their legal obligations under the CERD. The Committee consists of 18 persons who serve in their personal capacity. It meets twice a year at the United Nations in Geneva.

---

**4.4**

The ICERD committee concluded that the economic recession threatens achievements to combat racism and sends a clear message that racism must be back on the political agenda of the Irish government.

'The Committee notes with regret that the economic recession […] threatens to reverse the achievements that have been made [by Ireland] to combat racial discrimination at all levels. The Committee expresses grave concern over the disproportionate budget cuts to various human rights institutions mandated to promote and monitor human rights such as the Irish Human Rights Commission, the Equality Authority and the National Consultative Committee on Racism and Interculturalism.'

The 'persistent refusal' on the part of the State to recognise Travellers as an ethnic group is identified as a key concern. It recommends also that the State undertake concrete measures to improve the livelihoods of the Traveller community by focusing on improving students' enrolment and retention in schools, employment, access to healthcare and accommodation including transient sites.

On the issue of hate crime, the Committee makes a number of comments. It notes with regret that the review of the Incitement to Hatred Act 1989 has stalled. The Committee recommends that the Government pass legislation to declare illegal and prohibit racist organisations, in line with article 4(b) of the Convention. It also recommends that the racist motivation be consistently taken into account as an aggravating factor in sentencing practice for criminal offences. It also recommends that the State take appropriate steps to encourage the reporting of racist incidents and crimes.

Further information about CERD committee reports on Ireland can be found at http://www.cwc.ie/2011/03/cerd-committee-reports-on-ireland/

The European Commission has recently published an official 'communication' on early childhood education and care: *Providing all our children with the best start for the world tomorrow* (European Commission, 2011). This has the potential to inform Directives from Europe and also national legislation.

The policy paper calls for 'universal' childcare of all children and also states that the diversity of children in ECEC requires continuous reflection on pedagogical practice as well as a systemic approach to professionalism. It argues that many aspects of diversity are not sufficiently covered in ECEC training in many countries.

## Quality Targets in Services for Young Children

The European Commission Network on Childcare (1996) published *Quality Targets in Services for Young Children* in which the Network proposed a ten-year action programme with 40 targets to be achieved by 2006 to assist in the development and improvement of high quality childcare provision throughout the European Union member states. Targets 13, 14, 15, 18, 20, 34 and 36 concern access to services linked to diversity and equality approach to ECEC and are still relevant today.

### 4.5 Quality targets in services for young children

**TARGET 14:** All services should positively assert the value of diversity and make provision both for children and adults that acknowledges and supports diversity of language, ethnicity, religion, gender and disability, and challenges stereotypes.

**TARGET 15:** All children with disabilities should have right of access to the same services as other children with appropriate staffing assistance and specialist help.

**TARGET 20:** The education and learning environment should reflect and value each child's family, home, language, cultural heritage, beliefs, religion and gender.

**TARGET 36:** Services should adopt employment procedures that emphasize the importance of recruiting employees who reflect the ethnic diversity
(*Quality Targets in Services for Young Children*, http://www.childcarequality.ca/wdocs/QbD_QualityTargets.pdf)

In the following box you will find a variety of international organisations that have informed EU and national polices. Each instrument has a brief description with links for further investigation. Children are a minority in society, and legislation (as well as the lack of appropriate legislation) affects the child, the family and the community. It is often only when legislation or lack thereof affects us personally that we see the need for such legal instruments. Some countries need to be pushed by EU frameworks or international conventions and national pressure groups to support the rights of citizens. Unfortunately, legislation is sometimes the only way to ensure people are offered support and protection. Legislation can be limited depending on the view of a particular government and may not go far enough to offer citizens full rights or protections. Legislation can also negatively affect the rights of some citizens.

There are various European and national networks which bring allies together:

## 4.6 Support Networks

**European Network Against Racism (ENAR) (1997):**
ENAR is a network of European NGOs working to combat racism in all EU member states and represents more than 600 NGOs throughout the European Union. ENAR is committed to fight racism, xenophobia, anti-Semitism and Islamophobia, to promote equality of treatment between European Union citizens and third-country nationals. (Sign up and get the ENAR newsletter www.**ENAR**-eu.org)

**European Disability Forum (EDF) (1996):**
In 1996, European and national organisations of disabled persons and parents of disabled persons who were unable to represent themselves joined together to establish the EDF. EDF is an independent and unique platform in Europe, with a proactive role in dealing with the European Union institutions and decision-makers seeking to protect and defend the rights of disabled persons. Their aim is to influence and strengthen non-discrimination legislative measures in Europe, to ensure that the full integration of disabled persons in society becomes a reality. They represent the interests of 80 million Europeans with disabilities. (www.edf-feph.org)

**Diversity in Early Childhood Education and Training (DECET) (1998)**
DECET brings together a network of European organisations and projects with common goals about valuing diversity in early childhood education and training.

The network aims at promoting and studying democratic childcare, acknowledging the multiple (cultural and other) identities of children and families. DECET views early childhood provisions as meeting places where people can learn from each other across cultural and other borders and therefore as public provisions that can effectively address prejudices and discrimination. In this sense early childhood education makes a clear contribution to the construction of European citizenship.

(www.decet.org)

**Eurochild (2003)**
Eurochild is a network of organisations and individuals working in and across Europe to improve the quality of life of children and young people. The work of Eurochild is underpinned by the principles enshrined in the United Nations Convention on the Rights of the Child. Eurochild is funded by the European Commission.

(www.eurochild.org)

In your own time investigate the various Articles in the UNCRC below. Just being aware of children's rights is not enough. It is vital to make them a reality in your practice. In your own time, investigate the various Articles below and link them directly to developing your knowledge base and to practise with children.

## 4.7 Under the UN Convention on the Rights of the Child, the child has a right to*:

**Article 2**: Protection from discrimination
**Article 7**: A name and nationality
**Article 8**: His/her identity
**Article 12**: Have their opinions heard
**Article 19**: Protection from neglect and abuse
**Article 22**: Protection under Refugee Status
**Article 23**: Appropriate disability services
**Article 28**: Accessibility and dignity in Education
**Article 29**: Reach his/her potential in education with respect for cultural, identity, language and values for self and for culture and background and values of others
**Article 30**: Enjoyment of own culture and to practice religion and language

*There are 54 Articles in the UNCRC; this is a sample of articles linked to diversity issues.

## 4.8 Making connections

Link some of the Articles in the UNCRC to the implementation of the Anti-Bias Goals and to the Aistear Goals and Aims under the theme 'Identity and Belonging'.

For example: Goal One: to support children's identity and sense of belonging, connects to UNCRC Article 8, the right to identity, and Article 7, the right to a name and nationality.

Consider the possible links for the following:

- Aistear Aim 2: Children will have a sense of group identity where links with their family and community are acknowledged and extended
- Goal 1: Feel they have a place and a right to belong to the group
- Goal 2: Know that members of their and community are positively acknowledged and welcomed.

Continue with the other Anti-Bias Goals for Children and Adults and the Aistear Aims and Goals.

# National legislation

Equality Legislation at national level has been hard fought primarily through the efforts of NGOs working for the rights and recognition of marginalised groups such as Travellers, LGBT people, older people, people with disabilities, children and women. As already outlined, EU Directives are required by EU law to be addressed by national legislation. The knock-on effect of introducing legislation for marginalised groups is generally beneficial for all in society. 'Not only do large inequalities produce all the problems associated with social differences and the divisive class prejudice which go with them, but it also weakens community life, reduces trust, and increases violence' (Wilkinson and Pickett, 2009, p. 45).

In Ireland, equality laws have largely been informed by EU Directives. These include:

▶  Incitement to Hatred (1989)
▶  Gay Law Reform (1993)
▶  Unfair Dismissals (1993)
▶  Employment Equality (1998)
▶  Equal Status (2000 and 2004).

Building on this body of legal change over the past 20 years, the State recently recognised lesbian, gay and bisexual relationships for the first time through the Civil Partnership Bill. While this Bill is limited in its scope (for example, it doesn't recognize or support the children of same-sex couples) it is to be welcomed as a positive move towards gay rights. (See www.glen.ie).

In your own time, investigate the various national instruments below.

## 4.9 National instruments and institutions promoting human rights and democratic principles

- **Ninth Amendment of the Constitution Act (1984):**
  The ninth amendment extended the right to vote at Dáil elections to certain non-Irish nationals.

- **Irish Nationality and Citizenship Act (1985):**
  The Irish Nationality and Citizenship Act was in 1985 to give the Minister for Justice discretion to grant a certificate of naturalisation. The amendment resulted in applicants having to fulfil certain requirements, including having lived for at least five of the previous nine years in the Irish State. The Act allows the minister to dispense with the conditions in certain circumstances.

- **Prohibition of Incitement to Hatred Act (1989):**
  This Act aims to deal with actions, broadcasts or material likely to stir up hatred. This legislation was disappointingly ineffectual, as it requires proof of intent, which is virtually impossible in law; hence case law invoking this Act is negligible. This problem has now been acknowledged, and a review of this legislation was announced in 2000.

- **Homosexuality Decriminalised (1993):**
  On the 30 June 1993, the Irish Parliament passed a law to decriminalise sex between men. The main move to change the law in Ireland came from a ruling of the European Court of Human Rights in Strasbourg. In 1988, Ireland was found to be in breach of the European Convention on Human Rights on the grounds of privacy. The case was taken by Senator David Norris, a member of the Irish Parliament.

- **Refugee Act (1996):**
  The Refugee Act places the procedures for processing applications by asylum seekers for refugee status on a statutory footing. Two offices were established: a Refugee Applications Commissioner, who makes recommendations as to decisions; and a Refugee Appeals Tribunal to establish an appeals system for decisions about Refugee Status. All new asylum applicants over the age of 14 are now fingerprinted. The Act also sets out the rights of Refugees to work and receive social welfare benefits and medical care on the same basis as EU citizens. (Enacted fully in 1999.)

- **The Employment Equality Act (1998):**
  This act makes discrimination in employment unlawful on nine grounds: gender, marital status, family status, sexual orientation, religious belief, age, disability, race and membership of the Traveller community. The Act covers access to employment, conditions of employment, equal pay, promotion, training and work experience, all of which is relevant to employment within the childcare sector.

- **Ireland Ratifies Council of Europe Framework Convention for the Protection of National Minorities (1999):**
  The Council of Europe's Framework Convention for the Protection of National Minorities is the first multilateral human rights instrument devoted to the protection of national minorities. Ireland ratified the Framework Convention in 1999 on foot of a commitment in the Good Friday Agreement. In Ireland, the implementation of the Framework

Convention has been primarily focussed on the Traveller community, which is given specific protection and support under Irish legislation, but it is also relevant to other emerging minorities in Irish society.

- **The Equal Status Act (2000 and 2004):**
  Prohibits discrimination in the provision of goods, services, disposal of property and access to education on any of the nine grounds referred to under the Employment Equality Act 1998. It prohibits discrimination in all public and private services (subject to some exceptions) including educational establishments. Educational institutions have a duty not to discriminate in terms of admission, access, terms or conditions and expulsion. The Act has direct relevance for ECEC providers.

- **Housing (Miscellaneous Provisions) Act ('Trespass' Law) (2002):**
  The Housing (Miscellaneous Provisions) Act 2002 came into operation on 2 July 2002. When the Government introduced this legislation, it was promised that this legislation would not be used against Travellers living on the roadside and awaiting accommodation (this is not the case). Instead, it was promised it would only be used in instances of 'large-scale illegal encampments'. The legislation makes it a criminal offence to trespasses on and occupy public or private property. This offence is punishable by immediate eviction, a month in jail and/or a €3,000 fine and the confiscation of property. This Act has adversely affected the Traveller community's nomadic tradition and their way of life.

- **Ratification of UN Convention on Elimination of all Forms of Racial Discrimination (UNCERD) (2000):**
  Ireland ratified the UNCERD in 2000. The ratification of the Convention brings Ireland into line with all other EU Member States, sending out an important signal to the international community that Ireland is committed to tackling racism, and it provides an important mechanism through which progress to address racism in Ireland can be monitored and reviewed at UN level.

- **National Minimum Wage Act (2000):**
  The National Minimum Wage Act 2000 became law in Ireland on 1 April 2000. It was the product of a long trade union campaign to attack the problem of low pay. Over 163,000 employees benefited immediately from the statutory increase in the hourly rate. The Act covers all employees in the public or private sector, of any age who has entered into full- or part-time work. The minimum wage was revised down and restored in 2011 as part of Ireland's finance deal with the European Union, European Central Bank and the International Monetary Fund. Minimum wage rates can be the difference between staying afloat or living in poverty.

- **European Convention on Human Rights Act (2003):**
  This is an Irish law, which incorporates this EU Convention into our domestic law. This Act allows the Irish courts to interpret national law in terms of compatibility with the United Nations Commission on Human Rights (UNCHR). Higher courts can now declare a law incompatible with this Convention (although that law will remain on the statute books). All Irish domestic laws, including this one, remain subordinate to our Constitution.

## Policy

- **Task Force on the Travelling Community (1995):**

  This groundbreaking report was informed by active participation of Travellers and Traveller groups, in particular Pavee Point (1985) and Irish Traveller Movement (1990). The report recommended that the distinct culture and identity of the Traveller community be recognised and taken into account. The report made 341 separate recommendations concerning aspects of Traveller life. The report continues to shape Traveller policy today.

- **First Ethnic Identifier Question in the Census (2002):**

  A number of new questions were included in the 2002 census form, and again on the 2011 census form. One of these questions was on Traveller identity. Previously, efforts to distinguish Irish Travellers in the census had relied on enumerators identifying Travellers on the cover sheet during the fieldwork phase of the relevant census.

  The question used in the 2002 census was asked of the entire population and significantly, was based on self-identification. The census provides general information on numbers, age and gender profiles. A detailed analysis of the results was published by the Central Statistics Office (CSO) in January 2004.

## Institutions

- **Equality Authority (1999):**

  The Equality Authority is an independent statutory body set up to coincide with the passing of the Employment Equality Act, 1998. Established in October 1999, the Equality Authority replaced the Employment Equality Agency. The Equality Authority's mandate is to combat discrimination and to promote equality. The mandate covers the nine grounds of age, disability, race, gender, family status, marital status, sexual orientation, religion and membership of the Travelling community.

- **Irish Human Rights Commission (2001):**

  The Irish Human Rights Commission was established in July 2001. The commission is an independent body set up under the Human Rights Commission Act 2000 and Human Rights Commission (Amendment) Act 2001. The Commission was established as a result of a commitment under the Good Friday Agreement 1998. The function of the Commission is to promote and protect human rights in Ireland and ensure that Irish law and practice of the Irish state is in line with international agreements to which Ireland is a party and the Irish Constitution.

  There is a proposed amalgamation of the Equality Authority and the Irish Human Right Commission due to the recessionary times.

- **Office of the Director of Equality Investigations (1999):**

  The Office of the Director of Equality Investigations is a tribunal-type body contributing to the achievement of equality by investigating or mediating complaints of unlawful discrimination. The office investigates complaints of discrimination in relation to employment, access to goods and services, disposal of property and certain aspects of education. This protection against discrimination applies to all nine grounds. Where a complaint of discrimination is upheld, compensation and/or redress may be awarded.

- **National Disability Authority (NDA) (2000):**
  The National Disability Authority was established on 12 June 2000 under Section 6 of the National Disability Authority Act 1999. The role of the NDA is to act as a national body to assist in the coordination and development of disability policy, to undertake research and develop statistical information for the planning, delivery and monitoring of programmes and services for people with disabilities and to advise the Minister on standards for appropriate programmes and services provided or to be provided to people with disabilities.
- **Citizenship Referendum (2004):**
  The Irish people voted in favour of an amendment to the Constitution, which will remove the automatic right to citizenship for all children born in Ireland. The amendment states that 'A person who does not have at the time of their birth, at least one parent who is an Irish Citizen or entitled to be an Irish Citizen, is not entitled to Irish Citizenship or Nationality, unless provided for by Law'. This is now a matter for legislation, and means that some children may have less protection in terms of their fundamental rights under the Constitution.

## Childcare Legislation and Policy

In the past ten years there have been significant changes in policy development for children. You are familiar with the framework for quality, Síolta (CECDE, 2006), the curriculum framework, Aistear (NCCA, 2009), and the Diversity and Equality Guidelines for Childcare Providers (OMC, 2006). They all build upon the Government's White Paper, 'Ready to Learn' (Department of Education and Science, 1999).

Other important policy documents include the National Childcare Strategy (Department of Justice Equality and Law Reform, 1999) and the National Children's Strategy (Department of Health and Children, 2000).

## Childcare Regulations

A key document for early childhood services is the Childcare and Preschool Regulations (official title: Child Care (Pre-School Services) (No 2) Regulations 2006 and Child Care (Pre-School Services) (No 2) (Amended) Regulations 2006) (OMC, 2006). This document regulates accreditation and inspection of all childcare and preschool services in Ireland; you should familiarise yourself with its scope and content.

The Preschool regulations are based on the 'whole-child' perspective. This recognises the lives of children in a holistic and child-centred way. It allows for those working with children to understand children's development in the context in which they live.

The whole-child perspective focuses on three areas:

1. Children's innate capacity, which takes account of outcomes of children's development;

2. Formal and informal supports; and

3. Relationships around children's lives. (Child Care Regulations 2006)

The work of Bronfenbrenner (1979) and Ward (1995) has informed this perspective and it is in keeping with the spirit of the UN Convention on the Rights of the Child (1989). This emphasis supports an equality and diversity approach in ECEC and informs practitioners and inspectors of the necessity to support, among other things, children's identity, emotional and behavioural well-being and 'social presentation' ('children's growing understanding of their capacity to engage with others and realise the impact of their actions, appearance and behaviour on others') (Office of the Minister for Children, 2006, p. 69) within ECEC.

## 4.10 A Child's innate capacity

How the regulations view and value 'children's innate capacity' is outlined under nine 'domains':

- Physical and Mental Wellbeing
- Emotional and Behavioural wellbeing
- Intellectual Capacity
- Spiritual and moral wellbeing
- **Identity**
- Self care
- Family relationships
- Social and Peer relations
- **Social presentation**

They all form the basis for a holistic perspective on children and early childhood education and care. However, two of the nine domains are of particular relevance to the Anti-Bias Goals discussed in Chapter 7 of this book:

**Identity:** the diversity of children's experiences, culture, gender, social background and traditions should be nurtured and valued by the service provider. The provider and staff must actively promote **equality of opportunity, participation** and **anti-discriminatory practice** with regard to all children in their care. This includes the promotion of mutual respect between children in their care.

**Social presentation:** concerning children's growing understanding of their capacity to engage with others and realise the impact of their actions, appearance and behaviour on others. Service providers should support children in their understanding of others and learn to engage in social situations.

(OMC, 2006, p. 69)

Regulations 5 and 9 too are of particular relevance to the implementation of a diversity and equality approach. The Anti-Bias Goals will support your practice and help you meet the regulation criteria.

---

### 4.11 Regulation 5: Health, Welfare and Development of the child

A person carrying on a pre-school service shall ensure that each child's learning, development and well-being is facilitated within the daily life of the service through the provision of the appropriate opportunities, experiences, activities, interaction, materials and equipment, having regard to the age and stage of development of the child and the child's cultural context.

**Considering each child's development needs**
What service providers should do:

In planning activities to support each child's development, which are reflective of the philosophy and ethos of the service, as provided for in the Explanatory Guide to Regulation 14 (1) (f) and 25, each child's individual needs, interests and abilities should be considered. The provider should be pro-active in ensuring that appropriate action is taken to address each child's needs in co-operation with his/her parents and following consultation, where appropriate, with other relevant services.

Each child's learning, development and well-being needs should be met within the daily life of the service through the provision of the appropriate opportunities, experiences, activities, interactions and materials. In meeting these needs, service providers should recognise how children affect and, in turn, are affected by the relationships, environment and activities around them.

This approach is outlined in the National Children's Strategy (2000–2010) and is called the 'Whole Child Perspective'.

(OMC, 2006, p. 36)

---

Recognising each child's identity as both an individual and as part of a group in their daily life within the ECEC setting is one way to enhance the well-being of each child. Using the Anti-Bias Goals for children and adults will meet the requirement of Regulation 5 and the whole-child perspective.

## 4.12 Regulation 9: Behavioural management

(1)  A person carrying on a pre-school service shall ensure that no corporal punishment is inflicted on a pre-school child attending the service.

(2)  A person carrying on a pre-school service shall ensure that no practices that are disrespectful, degrading, exploitive, intimidating, emotionally or physical harmful or neglectful are carried out in respect of any child.

(3)  A person carrying on a pre-school service shall ensure that written policies and procedures are in place to deal with and to manage a child's challenging behaviour and to assist the child to manage his or her behaviour as appropriate to the age and stage of development of the child.

Child protection

9.(2) Within the framework of *Children First National Guidelines for the Protection and Welfare of Children*, clear written guidelines on identifying and reporting child abuse should be developed by the pre-school service.

In line with Article 2.2 of the UN Convention on the Rights of the Child:

1.  All childcare services and providers should consider the child's welfare to be of paramount concern.

2.  All children should be respected and treated with dignity at all times.

3.  Children's rights should be acknowledged and respected at all times.

4.  Children should never be subjected to any degrading or abusive behaviour.

(OMC, 2006, p. 42)

Children should be protected from prejudice and discrimination within services. Negative behaviour regarding a child's identity can be displayed by staff, children or parents on many grounds. Children should be pro-actively protected from such behaviour through policy development and practice.

## Summary

The lives of children and families are affected by many factors in society, including how we organise and regulate our living together as human beings. National and international legal frameworks, conventions and regulations play a major role in shaping the life circumstances of children. As ECEC practitioners committed to an Anti-Bias approach, to respecting diversity and to promoting equality, we should be knowledgeable about and critical of those influences. Becoming familiar with the legislation beyond ECEC that affects children's lives will build your confidence in proactively engaging with issues of diversity, equality and discrimination.

This chapter has introduced you to some key documents, legal frameworks and conventions that have influenced policy development in Ireland. While the information given is certainly not exhaustive, it should give you a good overview of documents you should be aware of from an Anti-Bias perspective.

## 4.13 Activity

Read the short scenario below. With your group of learners, discuss how the legal documents you have encountered in this chapter affect the child described below and his community in both positive and negative ways.

Owney Collins is four-year-old Traveller boy. He lives in a house in the west of Ireland. He is just about to start in an integrated pre-school. His grandparents live on a halting site in the town, where Owney loves to go there because his grandfather keeps lots of horses, which he brings to the horse fairs like Ballinasloe. Owney, like all Traveller children, is growing up in a different cultural context to settled children.

When Traveller children attend integrated services, it is generally the first time they come in close contact with both settled adults and children. It may also be the first time they realise they are different, and perhaps different in a negative way. Owney's parents recognise the benefits the education can bring their son, but they also know that it can be difficult, and that Travellers can be hurt in the education system because of their identity. Travellers have their own language, customs, values and traditions – their own culture. Despite a long shared history, they face on-going individual and institutional discrimination and opposition to their way of life.

There are approximately 30,000 Travellers in Ireland. Travellers are recognised as a minority ethnic group in England and Northern Ireland, but not in the Republic of Ireland.

Repeat this exercise with another example. Think of a child in an ECEC service and write down her or his scenario. You may look at some of the chapters in Section 3 for inspiration. How is their life affected, in positive or negative ways, by policy and legislation?

In this chapter we have explored legislation around and beyond ECEC, and made the argument that it is important to understand the legislative and regulatory frameworks that affect the lives of children and families. However, legislation per se is limited as it is always subject to interpretation. Childcare Regulation 5, for instance, is explicit about the well-being of every child. How this manifests itself for a child with a disability, from a marginalised group, or indeed for any child in daily practice in the ECEC service is a matter of interpretation and action by practitioners, managers and inspectors. Legislation and regulation can offer a necessary framework and orientation – it is up to us to bring it to life!

# SECTION TWO

# Re-thinking Early Childhood Education and Care

## Overview

The first section of this book introduced you to the historical and political context of diversity in present-day Irish society. The key message from that section is that early childhood practitioners need to have an awareness of the broader societal environment, and an understanding that the critical issues we are dealing with today have always been around in various forms. This second section focuses on how we interact with this context from a professional perspective. The three main questions we as early childhood practitioners will engage with in this section are:

1. **How do we think about children** and our professional practice with children, families and communities? How can we *critically reflect* upon our practice?
2. **How do we know what we know about children**? Where do the knowledge and the theories that inform our professional practice come from? How does this particular *way of knowing* affect our practice?
3. **What questions could we ask** and which orientations could we seek in order to do things differently, in ways that are more respectful to diversity and more equitable for all children and families?

While we look at the three main topics of this section – critical reflection, professional knowledge, and transformative practice – in three chapters, we need to keep in mind that they are interconnected: **thinking**, **knowing** and **doing** weave into each other in early childhood professional practice and cannot be separated.

Following an introduction to the theme of this section, Chapter 5 explores the notion of **reflective practice**. The importance of this concept of thinking about your practice is emphasised in key documents for the ECEC sector, e.g. Síolta and Aistear. We look at the possibilities and limitations of reflective practice and argue that in order to promote equality, the reflection needs to be critical.

Chapter 6 takes a closer look at how early childhood practice relates to the **professional body of knowledge** and the theories that inform this knowledge. Where does this knowledge come from, and how do we understand what knowledge means in the first place? We will examine one of the most influential underpinnings of early childhood practice critically – the concept of **development** and its consequences for ECEC practice.

In Chapter 7 we then ask what other possibilities might there be to orient professional practice with children, families and communities. What questions could we ask? Which professional, political and ethical stand could we take that would enable us to **transform professional practice** and to make early childhood care and education more equitable and just for all children. In this chapter we introduce the **Goals for Adults and Children** that underpin the **Anti-Bias Curriculum**. This concludes the section on *re-thinking early* childhood care and education and leads into the third section of the book, voices from the sector, which illustrate how these orientations and a critical awareness of children's and families' real-life experiences have become the starting point for early childhood services that make a difference.

## Early childhood practitioners know what's best for children – or do they?

Adults contribute hugely to shaping young children's everyday experiences in the childcare centre, pre-school or any other early childhood setting. We create environments, develop and 'deliver' curricula, structure times for activities and engage with children as individuals and groups, to name only a few examples out of a whole range of activities and interactions that occur in every early childhood setting every ordinary day.

Would you agree that as educators, we usually have a fairly good understanding of what we do in our daily practice? We seem to know what is appropriate for children in general – and for the children in our setting, our group, our community in particular. Depending on our experience (or our lack of it, if we are only beginning to work with young children) we might feel fairly secure about some or most aspects of our daily routine. We might feel more uncertain about others, for instance if we encounter new challenges like having to work to a new curriculum framework (Aistear), having to place our work in a new quality framework (Síolta), or being confronted with children from new and perhaps unfamiliar communities. Whether we are experienced educators or newcomers to the field, there will always be areas of uncertainty. In general, however, we usually have an understanding of what is 'right' for children and what 'good' early childhood practice looks like. Forget about curriculum frameworks and quality frameworks for a moment (we will have to come back to them) and imagine a visit to a childcare centre or preschool in your neighbourhood. As you walk through the door, look at the environment, listen to the sounds of children and adults involved in all sorts of activities, you will most likely get an impression of this centre within minutes. Depending on your experience (having worked in early childhood for a good while already, or having visited various settings during your studies), you will be able to make judgements about the quality of this centre, even though you never visited it before. There seems to be a common understanding, a common knowledge about the care and education of young children that enables us put things into perspective, and to judge whether or not we are doing things right. Where do you think this common understanding of what is good for children comes from?

## Practices – what we do, how we do it and how we think about it – are not givens.

What we see as 'good', or appropriate, depends crucially on its context and how we make sense of it. Early childhood practices are grounded in our understandings, for instance, what it means to be a child, what it is (or should be) like to grow up in our society, which happens to be twenty-first-century Ireland. Our judgements may depend a lot on our knowledge and understanding of how children 'develop' and learn, and how (and to what end) their development and learning can be best supported.

However, the key message of this book is that there are choices to be made, ethical and political ones, as Gunilla Dahlberg and Peter Moss remind us (2005), and very practical ones, too.

What it means to be a child in Ireland today depends a lot on where and how you grow up. Inner-city or rural, middle-class or working-class, Traveller or new immigrant community, girl or boy – it makes all the difference. How do you position yourself and what actions do you take to support children feeling OK about who they are? What actions do you take to stand up for those who don't?

### Practitioner's voice

Being from a minority group in Ireland, I can say that discrimination and racism are always part of my discussions with my friends and family. I am aware of how hard it is to be tolerant and how hard it is to accept. But I know that the biggest force creating the positive behaviours is being familiar with the differences, and what makes people discriminate is ignorance.

It is necessary to take action and stand up for yourself. It is also important to stand up for others, as sometimes they are too weak or simply have no tools to do that on their own. And of course there will always be people saying 'mind your own business', 'concentrate on your own life, that is his life', 'leave him alone'. But I know that these are not what we call mature, responsible members of the community.

(Student)

In order to understand what these choices are and how our own background influences the way we make sense of the world, we suggest it is necessary to 'unpack' some of the underlying assumptions of ECEC. In order to do things differently – as this is what this book is about – we need to question the big ideas that underpin early childhood practices, programmes and institutions. When we say 'we', it is to emphasise the responsibility of each individual involved in the care and education of young children to engage in this process. In ECEC however, like in any social practice, the 'we' reaches beyond the individual practitioner, teacher and childcare worker. It extends to all those acting in the system of ECEC: practitioners, students, trainers, lecturers, managers, academic researchers, policy-makers at the various layers of the system. We, the authors of this book, as we speak about early childhood practices from our particular perspective, are included in this system as well.

## Jargon Buster: Big Ideas

The concept of 'big ideas' was first used by postmodern philosophers including the French writer Jean-Francois Lyotard, who employed the term to describe the powerful assumptions that have underpinned modern societies for the last two hundred years. One of these 'big ideas' (or 'grand narratives', as they have been called as well) is that modern societies progress continuously, and therefore inevitably increase prosperity and individual freedom for everyone. Postmodern thinkers have been highly critical of these 'big ideas'. Continuous technological **progress** and growth, for instance, has become a risk to the survival of humankind as it consumes ever more irreplaceable natural resources, and the boundless pursuit of individual happiness has undermined the very fabric of our society. As the big ideas of the nineteenth and early twentieth centuries are no longer tenable, Lyotard and other postmodern thinkers postulated the end of **modernity** and described western societies as being in a state of **postmodernity**.

In this book we use 'big ideas' to describe the concepts that lie at the very basis of professional practice in early childhood care and education. Although we think they are important and students and practitioners should be familiar with them, we also think it is time to take them off their pedestals. One of them, which we discuss in more detail below, is **development**.

# SECTION TWO

## CHAPTER 5

# Reflective Practice and Critical Reflection

At this point in history, it seems that there are certain responsibilities that fall to us. Recently, reactionary forces have obtained success in proclaiming the disappearance of ideologies and the advent of a new history, one devoid of social classes and, therefore, without antagonistic interests or class struggle. At the same time, they maintain that there is no need to keep talking about dreams, utopia, or social justice. However, to me, **it is impossible to live without dreams**. How can we accept these neoliberal discourses which have been preached as if they were real and also keep alive our dreams? One way to accomplish that, I believe, is to awaken the political consciousness of the educators.

(Freire, 2007, p. 4)

## Overview

Reflective practice is *the* buzzword in early childhood. Many books are available to support you in becoming a **reflective practitioner** (among them the excellent *Reflective practice and early years professionalism* by Jenny Lindon (2010)). In this chapter we explore **reflective practice** and **critical reflection** against the background of changing expectations towards early childhood practitioners in the Irish ECEC context and with an eye on the Anti-Bias Goals for respecting diversity and working towards equality. The goals encourage us to become conscious and critical about diversity, and to engage confidently with difference and discrimination in all its forms. We begin our exploration with a close look at some expectations towards you, expressed in the curriculum framework. Aistear is underpinned by a holistic image of the child and it acknowledges that it takes reflective practitioners to realise this in everyday ECEC practice. While this is an important acknowledgement, which has many consequences for practice and professional preparation, we ask whether it is enough, considering the inequalities children and families face in this country. The short answer is that we think that the word *critical* needs to come into our understanding of reflection. We explore the concept of critical reflection from different perspectives and with different theoretical lenses.

Most of the time you will hear that it is the individual practitioner (you!) who needs to become **critically reflective**. We agree, but in the last part of the chapter we ask a question that is often neglected: what are the preconditions that you need as a practitioner in order to become reflective – and what are the responsibilities of those around you – the institutions, organisations and agencies that together with you comprise the early childhood education and care system. To encourage you to take a critical look at this system (in other words, to adopt a **systemic perspective**), we introduce findings of a recent European research project towards the end of this chapter. Some questions for discussion at the end of the chapter invite you to examine how well suited to critically reflective practice your work environment actually is.

## Introduction: Reflective practitioners needed

In your studies or on a training course, you will almost certainly have encountered an expectation that you be, or become a reflective practitioner. Aistear, the Early Childhood Curriculum Framework, endorses the notion of reflectiveness as a key feature of professionalism in early childhood:

> Thinking about what to do, how to do it and why, and then judging how well it went, is part of any professional's work. The reflective adult uses information about children's learning and development to think about his/her practice, and to identify how to improve it.
>
> (National Council for Curriculum and Assessment, 2009, p. 77)

Let us look at this statement in detail. What are its key messages regarding reflective practice? In the quote above, Aistear qualifies **reflection as a purposeful activity** at the very core of professional practice. Early childhood practitioners reflect upon – or think about – their practice. Doing so is by no means an add-on, or something you do 'on top of everything else'. Instead, reflection is an integral part of professional practice in early childhood care and education. Thinking and doing are two aspects of the same practice; one can't be done without the other.

The statement also combines and emphasises a number of important aspects or **purposes** of reflective practice, e.g. aiming to change and improve your practice, making use of what you know about children's learning, and exchanging and engaging with other practitioners, children and parents. Take a look at how Aistear describes what reflective practitioners do when they think about their practice:

## Thinking about practice ...

▸ **in order to improve it:**
The reflective adult uses information about children's learning and development to think about his/her practice, and to identify how to improve it.

▸ **with others:**
He/she may do this in partnership with colleagues and/or other professionals.

▸ **in order to do things differently:**
This reflection may result in the adult changing the way he/she interacts with children and their parents, re-organising the room, changing routines, planning particular activities, and providing specific materials and objects.

▸ **for purposes of assessment:**
The adult also shares assessment information with the children and their parents and uses the information to plan for children's progress

(National Council for Curriculum and Assessment, 2009, p. 77)

# Reflective practice is not enough

While Aistear recognises the importance of reflective practice as key to professionalism, it does so from a particular point of view. 'Reflection' is understood as a purposeful activity, undertaken by the practitioner, in order to improve their practice. It is grounded in a body of knowledge ('information about children's learning and development') which, we should assume, he or she has acquired through studies and training, and it aims at improving specific aspects of life in the ECEC setting (e.g. organisation of the room, provision of material, curricular activities).

No doubt, thinking about what you do, how you do it and sharing your thinking with fellow workers and parents in order to improve outcomes for children is important. But is it enough? Certainly not, we argue in this book. The problem is that this widespread understanding of reflective practice doesn't touch the big ideas – the values, theories and assumptions that underpin our understanding and knowledge. **Reflection** is very much about staying *in* the picture and asking whether we do things the right way, or how we could do things better. **Critical reflection** is about stepping *out* of the picture and asking whether we do the right things.

## 5.1 Jargon Buster: Reflective practice and critical reflection

**Reflective practice:**
Reflective practitioners systematically look at their practice, either on their own or with others. They think and talk about what they are doing in their day-to-day practice with children, and how it could be improved.

**Critical reflection:**
Practitioners who engage in critical reflection do this too, but they add a new dimension to their questions: more important than looking at how things are done is to ask why they are done the way they are, for what purpose and for whose benefit. Instead of asking how practice could be improved, they ask whether things could be done differently, based on different values, and in ways that would be more just and equitable for all children and families.

## Single- and double-loop learning: Two types of reflective practice

Thinking about professional practice in terms of *what* and *how* has been widely criticised by authors from different backgrounds, including management theory and adult education. In their 1996 book on the theory and practice of organisational learning, Chris Argyris and Donald Schön (1996) talk about two different kinds of learning in organisations as different as commercial companies, government departments, hospitals and educational institutions. In all of these organisations they identify a culture of dealing with challenges that could be described as reflective: members of the organisation look at their practices, or routines, in order to improve performance or to correct an error. They quite often do so within the existing goals, underlying values, plans and rules of the organisation. Here is what the reflective cycle looks like:

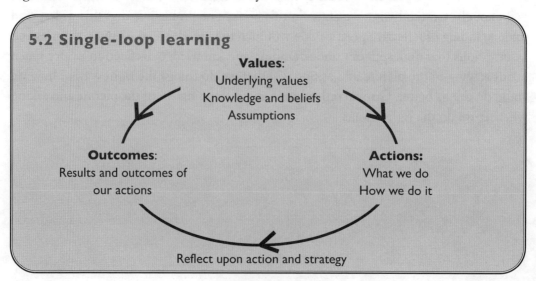

## 5.2 Single-loop learning

**Values**:
Underlying values
Knowledge and beliefs
Assumptions

**Outcomes**:
Results and outcomes of
our actions

**Actions:**
What we do
How we do it

Reflect upon action and strategy

This is alright as long as the outcomes of our actions are in line with what we had in mind. 'It worked', we might say, and feel reassured that we are on the right track. But what if the results and consequences are unexpected, surprising or challenging – if it didn't work the way we intended it to?

If we stay in the cycle above, we might reflect upon how to improve our results so we can get it right next time. Short-term, more-of-the-same solutions are regularly the result of such attempts to do things right (or better). Argyris and Schön refer to this common practice as **single-loop learning**.

There is an obvious problem with this approach: the goals, values and rules that govern the organisation – their frame of reference – are taken as givens; they are not questioned. Instead of reflecting whether we do things the right way, Argyris and Schön suggest we should systematically enquire whether we are (still) doing the right things. Conditions and contexts for the work might have changed dramatically, raising the question whether the guiding principles and values of our practice are still appropriate. This kind of questioning, which leads to changes in attitudes and values, is referred to as **double-loop learning**. In double-loop learning, reflection is on both the action (what we do or have done) and the implicit assumptions:

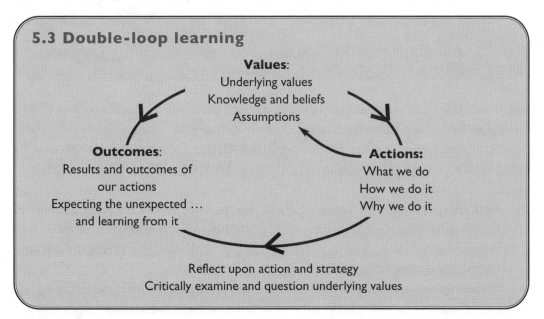

## 5.3 Double-loop learning

**Values**:
Underlying values
Knowledge and beliefs
Assumptions

**Outcomes**:
Results and outcomes of
our actions
Expecting the unexpected …
and learning from it

**Actions**:
What we do
How we do it
Why we do it

Reflect upon action and strategy
Critically examine and question underlying values

## 5.4 Further reading

As a concept, double-loop learning is closely related to understandings of learning developed by Gregory Bateson (1973, 2000) and to extended concepts of reflection (e.g. Boud, Keogh, and Walker, 1985).

# Introducing the 'critical' into reflection

Being able to reflect on your practice – 'what to do, how to do it and why' (Aistear) – is clearly an important part of becoming a professional in ECEC. But it is certainly not enough. On its own, reflection does not necessarily transform practice – what we do and how we understand it. In order to be **transformative**, reflection needs to be part of a constant process of questioning the presuppositions for our day-to-day work with children, families and communities. It involves **raising awareness, challenging our own views, assumptions and biases, and enabling all participants to develop new insights**. Jack Mezirow, the American educationalist who developed the **transformative learning theory** has described this as 'the process of becoming critically aware of how and why our presuppositions have come to constrain the way we perceive, understand, and feel about our world' (Mezirow, 1990, p. 14). Mezirow introduced a new, and crucially important concept: that **reflection has to be critical in order to change we way we think and act.**

## 5.5 Transformative learning theory

Critical reflection is about becoming aware of our presuppositions: how and why they shape and constrain the way we understand our world.

Critical reflection links to transformative practice: to challenge the way we think and to change the way we act.

(Jack Mezirow)

But critical reflection is not just about engaging with our own individual understandings. **Critical reflection is a collective exercise**: something that is best done in 'partnership with other colleagues and/or other professionals' (as Aistear rightly suggests), but also by engaging with children, families and members of the nearer and wider community.

▸ **Reflection** can be seen as thinking about your practice **within** the set boundaries of your setting, your daily routines, etc. It may help you to evaluate your work and improve it – but it does not fundamentally challenge the preconditions and underlying assumptions of that work.
▸ **Critical reflection** extends beyond the individual practitioner and beyond the individual ECEC service. As early childhood professionals we engage in critical reflection when we examine and question 'the social and political factors that that produce knowledge and practices, *together with the use of this knowledge to strategically transform education in socially progressive directions*' (Mac Naughton, 2003, p. 3, my emphasis).

Critical reflection is a key feature of our professional practice. As an approach to not only thinking about, but transforming practice, critical reflection is linked to political theories, e.g. Jürgen Habermas' theory of **communicative action** (Habermas, 1990) and Paulo Freire's concept of **conscientisation** (critical awareness) (Freire, 2000). They explore the emancipatory and empowering potential of questioning the 'big ideas' that underpin our practice.

Early childhood professionals and students are confronted with a whole array of big ideas or 'truths', about what it is like – or should be like – to be a child, and how children develop and how they should best be educated, to touch on only a few. It is our professional and ethical task to explore where those ideas come from and whose interests they serve. In a diverse and largely unequal world there is always more than one way of understanding the world. Yet some ways of knowing are valued more than others; some ways of understanding the world are deemed 'right' while others are often seen as irrelevant. Why, for instance, should we believe that all children normally develop the same way regardless of the circumstances in which they grow up? In other words, why should we believe that it is normal to be a white, middle-class child, and that being black, disabled, or from an immigrant family is not? The question we need to ask is **whose experiences and ways of knowing are valued** – and whose voices are silenced in the process of establishing our big ideas.

## 5.6 Critical reflection is about:

- asking questions
- becoming conscious
- not taking anything for granted
- moving from reflection to action

## 5.7 Becoming *critically* reflective, you might want to ask questions like:

- how have we come to do things the way we do?
- how have we come to understand things the way we do?
- who benefits from how we do and understand things the way we do?
- who is silenced by how we do and understand things?
- how many other ways could there be to do and understand things?
- which of those ways might lead to more equitable and fair ways of doing and understanding thing?
- what are we going to do about it?

  (Adapted from Mac Naughton, 2003. See Diversity and Equality Guidelines for Childcare Providers (2006) for more critical questions.)

## Systemic conditions for critical reflection

So far, we have looked at what it means to be, or become, a reflective practitioner, and how this is spelled out in the Irish ECEC context, e.g. the National Early Childhood Curriculum Framework, Aistear. We have argued that being reflective is necessary, but not enough for practitioners working in contexts of Diversity and Equality. Working towards more just and equitable outcomes for all children requires critical reflection in order to examine, question, challenge and transform the preconditions and underlying values of every day early childhood practice. We have looked at how critical reflection extends beyond the individual practitioner as it inquires into the preconditions, context and consequences of ECEC as organised by our service – and in Irish society in general. Critical reflection is a collective exercise, a way of working *together* in a critical learning community (Urban, 2010; Van Keulen and Del Barrio Saiz, 2010). Critical reflection, one might say, is all about *you* and your co-workers, and how you choose to look at your professional world.

Well, it is, and it isn't. While becoming critically reflective is a precondition for working towards respect for diversity, social justice and equality, there are also preconditions for critical reflection. Early childhood practitioners don't exist in a vacuum. They work within an early childhood care and education system that in itself is shaped by cultural, social, economic, historical and political conditions of present-day Irish society. We have explored some of these conditions and their origins in Section One of this book.

With so much emphasis on *your* values, views, questions and actions, there is a risk that the responsibility for becoming and being critically reflective is left with the individual practitioner alone. As soon as we take a **systemic perspective** – if we keep the 'bigger picture' in mind, that is – other factors and responsibilities become visible. Supporting critical reflection as a key element of early childhood professional practice is shared responsibility between many actors at all the various levels of the ECEC system.

### 5.8 The ECEC system

There is a multitude of components, institutions, agencies and people who, in their various roles, contribute to how young children in our society are cared for and educated. All of them are connected. They influence each other and ultimately the experience of every young child in early childhood care and education in this country. That is why we refer to them as a 'system':

- practitioners
- service providers
- FETAC
- the whole variety of early childhood settings, e.g. preschools, play groups, nurseries, crèches, Montessori schools, naíonraí, etc.

- local authorities, e.g. County and City Childcare Committees
- different government departments and agencies, e.g. Health, Education, NCCA
- professional associations and provider organisations, e.g. Early Childhood Ireland, Association of Childcare Professionals
- Colleges, Institutes of Technology and Universities
- policy and advocacy groups, e.g. Start Strong
- training providers
- trade unions

What are the contributions of all these different organisations to supporting **critically reflective and transformative practice** in Irish ECEC? And, more importantly, is this question of any relevance to your immediate work with children, families and communities in your setting? If we think it is (and indeed we do) then we need to include the entire system and its components into our critical analysis. Let's think back to the earlier sections of this chapter, and revisit the very basics of critically reflective practice.

**Critical reflection**, we said, means *thinking* about our practice, its underlying values, preconditions, consequences, etc., in order to *transform* ECEC so it becomes more just and equitable for *all* children and families. From a systemic perspective at least three key questions arise:

1.  **How are early childhood students and practitioners supported to become critically reflective?**

    Asking this question leads us, for instance, to the responsibilities of training institutions and colleges: is critical reflection part of the curriculum? If so, how do colleges, FETAC, etc., ensure that they create spaces for critical reflection within their courses so that it becomes a **lived experience** for students? How can students be expected to address issues of diversity and difference, inequality, discrimination and privilege with children unless they have a safe space for addressing these issues for themselves and with others?

2.  **What are the practical arrangements and conditions for critical reflection in the workplace?**

    This question leads directly to the often precarious working conditions of many practitioners in ECEC: is there paid time for all practitioners to participate in joint reflection, discussion, planning activities, etc.? Are these actively encouraged, supported and facilitated in the workplace? How are professional associations, trade unions, policy makers and others responsible for governing and regulating the sector ensuring that proper conditions be put in place for all early childhood practitioners?

3.   **If critical reflection is about transformation, what is the scope for real change?**
     Finally, if critical reflection is supposed to bring about transformation, we need to
     ask whether there is scope for *real* change. This, in turn, leads to the responsibility
     of management, regulation, funding and governance: does the way that the setting
     is organised encourage you to try things out and do things differently? Are
     practitioners and providers encouraged and supported to develop different services
     that meet the rights and needs of all children and families in the community?

The importance of a systemic perspective has been emphasised by a European research
project that explored what competences are required for working with young children,
families and communities. From in-depth case studies and a survey in different European
countries a recent research project on 'competence requirements in early childhood
education and care' (CoRe) (Urban, Vandenbroeck, et al, 2011) concludes that
'competence' in early childhood education and care has to be developed at all levels of the
system. The box below provides an excerpt from the CoRe report.

## 5.9 Competence in early childhood

A key finding of CoRe is that 'competence' in the early childhood education and care context
has to be understood as a characteristic of the entire early childhood system. The competent
system develops in reciprocal relationships between individuals, teams, institutions and the
wider socio-political context. A key feature of a 'competent system' is its support for
individuals' to realize their capabilities to develop responsible and responsive practices that
respond to the needs of children and families in ever-changing societal contexts. At the level
of the individual practitioner, being and becoming 'competent' is a continuous process that
comprises the capability and ability to build on a body of professional knowledge, acquire
practical skills and develop and show professional values. While it is important to have a 'body
of knowledge' and 'practical skills', practitioners and teams also need reflective competences
as they work in highly complex, unpredictable and diverse contexts. A 'competent system'
requires possibilities for all staff to engage in joint learning and critical reflection. This includes
sufficient paid time for these activities. A competent system includes collaborations between
individuals and teams, institutions (pre-schools, schools, support services for children and
families…) as well as 'competent' governance at policy level.

(CoRe, Urban, Vandenbroeck et al 2011)

The following table summarises the competence requirements at different levels of the
ECEC system:

## 5.10 Competence requirements in ECEC (CoRe)

| Level | Being capable to |
|---|---|
| **Individual competences** | Work towards social change<br>Communicate openly and enable reciprocal dialogue<br>Critically reflect: dealing with complex issues from diverse angles<br>Learn from disagreements<br>Deal with unpredictability and uncertainty<br>Co-construct new practice and knowledge with children, families and colleagues |
| **Institutional competences** | Arrange (paid) time for all staff to meet, plan, document, and reflect<br>Take part in action–research projects<br>Collaborate with research institutions |
| **Inter-institutional competences** | Network among ECEC institutions of the same district<br>Collaborate between ECEC institutions and health care and social services<br>Enable continuity between ECEC and primary education<br>Establish Partnership between ECEC institutions and training institutions<br>Connect ECEC institutions with local authorities and institutions |
| **Competences of governance at local, regional, national and European level** | Develop and promote a vision of ECEC as a public good<br>Ensure quantity and quality of provision<br>Arrange paid 'non-contact' time for all staff (for planning, documenting and reflection)<br>Facilitate opportunities for professional development for all staff<br>Design curricula and competence profile frameworks in consultation with stakeholders<br>Provide fair employment conditions<br>Coordinate interaction and collaboration between different governmental departments<br>Invest in qualified pedagogical support personal<br>Address the gender gap |

(Source: CoRe, Competence requirements in ECEC)

## 5.10 Suggestion for critical reflection

- Discuss the 'competences' that have been identified by the CoRe research project with your group of learners or your co-workers.
- How are these competences realised and supported in your learning environment, your workplace, in ECEC in locally and nationally?
- What gaps can you identify and who has the capacity to close them?
- Who are potential allies for working towards realising a fully 'competent system' in Irish ECEC?

# Summary

We began this chapter by examining a common expectation – that early childhood practitioners should be, or become, **reflective practitioners** in order to be able to fulfil their increasingly challenging tasks of supporting children's well-being and learning. This expectation is clearly stated, for instance, in the Early Childhood Curriculum Framework, Aistear. We explored different possible **purposes of reflection** upon your professional practice and found that **reflection on its own does not suffice** for working towards social change, respect for diversity and **more equitable outcomes for all** children and families. Taking a further step, we then looked at two different types of reflective practice, as described by Chris Argyris and Donald Schön: **single-** and **double-loop learning**. We discussed why it is important to include questions about the underlying values and assumptions for our work into the reflective cycle in order to make them visible and change them. We then introduced **the crucial difference between reflection and critical reflection** which aims to 'strategically transform' our care and education practices 'in socially progressive directions' (Mac Naughton, 2003, p. 3). Linking critical reflection to the work of critical theorists and educators, especially Paulo Freire's notion of **critical awareness** or **conscientisation**, we arrived at four interconnected components that characterise critically reflective practitioners: they ask questions, become conscious, don't take anything for granted, and move from reflection to action. In the final part of the chapter we extended the critically reflective framework from the individual practitioner to the early childhood care and education system – to the institutional, economic, historical and political conditions that shape the lives of children, families and communities, as well as the working environment of early childhood practitioners in this country. We asked how practitioners are supported to become, and be, critically reflective, and inquired about the scope for transformation – for meaningful change – of the way we organise and practice ECEC in our setting and, more generally, in Ireland. The chapter concluded by making a link between the Irish situation and the findings of a recent European research project (CoRe) that has identified responsibilities for change at every layer of the ECEC system: from the individual, to the institutional, the inter-institutional and governance level. A 'competent system', we concluded, actively addresses diversity and equality at each level.

## CHAPTER 6

# How do we know what we know about early childhood?

Why, anybody can have a brain. That's a very mediocre commodity. Every pusillanimous creature that crawls on the Earth or slinks through slimy seas has a brain. Back where I come from, we have universities, seats of great learning, where men go to become great thinkers. And when they come out, they think deep thoughts and with no more brains than you have. But they have one thing you haven't got: a diploma.

(*The Wizard of Oz*)

## Overview

In this chapter we will take a closer look at the **body of knowledge** that underpins our professional practice with young children, families and communities. As with the historical and political context of our work that we discussed that in Chapter 1, it is important to develop a critical approach to the knowledge and the theories that underpin our professional practice. In short, what we are encouraging you to do in this chapter is to take theory off the pedestal and start asking some critical questions. If you are new to the field of early childhood, e.g. if you are studying to become an early childhood professional, you will obviously want to find out what you need to know about early childhood education and care. In this chapter, we want to encourage you to go beyond the question of what knowledge you need. We start the chapter with an interrogation into how we understand what knowledge means in our field, how it relates to our professional practice, and where it comes from. This leads us to critiquing an approach to learning and education that Paulo Freire, the Brazilian educator and writer, has called 'the banking concept'. We ask how a different understanding of how knowledge is produced leads to an acknowledgement of the practitioners, children and families as active co-constructors of knowledge in our field. The chapter should give you an idea that the most important theoretical 'pillars' of our practice are not sacred, universal truths. On the contrary, they represent specific views, developed in specific historic, social and cultural contexts and they quite often serve specific interests. **Whose interests?** is one of the questions we encourage you to ask. **What other ways of** understanding, knowing and doing could there be? is another. We conclude the chapter by questioning critically, in some detail, one of the most important theoretical underpinnings of early childhood practice: child development.

---

### 6.1 Jargon Buster: Body of knowledge

The term 'body of knowledge' usually describes the complete set of concepts, terms and information that informs the way things are done in a particular profession (in this case, medicine, law, education and care. Yet the body of knowledge is much more than just a collection of information, books and articles; it is a way of looking at what counts as relevant knowledge in a profession and what doesn't. The relevance of knowledge can be contested even within a profession. For example, the medical profession has very different views on what is known about the human body depending on whether you are based in the western, 'scientific' or, for example the Chinese tradition (acupuncture).

Having professional knowledge enables us to do things right. In order to question and decide whether we do the right things, we need professional and personal values that give meaning to our knowledge. Professional values in early childhood education and care are based on children's rights, democracy and participation. Together, knowledge and values shape what we do: our professional practice.

Can you think of knowledge or values that are contested in the field of early childhood?

---

## Introduction: Coming to terms with what we 'know'

By now you might rightly say that we promised this book would be about practice – about doing things differently in early childhood – and all the first chapters talk about so far is history, concepts, knowledge and thinking. Fair enough. Perhaps we should have given you the health warning earlier. In order to do things differently, and to move from simply doing things right to doing the right things we will have to **engage with the knowledge that informs the way we act with children.** We will have to **explore where our knowledge comes from,** how, and by whom, it is generated and (being critically reflective) we will have to ask whether there are possible **other ways of knowing that might lead to other ways of doing.** So, yes (you saw it coming), this chapter deals with **theory and its relation to practice.** Are you still with us?

Let us come back to where we started this section: between adults, there seems to be a lot of common ground when it comes to talking about children. We know what children are supposed to be like – as girls and boys, aged, for example, two, three or six. Whatever way we look at it, **knowledge** and **understanding** plays a key role in informing our **actions,** our every day practices with children and families. But how do we know what we know about early childhood? The first and obvious answer to this question could be we acquire our knowledge through our professional preparation, in our studies at colleges and universities, and from those who are more **knowledgeable** than we are: lecturers, trainers, authors of academic books, etc. There is a lot to be read and learned out there. One might say the more of this knowledge we acquire, the better prepared we are for our work with children.

## The problem with knowledge

However, as you might have guessed, there are some fundamental problems with this answer. The first of these problems is not so much about *what* we need to know from the vast body of professional literature and theory – it is about the very nature of knowledge itself. The idea that knowledge is *produced* by scholars and researchers in a university somewhere, then *passed down* through lectures, books and trainings to those who first, as learners, *acquire* and then, as practitioners, *apply* knowledge, is deeply ingrained in our modern society and in our education system. This is, we all had to learn, how schools and universities work. They produce and transmit knowledge for you to take and apply. In our case, we apply it to our work with children and families.

The strange thing about this way of understanding what knowledge is all about is that it leaves us with a concept of knowledge that has little to do with real people and their roles in the knowledge-production-and-application process. Yes, we are talking about *you*, as you will see a bit further down in this chapter. It is almost as if knowledge were an object that could be handed from one person (the teacher, the adult) to the other (the learner, the child).

Knowledge, from this point of view, is something one can possess and accumulate in one's mind. Paulo Freire, the Brazilian educator and leading thinker of a critical pedagogy, has coined the term 'banking system' to describe our educational institutions that operate within this frame of thinking (Freire, 2000). His term resonates with other once well-established ideas about learning, e.g. that children are empty vessels, waiting to be filled with knowledge by the adult. The real banking system produces and maintains huge inequalities between those who have and those who have not. The same is true for the 'banking system' of education: this understanding of knowledge, learning and teaching produces and maintains inequality, privilege and exclusion. As we can see anywhere around us, the possession of the right kind of knowledge is a powerful determiner of inclusion or exclusion, of our place in society.

> ### 6.2 Discuss
>
> Educational institutions (preschools and schools, FE and HE colleges and universities) are **gatekeepers**. As educators working in these institutions, including early childhood institutions, we have to take a stand: Do we want to keep the gates tightly shut for those not deemed fit – or do we struggle to push them wide open for an inclusive education for all?
>
> - With your group of learners, share your own experiences as a learner in preschool, school or college
> - Can you think of any examples of exclusion or inclusion through educational institutions?

## Another problem with knowledge – and a glance of hope

A second problem with this prevalent understanding of knowledge and the roles of learners is that it leaves us stuck in the past. Knowledge, it suggests, is static and representative of the world as it is, or as is was at the time of its creation. Organising schools the way we do in most modern societies, we are prone to reproduce and apply yesterday's solutions to today's and tomorrow's problems. This has widely been criticised as inappropriate. Some authors, including the American anthropologist Margaret Mead, explain that in our rapidly changing modern societies, adults simply cannot know what to teach their children because their experience is grounded in the past. She suggests we need a radical new relationship between adults and children, teachers and learners, one that 'keeps the future open' and she claims 'we are all immigrants into a new era' (Mead, 1978). Others, writing about the epistemological foundations of modern schooling, identify a shift in thinking about knowledge. Instead of knowledge being static, Gert Biesta and Deborah Osberg write that it is 'caught up with the activity and situations in which it is produced' (Biesta and Osberg, 2007).

---

### 6.3 Jargon Buster: Epistemology

Epistemology is the study of knowledge and justified belief. As the study of knowledge, epistemology is concerned with the following questions: What are the necessary and sufficient conditions of knowledge? What are its sources? What is its structure, and what are its limits? [...] Understood more broadly, epistemology is about issues having to do with the creation and dissemination of knowledge in particular areas of inquiry.

(http://plato.stanford.edu/entries/epistemology/)

The question is: how do we know what we know?

---

Paulo Freire, in his classic *Pedagogy of the Oppressed*, first published in 1970, has an almost poetic way of making the same argument that Gert Biesta and Deborah Osberg picked up many years later. Here is how Paulo Freire wrote about the banking system of education – in his own words:

> In the banking concept of education, knowledge is a gift bestowed by those who consider themselves knowledgeable upon those whom they consider to know nothing. Projecting an absolute ignorance onto others, a characteristic of the ideology of oppression, negates education and knowledge as processes of inquiry. The teacher presents himself to his students as their necessary opposite; by considering their ignorance absolute, he justifies his own existence. The students, alienated like the slave in the Hegelian dialectic, accept their ignorance as

justifying the teachers existence – but unlike the slave, they never discover that they educate the teacher.

(Freire, 2000, p. 53)

> ### 6.4
>
> For apart from inquiry, apart from the praxis, individuals cannot be truly human. Knowledge emerges only through invention and re-invention, through the restless, impatient continuing, hopeful inquiry human beings pursue in the world, with the world, and with each other.
>
> (Freire, 2000, p. 53)
>
> Can you connect Freire's thoughts with your observation of a two-year-old exploring their world?

Let us get 'epistemology' back on the ground. If we understand knowledge as something that is static, decontextualised from real people's lives and produced in universities, then you, as practitioner, are out of the picture, and so are the children and families with whom you work. If, on the other hand, we can understand knowledge as deeply embedded in real-life situations and as something that emerges from our active engagement with the world, you, as practitioner, are *in* the picture. All of a sudden we can see how practitioners, children, families all contribute to what we know about children, their lives and our professional early childhood practice.

## Taking theory off the pedestal

We tend to put theory on a pedestal, especially in contrast to practice. Practice, we might say, is about *doing* something, while theory is the abstract knowledge about it. Theory, then, is meant to inform practice, as a kind of universal blueprint for actions we take in our professional work. While we might admire the apparently superior role of theory in the hierarchy of knowledge, we also nurture our suspicions about this top-down relationship between theory and practice. We say, for instance, 'this should work, in theory', actually expecting it to fail, because what we perceive as theoretical knowledge often fails to take into account the complications and the messiness of real life.

Early childhood education and care and its professional practices are informed, to a large extent, by theories that promise to provide us with universal insights and guidance for our professional practice. Sometimes these theories, or 'big ideas' as we might call them, are so deeply ingrained in our understanding of the world that we take them for granted. We don't even think of questioning them because we believe them to be universal truths. Don't worry – this is not a specific flaw of the early childhood profession. Authors from a wide range of disciplines have pointed out the problems with the notion of universal truths that underpins much of modern science and society.

Michel Foucault, the French philosopher, links these theories to an accepted way of talking about something. There are **dominant discourses**, he explains, that are so powerful that they result in a **regime of truths** that can't be questioned. Postmodern and poststructuralist thinkers have long urged us to question these universal beliefs, arguing that, to take one example, western science is only one way, albeit a powerful one, of explaining the world, and that all our knowledge has to be seen in its political, historical and cultural contexts. There are, they suggest, always many perspectives on what counts as true and we must actively seek them and encourage those who are usually silenced and marginalised. In doing so we need to explore where these so-called truths have come from, which inevitably leads us to the question of who has created them and whose interests they serve.

Consider, for example, the passage from Gaile Cannella's and Radhika Viruru's book *Childhood and Postcolonisation* below and discuss it with your learning group. How come academic research on children seems to have favoured some research questions over others? In whose interest do *you* think this is?

---

### 6.5

If one believes that there are fundamental truths about human beings that exist and that rigorous study is the way to reveal those truths, then the Western scientific study of childhood that has taken place and that forms the basis for many of our current understandings of childhood makes some sense. If, instead, one focuses on power (e.g., colonialist, imperialist, capitalist, psychological, adult, and otherwise) and what to do in situations when one group has more power than another, entirely different questions and knowledges are enacted. For example, why have we (in fields concerned with younger human beings) not focused more on ways in which to make children's perspectives a much larger part of the discourse on childhood? Or, rather than exhaustive studies on whether children can tell if a tall, thin glass has more liquid than a short, fat one, why haven't questions like possibilities for lowering the voting age been looked at in more detail?

(Cannella and Viruru, 2004, p. 7)

---

## A 'big idea' at the foundation of ECEC practice: The dilemma with development

One of the most powerful and influential 'big ideas' in our field, for instance, forms the very core of our professional practice: that there is a distinction between children and adults; that children develop (progress) towards adulthood, and that adults (e.g. parents, teachers or experts) possess knowledge and judgemental power over children. If it weren't for our firm belief in this distinction, wouldn't it be hard to legitimise educational institutions, curricula and, not least our own profession? However, for critically reflective early childhood professionals – as discussed in the previous chapter – the theoretical question of how we understand and explain child development becomes a very practical one when we decide how to engage with diversity and how to actively promote equality in our practice with children, families and communities.

When we conceptualise **children as becoming instead of being**, as people who have yet to arrive at being fully developed adult human beings, we reinforce the distinction between adult and child, teacher and student. Paulo Freire identifies this distinction as the core of oppressive education: '**by considering their [the children's] ignorance absolute, he [the teacher, practitioner who is most likely a she in our field] justifies his own existence**' (Freire, 2000).

There are some critical questions for early childhood practitioners in there: Can we understand ourselves as professionals and build a strong professional identity *without* having to construe others (children, parents) as inferior? Can we move proactively from unequal to more equitable power relationships in our practice, and build our professional identity on respect and mutual acknowledgement? We will come back to those questions in the following chapter when we discuss approaches to diversity and equality and introduce the Anti-Bias Goals for children and adults.

## 6.6 Jean Piaget and developmental psychology

Below is an excerpt from a student's critical examination of Jean Piaget's influence in early childhood practice and theory:

> One of the most prominent figures in the history of early childhood developmental thinking was that of Jean Piaget, a Swiss developmental psychologist. Jean Piaget's theory has had such an impact on the territory of early childhood development that it has informed educational practices and policies. Neither a child psychologist nor expert upon the field of childhood education, it is remarkable that such a figure in history has had a fundamental effect on child development and the discourse of the latter. It is not uncommon to hear either teachers or parents make the remark, 'it is a stage that she is going through, which is common for their age group...!' Such thinking and perspective of early childhood development has dominated the landscape of early childhood development.
>
> Jean Piaget was interested in the way that children learnt, thought and how they acquired knowledge; thereby formulated stages to illustrate the 'Phases of cognitive thinking', sometimes referred to as the developmental milestone theory (Piaget, 1952, 1954).
>
> (Student, 2010)

Although we often identify developmental theory with the work of Jean Piaget, the idea that children pass through a series of predictable 'stages' on their way to adulthood has been accepted knowledge in western society for hundreds of years (Walsh, 2005). Comenius (1592–1670) compared children's development to the growth of plants; Pestalozzi (1746–1827) wrote about the **laws of human unfolding** and Friedrich Froebel, the nineteenth-century pioneer of early childhood education, introduced the definition of early childhood we still use today – as being a distinct period from birth through age eight.

The 'truth' that children develop makes early childhood education as a profession possible:

> Because it was thought that young children differ developmentally, it necessarily followed that they learn differently from older children and adults. Consequently, it was thought that schooling for young children should differ from schooling for older children and adults.'
>
> (Chung and Walsh, 2000)

Establishing the difference between children of different age groups, and most important, between children and adults, has a number of drastic consequences (besides legitimating our profession, that is!). From such a vantage point, it is easy to see and treat children, especially very young children as

▸ inferior to adults, because they are not yet fully developed
▸ 'becomings' rather than beings
▸ future members of society, instead of as citizens and bearers of rights in the here and now.

## Are you normal?
Another drastic consequence of our supposed ability to predict how (all) children (should) develop is that it introduces the notion of normality. The 'normal' child is the one who develops according to the prescribed stages, goals and predetermined outcomes. When children fall into the many categories of abnormality and pathology we have invented for them (and there are many such children) – we make ourselves believe that there must be something wrong with their

▸ bodies
▸ minds
▸ behaviour
▸ family.

What other categories can you think of? Each of these categories and labels define difference in a negative way, establish 'special' educational 'needs' and call for all sorts of professional intervention.

## Beyond Piaget

Piaget's notion of universal, predictable stages undergone by all children has been challenged widely by authors who took another angle on 'development': Lev Vygotsky has pointed out the **influence of the cultural and historical context** in which children grow up (Vygotsky, 1978); Urie Bronfenbrenner, in his **ecology of human development**, reminds us of the complexity of individuals' experiences in the **micro- and macro-systems of society** which he described as 'a set of nested structures, each inside the next, like a set of Russian dolls' (Bronfenbrenner, 1979).

Developmental psychology, as a discipline, has moved beyond early twentieth century concepts that described children's development in universal and absolute terms. Instead, contemporary developmental psychologists tend to describe development as a result of complex interactions between influences of nature (biology) and social context (culture, history, etc.). See for instance Richard M. Lerner's definition in a handbook of child psychology:

---

**6.7**

These mechanistic and atomistic views of the past have been replaced by theoretical models that stress the dynamic of multiple layers of analysis, a perspective having its roots in systems theories of biological development [...]

In other words, development [is] understood as a property of systemic change in the multiple and integrated levels of organization (ranging from biology to culture and history) [of] human life and its ecology.

(Lerner, 1998)

---

Strangely enough, this conceptual and theoretical shift from a universal understanding of children's development (definite stages that are the same for all children, regardless of the context of their upbringing) towards recognising the influence of the very different realities of children's lives was made by mainstream developmental psychology a good while ago, from the second half of the twentieth century, but it is yet to make its way into early childhood programmes that consider themselves to be developmental.

### Questioning the universal child

Ideas about child development, it seems, have become one of the 'truths' of our practice and profession. A 'good' early childhood programme, we all seem to agree, is one that is developmental. This consensus extends across the board to include practitioners, early childhood professional preparation courses at colleges, as well as large international organisations that fund early childhood programmes in developing countries of the world like the World Bank.

Early childhood programmes, curricula and practices, the story goes, can be determined by knowledge of children's development. Once we know how children develop, we can apply this knowledge to deliver **developmentally appropriate practices**.

## 6.8 Jargon Buster: Developmentally Appropriate Practice (DAP)

DAP is promoted by the American National Association for the Education of Young Children (NAEYC).

As NAEYC defines it, DAP is a framework of principles and guidelines for best practice in the care and education of young children, birth through age eight. It is grounded both in the research on how young children develop and learn and in what is known about education effectiveness. The principles and guidelines outline practice that promotes young children's optimal learning and development.

(National Association for the Education of Young Children, 2009)

Assuming that you have read this chapter from the beginning, there should be some alarm bells ringing now. Remember our excursus to understandings of knowledge and how we think it is generated (**epistemology**)? Here are some questions you might want to ask yourself – perhaps you can discuss them with others, too:

## 6.9 Discuss

**Where does your knowledge about children's development come from?**
From lectures, textbooks, lessons taught at college?
From your own personal experience of being a parent, being your parents' child?
From your own professional experience in working with a particular group of children, their families and community?

**Who participates in creating this knowledge – and who doesn't?**
Academic authorities, theorists and writers?
Families and local community?
Children?
You and your fellow workers?

**Who is the child we have in mind when we say our practice in the nursery is developmentally appropriate?**
An idea of a 'universal' child?
A real girl or boy in your setting?

# Deconstructing developmental psychology

Where does your knowledge and understanding come from, and what is your own role in developing understandings about children? Erica Burman undertook a close examination of developmental psychology, its history as a scientific discipline and its specific way of constructing knowledge about children. Her book is called *Deconstructing Developmental Psychology* (Burman, 2008). She explains that in the nineteenth century, the pioneers of developmental psychology in Europe had to prove themselves in a very specific academic climate. Natural sciences – physics, chemistry, biology – were still struggling to develop their distinct identities as scientific disciplines. They were eager to define their boundaries (what counts as scientific, in a particular discipline) and their methods, and they were competing for recognition. Moreover, science, in western, industrial societies was about factual knowledge that could be discovered by applying scientific methods. The world, nineteenth-century scientists believed, was waiting to be discovered, measured and counted. If you see the world as giant clockwork, then science can tell how exactly how it ticks.

In order to be taken seriously, early psychologists had to model themselves and their young discipline in a particular way. Most important, they had to have a distinct object of their studies and agree on a set of scientific methods and come up with a coherent frame of thinking (a theory) that allowed for rational explanations of their findings.

It was in this time and climate that the universal child was invented. Not that it ever existed, in the real life of highly diverse and unequal nineteenth-century Europe, but it proved extremely helpful to build developmental psychology as an accepted scientific discipline. The idea of the universal child worked so well because it assumed that all children were the same, regardless of where and how they grew up. This theoretical construct was useful for the development of the new scientific discipline (developmental psychology), but it also had major implications for another relatively new field of practice: that of early childhood care and education. In our field, the universal child, as a theoretical construct, translated into the idea that all children of a particular age should be treated the same, regardless of where and how they grow up.

This is of course a highly problematic notion. Here are two of many reasons why:

- First, the notion of universality and sameness completely ignores the **diversity between children** (just take a look around your classroom, your service), making it difficult if not impossible to a) embrace difference and diversity and b) to address the existing inequalities within this diversity. This is a major concern for current ECEC practices in Ireland.
- Second, grounded in the western socio-cultural context (the minority of the world), practices and programmes grounded in the notion of the universal child tend to be

imposed onto socio-cultural contexts elsewhere (the majority of the world), largely ignoring the **diversity of the contexts of growing up**. Alan Pence and Kofi Marfo (2008), writing about early childhood programmes in a number of African countries funded or set up by international agencies, express their concern about the 'uncritical adoption of program and service delivery models grounded in value systems and knowledge bases that may not be appropriate for the continent'. The 'implantation of Minority World ECD services and practices in the Majority World', they argue, 'is symptomatic of the failure of Minority World systems and frameworks to fully understand and embrace diversity of cultural contexts'.

## Summary

How do we know what we know about early childhood? The main message of this chapter is that knowledge and theory are always produced in particular circumstances and by particular people. What we know is tied up with the situations in which the knowledge is produced. It is tied up, too, with the people who contribute to the knowledge – and to those who are excluded because their knowledge and experience is seen as not relevant, not scientific, etc. With every idea and theory there is a vast hinterland of political, historical, philosophical, social, cultural, economic conditions that shape them. It is important to understand these connections because once they become visible, they open up the possibility of different **ways of knowing** which, in turn, open **alternative ways of being and doing**; i.e. alternative ways of developing your professional practice. These different **epistemologies** (how we think about knowledge) are particularly relevant when working towards embracing diversity and promoting equality for all children, families and communities. Understanding that **knowledge and theory are never neutral** allows critically reflective practitioners to actively write themselves, children and families into the story of the production of the professional body of knowledge. They can examine, discuss and document their experiences as complementary, not inferior to the knowledge, theory and evidence produced by scientific research.

Theory and practice are two inseparable aspects of our profession. As critically reflective practitioners, we contribute to both.

### 6.10

The fundamental certainty is that I can know. I know that I know. In the same way, I also know that I do not know, which predisposes me to know the following: first, that I can know better what I know; second, that I can know what I do not know yet; third, that I can produce forms of knowledge that do not exist yet.

(Freire, 1997, p. 37)

## Questions for critical reflection

Becoming and being professional in an early childhood care context, we have argued in the previous chapter, is about becoming critically reflective and about asking critical questions. Becoming critically reflective, as we have discussed in this chapter, is closely interconnected with the way we understand and approach the body of knowledge that orients our professional practice. One of the most important critical questions to ask, we suggest, is the question about our knowledge and understanding of children, their lives and realities. There are other questions to ask as well, and they are closely related to our own identity as professionals in early childhood care and education. They include:

▸ Are we ready to accept, embrace and cherish the diversity and messiness of children's and families' lives?

▸ Are we open to the constant uncertainty that is the result of not taking anything for granted?

▸ Can we be (and support others to become) researchers, inventors and experimenters in our work with children and families?

▸ Do we see ourselves as activists working towards changing children's lives for the better?

## CHAPTER 7

# Approaches to Diversity and Equality

It is necessary to take action and stand up for yourself. It is also important to stand up for others, as sometimes they are too weak or simply haven't the tools to do that on their own. And of course, there will always be people saying 'mind your own business', 'concentrate on your own life, that is his life, leave him alone', but I know that these are not what we call mature, responsible members of community.

(Learner, 2009)

## Overview

Following the critique and **deconstruction** of some of the assumptions that are often taken for granted that underpin early childhood education and care in the previous chapter, we now turn to something more cheerful (if you want to put it that way). In this chapter we ask what possibilities are there to orient our professional practice with young children, families and communities. What choices do early childhood professionals make when dealing with diversity and working towards more equitable experiences and outcomes for *all* children? We begin the chapter with an overview over **three different approaches to diversity** that you are likely to find in services. Most likely, you will recognise them from your studies and your visits to early childhood settings. We will then explore in more detail a fourth approach based on the **Anti-Bias Curriculum** and the diversity and equality practice as developed by the '*éist*' project in Ireland. The Anti-Bias approach informs key documents for the Irish ECEC sector, including Síolta (Centre for Early Childhood Development and Education, 2006), Aistear (National Council for Curriculum and Assessment, 2009) and the Diversity and Equality Guidelines for Childcare providers (Office of the Minister for Children, 2006). It is an activist approach with clear goals for adults and children that orient professionals in early childhood practice. Discussing different possible approaches will support you in making choices and taking a stand as an early childhood professional that embraces diversity and works towards equality and social justice. This chapter concludes the section on **re-thinking**

**early childhood education and care** and leads you into the third section of this book which is about choices made and changes introduced by ECEC practitioners in Ireland.

> ## 7.1 Jargon Buster: Social Justice
>
> Social Justice is a process, not an outcome, which (1) seeks fair (re)distribution of resources, opportunities, and responsibilities; (2) challenges the roots of oppression and injustice; (3) empowers all people to exercise self-determination and realize their full potential; (4) and builds social solidarity and community capacity for collaborative action.
>
> Working definition of social justice, collectively written by students attending the Social Justice Symposium at University of California, Berkeley. (http://socialwelfare.berkeley.edu/sjs/)

# Introduction: Approaches to Diversity

People can have different beliefs and assumptions about how best to deal with the undeniable reality of diverse societies. As we have explored in the previous chapters, those beliefs and assumptions influence our behaviour towards others. A first and most important step towards developing a professional stance is becoming conscious of our assumptions and belief systems. This is a real challenge for many as the process of becoming a critically reflective practitioner (see Section Two, Chapter 5) starts with turning the focus from others (who they are, what they need and how to teach them) to ourselves. The first question we can ask ourselves is, '**How have I come to see and understand things the way I do?**'

Just as individuals have belief systems and assumptions that shape the way they engage with the world, so too do organisations, professions and politics. In the case of the Irish ECEC system, these underlying beliefs have had (and continue to have) crucial influence on policies towards children and families (see Section One, Chapter 1).

Over time, different approaches to addressing the fact that people are different have been developed. All of them have left their traces in early childhood education and care practice.

In this chapter, we are going to look at some of them – and we ask you to develop your own conscious and informed professional and personal understanding of how you are going to approach the diversity and inequality in our society – starting with the early childhood setting you will be working in.

The definitions of approaches to diversity and equality in this chapter build on material first developed by the '*éist*' project. They have previously been published in various '*éist*' resources and publications, e.g. Murray, 2010 and Murray and O'Doherty, 2001, and, recently, in a chapter by Colette Murray in *Early Childhood Education and Care: An Introduction for Students in Ireland* (Taylor, M. and Mhic Mhathúna, M. (ed. 2012)).

# Where to begin?

Aistear, the early childhood curriculum framework (2009), Síolta, the quality framework (2006) and the Diversity and Equality Guidelines for Childcare Providers (2006) are good starting points for beginning your process of addressing diversity and equality. However, **approaches to diversity are not 'how-to' prescriptions for diversity and equality**. Your approach to work is closely tied to your own understanding and acceptance of diversity. Having a knowledge base of the approaches will give you tools to recognise, evaluate and eventually change what is happening in a setting. It will change your thinking on how diversity can be approached in ECEC practice.

---

### 7.2 Equality and Diversity: Aistear

Nurturing equality and diversity is important in early childhood. Promoting equality is about creating a fairer society in which everyone can participate equally with the opportunity to fulfil his/her potential. Diversity is about welcoming and valuing individual and group differences, and understanding and celebrating difference as part of life.

### Equality and Diversity: Síolta

Equality is an essential characteristic of quality ECEC. Quality early childhood settings acknowledge and respect diversity and ensure that that all children and families have their individual, personal, cultural and linguistic identity validated.

(CECDE, 2006)

---

Diversity is a reality, and so is social exclusion. There are different ways we can respond to this reality: we can aim to make the differences go away – usually by forcing those who we perceive to be different to become like us. This is called an **assimilationist approach**, and it is totally unacceptable, for reasons we will discuss below. A slightly more sophisticated approach to the fact that people are different would be to celebrate all the new and interesting experiences of 'others' (members of the minority culture) can bring to our environment: a **multicultural approach** encourages children to become tolerant of 'exotic' minority cultures in our society. That being different is not just an issue for others, but for the dominant, majority culture as well, is the underpinning of the **intercultural approach**, which aims at fostering understanding and respect between minority and majority cultures. After having have read through the first chapters of this book you will be able to point out the key problem of the three approaches mentioned above. You're right – they are all about culture, as if the only way that people differ from each other was as members of their ethnic groups, or as if culture were the only feature that determined people's identity.

In fact, people differ from one another in many ways, and who we are – our identity – is a kaleidoscope of many different features. People have a lot in common, too.

They share, for instance, the same humanity and are bearers of the same human/children's rights. The **Anti-Bias Approach** takes *all the ways people differ* as a starting point for an activist approach to education that aims at ensuring these human rights are respected for all children in our services. It works proactively towards achieving change in the ECEC setting and society. Therefore, in this chapter, we will focus on the Anti-Bias Approach in more detail.

## Assimilation in ECEC

If you follow an assimilationist approach, you believe that it is better for minorities to be absorbed into the main or dominant culture. The assumption underpinning assimilationist practices is that it is important for all children to share the same values – our values, that is. From an assimilationist point of view, ethnic diversity in society can only be divisive. **Assimilationists tend to assume that minority groups are inferior, deficient or lesser in some way.** Therefore, the expectation is that the members of minority groups change and adapt to the values that are prevalent, e.g. in the education system or the preschool. While assimilationist early childhood practitioners would need some tolerance and awareness for minority groups, there is no real demand for changing practices or the education system if you come from this perspective. It is easy to see why this approach has been criticised for being patronising, dismissive of other cultures and racist. Apart from that, it simply doesn't work. The expectation that minority communities, their needs and culture disappear over time, become invisible and absorbed into the majority culture has nothing to do with the reality of our society.

### Questions for exploration:
▸ Is this approach practiced today?
▸ Can you give an example of where it has been, or is practiced?
▸ Can you think of examples beyond Ireland?

## Multicultural approach

### 7.3 Jargon Buster: Multicultural approach
'Multicultural' refers to a society, group, school or organisation where people of different ethnicities, cultures and religions live, work and communicate with each other.

Most people tend to acknowledge that 'new' communities are now part of our society and that immigration is a reality (see Chapter 1). Fortunately, there is broad acknowledgement, too, that immigration has made a positive contribution to our society and economy, and quite often this recognition is paired with a genuine curiosity about the cultures of the new communities. Educators have long responded positively to new cultural diversity and have sought to celebrate the different cultures in an educational setting. Multicultural practices are widely accepted in early childhood education and care: we encourage families to bring in traditional food, put up pictures of people wearing exotic clothes and celebrate cultural or even religious festivals

▸    The multicultural approach to diversity acknowledges the need for recognition and celebration of different cultures in an early childhood education and care setting.
▸    It focuses only on **cultural diversity** and specifically on the **exotic** or **touristic** cultural aspects such as food, festivals, dress, horse-drawn caravans, etc.

---

### 7.4 Discuss

Consider the following:

In Dublin's inner city, in an endeavour to welcome new communities many schools engage in the celebration of various cultures. Irish children remarked on the lack of celebration of the Irish children from the community.
Discuss with your group of learners:

- Does this scenario sound familiar to you?
- Can you give other examples of multicultural practices in early childhood education and care?
- What does it tell us about our understanding of culture? See the *Diversity and Equality* page on www.gillmacmillan.ie.
- What other ways of engaging with the reality of different cultures in one setting could there be?

---

There is a certainly a value to multicultural thinking and practice with regards to diversity. It encourages curiosity and acknowledges the need for broadening the content of the curriculum and for addressing specific needs of minorities. However, its focus on solely **cultural** aspects, particularly on those aspects of culture that appear interesting, exotic and different, makes it problematic, too. Multicultural practices have tended to be found in settings where there are mainly children from minorities and not addressed in settings where there are mainly majority children. This is most likely a consequence of celebrating the exotic elements of culture when addressing diversity.

In the UK in the 1960s the multicultural approach was initiated to support inclusion and break down barriers between new immigrant communities. It set out to change negative attitudes and practices around difference. Multiculturalists believe that if children are exposed to diversity through other cultures, languages and customs at an early stage, it will have a positive impact, and that children will become more tolerant and less likely to develop prejudiced ideas.

However, focusing on the exotic aspects of other cultures has the potential to confirm, or even cause, stereotypes, i.e., 'all Africans play drums and are brilliant dancers'. What is airbrushed from the picture, in a multicultural approach, is usually the broader societal context in which diversity – and inequality – exist. Issues of prejudice, discrimination, racism and power are not addressed.

# Intercultural approach

Unlike the multicultural approach that focuses on the exotic aspects of minority cultures and thus perpetuates their being different to what is 'normal' (the majority culture), the **intercultural approach** is about fostering understanding and respect *between* majority and minority cultures. It starts from the assumption that **culture and equity are not just issues for members of minority groups**. Addressing issues of diversity and equality is equally important for all children, be they members of the majority or minority group in society. One way of doing so is to start developing an awareness for one's own cultural identity (see the *Diversity and Equality* page on www.gillmacmillan.ie).

Intercultural approaches to education aim to:

- ▸ acknowledge the importance of assisting all people within early childhood education and care to become aware of their own cultural identity.
- ▸ emphasise the need to remove the blinkers that hinder people's ability to reflect on diversity issues.
- ▸ promote the necessity for diversity to be incorporated across all areas of the curriculum.
- ▸ acknowledge the need to look at racism and power relations.
- ▸ challenge stereotypes.

Developing intercultural early childhood education and care systems is about inclusion by design – not as an add-on or afterthought. In every aspect of their practice, policies and routines, ECEC practitioners should think about how to support diversity and inclusion, and how to address issues of stereotyping or prejudice.

The intercultural approach to ECEC is essentially about **creating the conditions for provision, participation, protection, interaction, respect and recognition** (NCCRI, 2008).

**7.5 Discuss**

- Is the intercultural approach practised today?
- Can you give an example of where it has been, or is practiced?
- Re-read the scenario about celebrating different cultures in Dublin's inner-city schools. How could you approach this situation from an intercultural perspective?

# The Anti-Bias Approach

Culture plays an important role in determining who we are, how we see ourselves and how we distinguish ourselves from other individuals and groups. But is it the only way people form their identity – both as individuals and groups? Is being a member of a particular cultural group the only way that people differ? Certainly not. Think about yourself for a moment and look in an imaginary mirror: what would you say determines who you are, where you feel you belong and how others see you and how you see yourself? I can only assume that what you see in the mirror is a person of a certain **age**, a specific **gender** (male, female or transgender) and yes, almost certainly, of a particular **ethnic or cultural background**. What if this 'ethnic and cultural background' happens to be 'Irish'? Well, remember what you read in chapter one about the diversity at the very core of Irish society over the centuries? Even being culturally Irish can mean having many different roots, and is diverse in itself.

There are many more aspects of your identity than can be seen in the mirror, which can only show what's on the surface. Beyond that is a person who may belong to a **family** and **community**, who has certain **abilities**, is a member of a **social class** and has a **sexual orientation** (e.g. hetero-, bi- or homosexual). All these aspects mix and come together to qualify **who you are**. How would you feel if all the complex aspects of you would be ignored and reduced to just one – your membership of a particular 'culture'?

In early childhood education and care, the **Anti-Bias Approach** offers an opportunity for addressing all areas of diversity (e.g. gender, (dis)ability, GLBT, class, etc.), not just culture. It was developed in the US by Louise Derman-Sparks and the ABC taskforce (Derman-Sparks, 1989), and adapted for Australia by Glenda Mac Naughton and her team, for South Africa by Brenda Gaine, by Babette Brown for the UK, and by the DECET network across Europe. It was introduced to and adapted for the Irish context by the '*éist*' project (Murray and O'Doherty, 2001). It is an activist approach and recognises the societal context and its influence on generating equality or inequalities. At the heart of the Anti-Bias work is a vision of a world in which each child is able to blossom and each child's particular abilities and gifts can flourish.

## 7.6 Why Anti-Bias?

Why an Anti-Bias Curriculum? Because children develop biases against people of colors and cultures other than their own, and against people with abilities different from their own, when they are very young. At an early age children have ideas about what boys are 'supposed' to do and what girls 'can't' do. Most of us are uncomfortable seeing these biases develop.

It's not enough to teach tolerance. Pretending not to have heard a hurtful remark one child makes to another just isn't enough. Adults must make it clear that it is not OK for a child to say or do unkind things to another person and that, if this happens, the adult will firmly step in.

As teachers and parents, we inadvertently teach our own biases. It's important for each of us to examine our possible biases and learn how they may influence children – and how to reduce, handle, or even eliminate them.

(From the original Anti-Bias Curriculum, published by Louise Derman-Sparks and the ABC Task Force in the US in 1989.

## Key characteristics of the Anti-Bias Approach to Diversity and Equality in early childhood:

▶ It is value-based: differences are good, oppressive ideas and behaviours are not. It asks practitioners and children to confront troublesome issues rather than covering them up. The approach is integral to all aspects of daily life in the setting and is not just activity-based (Murray and O'Doherty, 2001).

▶ It recognises that celebrating diversity alone is not sufficient to address the issues that go hand in hand with diversity, such as discrimination and inequality. The approach focuses proactively on minority and majority children.

▶ It is proactive and recognises and acknowledges inequalities, stereotypes and power issues in society and in ECEC settings.

▶ It actively supports children to deal with diversity.

▶ It is an activist approach that focuses on addressing the social context for growing up as well as the educational context in the ECEC setting.

▶ It aims to empower all children to develop to their full potential in a diverse society.

▶ It has four clear goals for adults *and* children (see below). The goals can orient your thinking and practice, yet they are not prescriptive.

▶ It supports the implementation of Síolta Standards (2006), Aistear (2009) Themes and the Diversity and Equality Guidelines for Childcare Providers (2006).

## Anti-Bias Goals

The Anti-Bias Approach offers a structure of four clear Goals; they address adults as well as children. The Goals build on one another, like stepping stones, which means that before you can actively address Goal 4, you should have worked through Goals 1, 2 and 3.

▶ The **Goals for Adults** support you to raise your own awareness, knowledge and understanding of diversity and equality, in order to engage effectively with children and adults.

▶ The **Goals for Children** support you to ensure that each child be recognised and actively respected in the ECEC setting, and can engage comfortably with diversity issues. This includes being able to stand up for themselves and others in difficult situations.

---

### 7.7 Anti-Bias Goals for Adults and for Children

**Goals for Adults:**

1. To be conscious of one's own culture, attitudes and values and how they influence practice

2. To be comfortable with difference, have empathy and engage effectively with families

3. To critically think about diversity, bias and discrimination

4. To confidently engage in dialogue about issues of diversity, bias and discrimination. Work to challenge individual and institutional forms of prejudice and discrimination.

**Goals for Children:**

1. To support each child's identity (individual and group) and their sense of belonging

2. To foster children's empathy and support them to become comfortable with difference

3. To encourage each child to critically think about diversity and bias

4. To empower children to stand up for themselves and others in difficult situations.

(Murray et al, 2010, OMC, 2006)

---

## Goals, questions and critical reflections

Deepening our understanding of who we are now and how we came to *be* that person is at the heart of becoming a strong Anti-Bias teacher.

(Derman-Sparks, 2010, p. 22)

Working with the four Anti-Bias Goals requires a critical attitude and openness to asking questions. In Chapter 5 we discussed why it is important for ECEC practitioners to develop such an attitude, and how to move from reflection (as in reflective practice) to

**critical reflection**. We defined critical reflection as something to do with **asking 'why' questions**:

More important than looking at how things are done is to ask why they are done the way they are, for what purpose and for whose benefit. Instead of asking how practice could be improved, they ask whether things could be done differently, based on different values, and in ways that would be more just and equitable for all children and families.

Working with the Anti-Bias Goals for adults and children is a good way to orient your critical 'why' questions.

Each Goal should initially be considered separately by asking many why and how questions. This can happen at both individual and team level. We offer some critical questions as starting points for your own analysis below. The Diversity and Equality Guidelines for Childcare Providers (2006) offer further information and more critically reflective questions. Explore each set of questions for adults – on your own or, preferably, with your learning group – and then **discuss how you can engage effectively with this Goal for children.**

▸ For **Goal 1 for adults**: 'Can I stand back, examine and discuss objectively my own ethnicity and culture?'
▸ For **Goal 1 for children**: 'Do I have the skills to create a setting which reflects and includes all children in the setting?'

Through consultation and equality-proofing by the '*éist*' project (www.pavee.ie/edenn), the essence of the Anti-Bias Goals is also embedded in Aistear and Síolta, particularly under the Standard and Theme of Identity and Belonging).

---

## 7.8 Jargon Buster: Equality-Proofing

Equality-proofing involves incorporating an equality perspective in all aspects of policy development (NESF, 1996) (i.e. Aistear, Síolta). The ultimate objective and potential of equality proofing is to promote the development of a more equal society. Equality proofing is about recognising diversity and acting to ensure fair treatment and non-discrimination. It is about providing appropriate services to workers and end users. It is about meeting real needs.

(CWU, 2008)

---

The remaining part of this chapter focuses on you beginning to engage with some of the Anti-Bias Goals for adults and some for children.

We offer you the opportunity to start to explore your own personal beliefs and attitudes and to further build your knowledge base, all of which will inform how you acknowledge, recognise and engage effectively with diversity issues. We offer some scenarios for reflection on working with children. We provide some questions for reflection, which may seem awkward at first, but by posing and listening to questions that put you on the spot, we can begin the process of working towards Goals of the Anti-Bias Approach.

To that end, there are also four areas to keep in mind when working with the Anti-Bias Goals. Already touched on, they include being personally reflective, building your knowledge base, developing skills and working with others to critically reflect on diversity issues and implementation.

## Four areas for engagement

▸ **Personal reflection and understanding:** being aware of your own values and attitudes and how they affect your practice (Refer to discussion questions in Chapter 2 and below).

▸ **Building your knowledge base:** exploring the historical context, research, approaches to diversity and understanding diversity terminology: how stereotyping, prejudice, discrimination, oppression, racism, sexism and homophobia operate and the resulting consequences for a child's self-identity, both individual and group, self-esteem and well-being (Refer to Chapters 1–4 for building your knowledge base).

▸ **Building your skills for practice:** recognise that embracing children in all their diversity means creating an appropriate physical environment, addressing difficult situations in practice with adults and children, and figuring out what actions to take (Refer to Section 3).

▸ **Critical reflection:** build learning communities in your teams or externally to explore concepts, attitudes and practice actively (Refer to Chapters 5 and 6).

Under the four areas we now analyse some of the Anti-Bias Goals. It is not possible to address each Goal in detail here, but the vignettes below offer ways to progress. Reflective practice is ongoing and requires an active engagement and commitment. Transforming practice is largely about a change in mindset and belief in a more just society for all. It is rather about being actively involved in tackling inequalities rather than reproducing inequalities.

## Personal reflection and understanding

Ultimately 'the most important thing we bring to our practice is who we are' (Derman-Sparks, 1989, p. 22) which is often an overlooked resource (Urban, 2010b). As adults we are affected by our own social conditions and our identities. For instance, our own class, race, ethnicity, gender, sexuality, ability, etc., will affect how we reflect critically on the way in which our biases influence our choice of curriculum goals. How we see and understand the world may restrict our ability to develop practices that are inclusive and transforming for particular groups of children. This engagement with ourselves is not an easy one, but necessary if we are to uncover and change our conceptions and truly accept others in their diversity. When we see things differently we can choose different actions.

### *Personal reflection using Goal 1 for adults:*

To be conscious of one's own culture, attitudes and values and how they influence practice.

Consider the following comment:

> I never considered myself to be racist or biased towards other people but I find myself challenged now on a daily basis. Am I judging other people by their behaviour or looks? Do I really think, 'Travellers are—', 'Roma are—', 'the English are—'? But now I am learning to look beyond the prejudice and see the person. I am learning the hard way about biased behaviour. I have to re-think my own views on people. [I have to consider] not what society thinks but what am I going to do to change my way of thinking.
>
> (Practitioner attending Anti-Bias training)

What do you think was going on for this practitioner?

Take some time to explore the personal reflection questions below and to engage with **Goal 1 for adults.** This can be done with a friend, colleague or part of your learning community.

### *Personal reflection questions:*

▸ How did I first learn about difference? What messages did I receive?
▸ Where did the messages come from?
▸ Were they positive, negative or mixed?
▸ Do I believe some of the messages about particular groups in society (Traveller, lesbian mothers, girls, boys, etc.) that declare them to be inferior in some way? If so:
  — What are the messages?
  — Where did I learn them?
▸ How might my belief of the messages affect my work with children and families?
▸ How do I now go about dealing with them?
▸ Recall ways in which someone (teacher, adult) helped you learn about how to deal respectfully with difference.

Responses from learners engaging with the above questions:

> I have never had to question my own opinion to this extent before. I've never thought about diversity this deeply before and I feel I will spend a lot of time thing about it now.

> Everyone has a story or a life experience that is relevant to diversity in a positive way.

> I ask myself what values have been installed in me and whether I have confidence in my identity because of my life experience.

> I guess I feel now I have to put myself in the place of the children I care for before I make any judgement.

(Practitioners, 2011)

---

### 7.9 Links: Goal I for adults

Síolta Component 14: 14.2.2; 14.2.4; 14.3.2; 14.3.4
Aistear Theme Identity and Belonging, Introduction

---

## Building your knowledge base

To engage confidently in dialogue about discrimination and other critical issues with adults and children it is necessary to have an understanding of diversity terms that are both descriptive ('Black', 'refugee', etc.) and conceptual ('stereotype', 'prejudice', etc.).

Build your knowledge base using **Goal 2** for adults, 'to be comfortable with difference, have empathy and engage effectively with families', and **Goal 3** for adults, 'to think critically about diversity, bias and discrimination'.

> I am learning the importance of applying the Anti-Bias Goals to myself as well as the children. Personally, I do use opportunities at home with my own children to correct them if I hear them using various words. My six-year-old was saying 'a brown boy started in my class today'. I chatted with him about the boy and the use of 'black' instead of 'brown' to refer to the boy. These little opportunities or 'teachable moments' can be used to have a conversation with the children in the playschool. By knowing the correct meaning of all the terminology I feel more equipped with the tools to deal with issues as they come up with adults. This also depends on the situation at hand, but everyday chat can be very stereotyped

about groups of people and maybe I could say something about the words people I know use and let them know I don't like it or appreciate it being said.

(Learner implementing a diversity and equality approach, 2009)

*Exploration exercises:*

**Using Goals 2 and 3 for adults**

Work with a colleague or learning community using the diversity and equality guidelines glossary (Office of the Minister for Children, 2006) and begin to explore your understanding of diversity concepts, or use Chapters 2 and 3 to explore concepts and terms. Sharing this exploration with others deepens understanding of concepts and of how they influence the way you look at situations and how they affect people's lives.

---

### 7.10 Links: Goal 2 and Goal 3 for adults

Síolta Component 14: 14.2.4; 14.2.5; 14.3.1; 14.3.2; 14.3.4
Aistear Theme Identity and Belonging, Introduction
    Equality and Diversity Principles: p. 8; p. 9, the adult's role
    Thinking about My Practice: pp. 15, 27, 51, 55, 59

---

## Building your skills for practise and critical thinking

How we interpret the diversity and equality principles in ECEC policy documentation and how we work with diversity is what counts. Remember that it is not the human differences that cause problems; rather, it is how we react and how we treat those differences. Providing an appropriate equitable 'physical environment' (Office of the Minister for Children, 2006, p. 34), working through observation of the children and families, and planning the implementation of curricular goals is essential in addressing diversity and equality in practice.

---

### 7.11 Links: Goal 1 and 2 for children

Build your skills and critical reflection using **Goal 1 for children**, 'to support children's identity (individual and group) and their sense of belonging' and **Goal 2 for children**, 'to foster children's empathy and support them to be comfortable with difference'.

#### 'People in wheelchairs can't really do much'

Children in one centre were given access to a wheelchair for a number of weeks. The staff told the children that the wheelchair was a prop for their play and that they were to use if safely and as if they really had to use a wheelchair. All the children were reminded that they needed to ask the person in the wheelchair if it was OK to push them, etc.

The children were observed in their use of the wheelchair and their comments were recorded, including 'people in wheelchairs can't really do much', 'I'd hate to be in a wheelchair because I wouldn't be able to play with my friends anymore.'

The staff challenged the children on their comments and asked why they thought that a person in a wheelchair couldn't do anything, and what is was the you couldn't do while you were in a wheelchair.

Next, the staff teased out what they would need in order to be able to do the activities they wanted to do while in the wheelchair. Examples were 'a higher table to fit in closer so I can get the paint and things I need', 'stronger arms to push myself up the garden', 'wider doors to fit through' and 'toys lower down so that I can reach them myself'.

By the time the wheelchair had to be returned, the children had made a book with pictures of themselves engaging in numerous activities while in the wheelchair, along with the children's observations, which included, 'If I built my own school I would have everything right for me and then it wouldn't be so bad being in a wheelchair'.

(Practitioner implementing an Anti-Bias approach 2010).

## 7.12 Links: Goals 1 and 2 for children

**Goal 1 for children**
Síolta Component 14: 14.1.1; 14.2.1; 14.2.2
Aistear Theme Identity and Belonging: Aim 1, Goals 1–6

**Goal 2 for children**
Síolta Component 14: 14.2.2; 14.2.2; 14.3.5
Aistear Theme Identity and Belonging: Aim 2, Goals 1–6; Aim 3, Goals 4–5

## Critical Reflection

Working together to explore diversity issues is both challenging and rewarding. There is no 'one-size-fits-all' approach to diversity work. It is 'messy' (Urban, 2010a) and complicated, so working together strengthens confidence in addressing new and complex issues.

*Critically reflect on the following three scenarios using Goal 4 for:*
**Adults:** to confidently engage in dialogue about issues of diversity and discrimination. Work to challenge individual and institutional forms of prejudice and discrimination.
**Children:** to empower children to stand up for themselves and others in difficult situations.

▸   John's birthday party was coming up at the end of the week. He was overheard saying to David (Black Irish boy) at the sand box 'Blackies can't come to my party'.
(Practitioner, 2009)

▸ All children are given sausages at various snack times. Some parents' religious beliefs prohibit eating pork, but the playgroup leaders discount this, saying 'Oh for God's sake, all children eat sausages. They're in Ireland now, so they can eat what we eat.' This student was unsure how to respond or deal with the issue.

Student, 2010

▸ Every parent wants their child to be normal and they won't accept that their child should be in a special school. We just don't have the facilities for them and it slows down the normal children. It makes things very hard for the teacher.

Trainer, 2009

Work through these scenarios. To begin, outline what you think is happening in the scenario. Then consider what you might do in these situations for children, families and staff.

Using the Anti-Bias Goals outlined above, identify what knowledge/skill you might need to acquire to address these issues appropriately.

---

### 7.13 Activity: Link to the Anti-Bias Goals, Síolta Components and Aistear Goals

Take the four Goals for Children and analyse each Goal separately.
Identify actions that could be carried out to develop each Goal in the setting and with the children.

---

## Summary

We started this chapter by looking at three different approaches that early childhood educators have taken – and are taking – in order to engage with the fact that diversity is a reality in society. We explored why it is totally unacceptable to expect minority groups to **assimilate** into the majority culture; we discussed the naivety of many well-meaning **multicultural** practices and looked at the possibilities of **intercultural** approaches to working with young children. As part of our exploration, we identified the main problem with these approaches, including that they tend to focus on culture only. There is a lack of recognition of diversity in all its aspects (gender, ability, class, ethnicity, etc.) and of the 'shadow side' of diversity – discrimination, exclusion and racism, as well as other '-isms'. The Anti-Bias Approach, developed by Louise Derman-Sparks (1989) and adopted for the Irish ECEC context by the '*éist*' project (Murray and O'Doherty, 2001) offers an activist, goal-oriented framework for addressing these critical issues with children and adults. The chapter introduced the four Anti-Bias Goals for adults and children, and suggests a number of critical questions you should ask and discuss when you embark on your personal and professional learning journey. In asking these questions, link your engagement with the Anti-Bias Approach to broader issues of **critical reflection** as discussed in Chapter 5. Understanding the Anti-Bias Goals will offer you insight into inspiring practice in Section Three of this book.

# SECTION THREE

# Voices from the sector

We began this book with an overview of the historical events and political conditions that have shaped, and continue to shape, Irish society today. As we have discussed in the chapters of the first section of this book, early childhood practitioners may not need specialist knowledge in all these areas. They do, however, need an awareness of the wider societal factors that form the context and the reality of growing up in this country today, and they need **concepts** and a shared language (**terminology**) that enables them to make sense of their world. Being aware of the political, social, historical and socio-economic world outside the early childhood setting helps us better understand the world inside. The two worlds are inseparable; in fact, they are one. Crucial questions that arise from our exploration are:

▸ **How are we going to develop inclusive practice** in ECEC that builds on and relates to the real-life experiences of children, families and communities?
▸ **What do we need to ask** and to know in order to understand children's realities?
▸ **How can we take action** as individual practitioners and as a growing early childhood profession on the whole and proactively address diversity, inequality and discrimination?

We have looked at these – and other – critical questions in the chapters in Section Two. We discussed the importance of critical reflection, explored difficulties and possibilities around the way we build our professional knowledge base and linked our exploration to practical and conceptual approaches to diversity and equality in early childhood education and care. We introduced in more detail the Anti-Bias Approach, based on the work of Louise Derman-Sparks (Derman-Sparks, 1989) and developed for the Irish context by the '*éist*' project (Murray and O'Doherty, 2001).

▶  How can we, as reflective practitioners, ask and explore *critical questions*?
▶  How can we *critically engage with theories and knowledge* that underpin our professional practice?
▶  How can we use our reflection and knowledge to engage with the Anti-Bias Goals and to **develop our anti-discriminatory practice**?

The third section of the book builds on both the contextual and conceptual explorations discussed in the two previous sections. The chapters in this section are different to what you have read so far. They are the result of longstanding collaborations with practitioners, learners and trainers with the '*éist*' project and the EDENN network (http://pavee.ie/edenn). They work in different settings and organisations in different parts of the country. What they have in common, though, is a commitment to inclusive and anti-discriminatory practice in early childhood education and care. They have come together in training, seminars, joint projects, etc., and they all build on the Anti-Bias Goals for Adults and Children to orient their practice.

We have come together in this book to share experiences of working with the Anti-Bias Approach in the Irish early childhood sector. The purpose of bringing the voices from the sector together in this section is twofold: first, the chapters in the section provide an insight into the reality of Anti-Bias work in ECEC in this country. The examples illustrate what can be done and achieved under real-life conditions, so to speak. The scope of the following chapters is broad but certainly not exhaustive. While the contributions cover many different aspects of working in a context of Diversity and Equality from an Anti-Bias perspective, many others could have been added. To be very clear: the choices we made for this book are not about *which* 'diversities' (e.g. gender, ethnicity, ability, etc.) are relevant, let alone more relevant than others. There is no diversity hit list! We have chosen the contributions for this book because they offer different and individual voices that are closely connected by their commitment to bringing the Anti-Bias Goals to life in all aspects of ECEC practice and training.

The second purpose of bringing voices from the sector together in this book and in this section links back to the discussion we had in the earlier chapters on critical reflection and the professional body of knowledge (Section Two, Chapters 5 and 6). The contributions in this section are not 'how to' instructions. They are based on experiences and reflections of practitioners, trainers and students; each one of them asks you to critically engage with your own practice in order to develop and change it. Moreover, the chapters represent genuine voices from the ECEC profession in Ireland. None of them are written from the height of an ivory tower; they are well grounded in everyday practice. Here are professionals and practitioners making important contributions to co-constructing the professional body of knowledge in their field, and sharing their knowledge, experience and reflections with their professional learning community. It is an excellent example of a profession 'speaking and thinking for itself' (Urban and Dalli, 2011). As you will discover when you work through the chapters, none of this is rocket science, but all of it is informed, critical and reflective practice.

We have asked all contributors to link their examples to the Anti-Bias Goals for Adults and Children, and to suggest questions for reflection, points for discussion and activities for you and your group of learners.

## 13.1 Anti-Bias Goals for Adults and Children

### Goals for Adults

1. To be conscious of one's own culture, attitudes and values and how they influence practice.
2. To be comfortable with difference, have empathy and engage effectively with families.
3. To think critically about diversity, bias and discrimination.
4. To engage confidently in dialogue around issues of diversity and discrimination, and to work to challenge individual and institutional forms of prejudice and discrimination.

### Goals for Children

1. To support children's identity and sense of belonging.
2. To foster children's empathy and support them to become comfortable with difference.
3. To encourage each child to think critically about bias.
4. To empower children to stand up for themselves and others.

We invite you to join this conversation among professionals and enrich it with your own thoughts, questions and experiences.

# SECTION THREE

## CHAPTER 8

# Do 0–6-year-olds need lessons in gender equality?

There's one boy who comes in with his Power Ranger outfit on. That's just who he is. There is no way he will play in the home corner. He says that's 'girls' play'. He can't stay still for a minute. I try to get him involved in quieter activities but he can be disruptive. I just let him get on with his own play as long as he doesn't disrupt the quieter children who are engaged in constructive activities.

(Team Leader, Early Childhood Centre)

## Overview

In this chapter we will take a look at gender and how it affects play and opportunities for children in later life.

## After reading this chapter you should be able to:

▶ explore how gender differences affects children's lives both now and in their future;

▶ get an understanding of how the experiences of children might be changed through intervention;

▶ find ways to be inclusive and support the best development of both boys and girls; and

▶ ask some questions regarding our practice as early childhood practitioners with regard to gender issues.

## Introduction: Gender and the very young

With regard to diversity and equality in early childhood, gender is probably one of the most difficult areas to manage. There are a number of reasons why I believe this is the case. Firstly, people tend to think that biology overrides all attempts at trying to make things equal, and an attitude of 'boys will be boys' prevails. Secondly, I think early childhood educators are not so horrified when girls or boys exclude each other because of gender as we would if a child were excluded because of a disability or skin colour. One reason for this may be that gender discrimination is common practice in all of our cultures, and it is not surprising when children display behaviour that is so pervasive. Another reason for the complexity of gender equality put forward by Glenda MacNaughton (2000) is that challenging gender concepts within early childhood requires challenging how practitioners are informed by the perspective of Developmentally Appropriate Practice (DAP) (MacNaughton, 2000). MacNaughton and others have challenged DAP, which seeks to support the development of the 'homogenous individual child', yet fails to take into account the cultural and gender difference which are affecting the identity and experiences of that child. DAP does not prepare the practitioner for dealing with this.

Jipson (1998) suggests that DAP ignores issues of cultural diversity when determining what constitutes what is appropriate, and Mallory and New (1994) also question the principles of DAP in relation to the education of children with disabilities.

MacNaughton proposes that other perspectives are valid ways of interpreting children's behaviour, and that teaching in a way that contradicts the DAP approach can therefore be justified. For example, intervening in children's play that a practitioner deems to be sexist and controlling behaviours that favour one gender over another or disempower.

---

### 8.1 Jargon Buster: Developmentally Appropriate Practice (DAP)

DAP is promoted by the American National Association for the Education of Young Children (NAEYC).

As NAEYC defines it, DAP is a framework of principles and guidelines for best practice in the care and education of young children, from birth through age eight. It is grounded both in the research on how young children develop and learn and in what is known about education's effectiveness. The principles and guidelines outline practice that promotes young children's optimal learning and development.

(National Association for the Education of Young Children, 2009)

---

## 'Is it a boy or a girl?'

From the moment children are born, boys and girls are treated differently in most cultures. One of the first questions asked is the sex of the baby, even before it is born. This is important information for parents and relatives and friends so they will know what clothes and presents to buy and what names are acceptable for each sex. Whether or not there are differences, adults treat newborns in different ways; they make different comments about babies depending on whether they think they are looking at a boy or a girl. As children develop, the different approaches and expectations for boys and girls become more marked. The style of dress, hair, choice of toys and interests that are supported by the adults around them differ greatly for boys and girls. In the Republic of Ireland we even have segregated boys and girls primary schools.

By the time children come to early childhood care and education there are common beliefs about gender (Honig and Wittmer, 1983) that boys are noisy, competitive and aggressive and love construction-related and rough-and-tumble games. Girls are quiet, compliant and play co-operative games in the home corner and would do arts and crafts all day long if they could.

> Caregivers and parents differences in treating and responding to male and female children seem to differ from birth onwards in ways that reflect what adults believe to be typical or desirable pathways and behaviours for each sex. Some of these differences reflect a bias toward expecting males to be agentic – to be active, decision-makers – and expecting girls to be nurturant, submissive and interpersonally sensitive to others.
>
> (Alice Sterling Honig, 1983, pp. 67–8)

While there is some scientific research that asserts that differences in male and female brains affect their interests and behaviours (Cahill, 2005) there is an important question that should be asked: should biology determine life outcomes for people? It must be remembered that differences in abilities within genders each is often more marked than across the genders. Maccoby and Jacklin (1974) maintain that physical and behavioural difference vary greatly across different ethnic and cultural groups. Gender difference in itself is unproblematic, but when one group gains and one loses out because of the differences, then the issue becomes political.

Modern Ireland does not present equal opportunities for boys and girls. Men earn 30 per cent more than women and women are severely under-represented regionally and nationally within decision-making structures (CSO, 2010). While there have been improvements in the past 40 years women still are under-represented in positions of power within all sectors, even one that is female-dominated such as primary school teaching. Those women who have 'made it' struggle within structures that support the lifestyle and priorities of men. Rarely do men have to make the choice between family and work, and rarely would they opt to make that choice; for those men who do, they are deemed newsworthy (*Irish Times*, 17 May 2011). For those women who need to or choose to work, the obstacles they meet can seem insurmountable: inadequate maternity and parental leave; insufficient and costly childcare; and non-family-friendly work practices. Fathers in families suffer from being cast in the role of breadwinner, and when a separation takes place they are often left playing a minor role in the rearing of their children (Murphy and Caffrey, 2010), depriving them and their children of a valuable connection.

These lessons that children learn about who they can possibly be and what roles they will play in society are learned from the day they are born. They receive input from family and the media, and they are at the mercy of commercialism in all its forms. When a boy chooses to identify with Ben 10, or a girl wants to be a fairy princess, who or what is influencing their choices? Who designs the toy catalogues with red and black pages for boys and pink ones for girls? (Valiulis, O'Driscoll and Redmond, 2007). Who decides to print flimsy girl jeans and t-shirts with *Babe* written across the chest or bottom? What inspires people to buy those for their girl children and strong, sturdy, warm clothes for the boy children? Are boys learning here that they are expected to be tough on their comfortable clothes, which come in toned-down blues, browns or black, and what are girls learning about their identity from wearing skimpy, fussy or sexualised clothing?

## But girls can be fire fighters!

For early childhood practitioners it can seem like an uphill struggle to confront gender attitudes that already exist in children as young as 2 years (Derman-Sparks, 1989) and which have been reinforced by the media and perhaps also by family values. Working with issues of gender is not about making children into something they are not, it is about recognising that maybe they have not had real choices, and that how we interact with them around gender issues and how we create a gender-positive environment has the possibility of opening up doors for them. It might mean correcting misinformed statements such as 'girls can't be firemen' with 'but girls can be fire-fighters!' and bringing in an example from a book, a photo, a puzzle or asking a woman who does work at the fire station to visit in her uniform.

In a gender-safe environment, boys and girls are comfortable with themselves and with others of the opposite sex. They play together and allow each other to play in all sorts of games. In order to create a gender-positive environment, early childhood practitioners must start by observing closely how children play together and how they play with different equipment. This should not be done in a cursory fashion, as practitioners tend to underestimate the gendered play of children (MacNaughton, 2000). Whether there is as much space for adventurous and boisterous play as there is for quiet sedentary play should be considered.

MacNaughton (2000) gives an example from a practitioner who, prior to their action research group, viewed block-playing as something that both boys and girls did in her centre. When she viewed the play from a feminist perspective rather than a developmentally appropriate practice perspective, she observed how both sexes played differently with the blocks and how often the boys' behaviour inhibited the girls' play.

Consider the following:

▶ Are the home corner and the construction areas closely connected? This encourages cross-gender play.
▶ Are the adults supportive and encouraging of all kinds of play, including loud and rough-and-tumble play?

▸ Are children who might be intimidated or disturbed in their quieter play protected from noisier play, and supported in skills to speak out about what they need?

▸ Are all types of femininity and masculinity supported, i.e. both girls and boys who like to dress up, play in the home corner and be involved in quiet imaginative play, and girls and boys who want to play adventurous, physically risky and noisy play?

▸ Are children who don't fit the gender stereotypes being excluded or teased by other children?

Children need all kinds of play to succeed in life. What are the effects of the different types of play on later skills and life experiences? Co-operative play develops skills in communicating and social awareness, which are very necessary skills and the basis for the survival of human society. Caring and nurturing types of play are equally important, developing skills in empathy, protectiveness and sensitivity to the needs of others. Physically risky play helps children develop a sense of their bodies and its capabilities and supports physical competence and strength. It promotes a sense of adventure, excitement, anticipation and achievement. These skills are equally important for society as they promote entrepreneurial skills and a desire to discover new horizons. Construction play is the basis for many mathematical, logical, depth perception and engineering skills, and promotes imagination, visualisation and problem-solving.

## 8.2 Discuss

**Changing the environment**

We put the construction area and the home corner beside each other and made sure that the home corner had plenty of tools as well as household utensils. In the dress-up area beside it we put hard hats and 'hi vis' vests and other types of dress-up clothes as well. We cut down on the princess dresses and put in a lot more neutral things like scarves and fabric and different textured materials that are open-ended.

A diversity and equality Anti-Bias philosophy in the ECEC setting supports children to get involved in all kinds of play and the breadth of what the daily routine offers. If early childhood practitioners discover that their practice or environment seems to be contributing to gendered play, i.e. boys tending to play in construction or loud and boisterous games and girls tending to play in the home corner or quiet and co-operative play, what should they or could they do to change this? Being willing to change the environment around and observe the results is a start. Bring artistic artefacts or home corner equipment into or close to the construction area. Model playing with construction toys in the home corner, and with decorative materials, such as shells, cloth or ribbons, in the process of construction play activities. Sit with children and model how to construct play activities with decorative material such as shells, cloth or ribbon.

Support both genders to become involved in boisterous, imaginative games such as wild animals, super heroes, or fighting games by modelling boundaries and what is acceptable pretend play and what is hurtful. Allow all children the space for contact but ensure that the rules of the games are agreed with children beforehand. Intervene and support children to set and reset limits that are being broken and uphold the consequences to breaking rules. Adults getting down on the floor and getting involved in construction will attract more children to a given area of play, which is important for girls who might perceive boisterous play as boys play. It is good to support and encourage children who do not fall in to the stereotypes of masculine and feminine play and help them to stand up for themselves in the face of exclusion or teasing (Anti-Bias Goal 4 for Children).

Finally, as early childhood practitioners, have we looked at the effects of stereotyping on our own outlook and perceptions? Do we examine and challenge our own perceptions in discussions with colleagues. Do we welcome men into a field of work that has largely been the domain of women? If we are resisting, what is that founded on? Have we made equality and diversity policy clear to parents? Are they aware of what a gender-safe environment means? What happens when a parent questions our policy or our practice?

## Summary

Research and anecdotal evidence shows that boys and girls play differently and are treated differently in their early years. Different types of play and experiences have an effect on skills and opportunities in later life. Children themselves will discriminate against each other if they cross the perceived gender lines. Our job as early childhood care and education practitioners working in an equality and diversity/Anti-Bias setting is to ensure opportunities for children to develop a healthy gender identity. There is an onus on society to provide equal opportunities for all, while children are developing their skills and strategies as they progress through the education system and into adult life.

### 8.3 Discuss

1. Can you identify some gender roles that are associated with men and women? How would you explain to a three-year-old that being a man does not mean that you cannot cook and being a woman does not mean that you cannot drive a truck?
2. Write a list of words that you would describe as 'feminine' adjectives and a list of words that you would describe as 'masculine' adjectives. Is there any reason why these cannot belong to either gender? How would you explain these culturally formed ideas to a four-year-old?

## CHAPTER 9

# The Family Wall Project

I am continuously thinking about the idea of identity and belonging with the children in the room. We have made a start on the Family Wall and the self-portraits with the children. These are some of the activities recommended from the literature from Pavee Point and I can already see the benefits to the children. They enjoy talking about themselves and who they are, and looking at each others' pictures.

(Learner, 2009)

## Overview

In ECEC we all enjoy taking photos of events and showing them to children and parents. We also make individual books of children working in the setting. So what's so special about the Family Wall? Is it not just about taking more photos and displaying them? In this chapter we hope to engage you with an account of the experiences of practitioners from ten ECEC settings across Ireland. All ten settings introduced the Family Wall as part of a project initiated by the Equality and Diversity in Early Childhood National Network (EDENN). The practitioners documented their own learning journey and the children's reactions and shared their experiences through interviews, written records and photographs.

The aim of the Family Wall project was to capture the voices of Irish practitioners and children working with diversity and equality tools to inform Irish practice. To date we have been largely informed by work carried out in the US, UK and Australia, whereas this work draws on the social context and the voices of practitioners and children in Ireland. While this is a small project, it has been far-reaching in capturing the experiences of practitioners and children from 0–5 years in ECEC services nationally, and we hope that the experience will inform future research in the Irish context.

The chapter begins with an introduction to the idea behind the project. It then presents the Family Wall as a practical tool that can be integrated into the everyday life of children in the setting. Experiences and reflections documented by participating practitioners illustrate the transformative potential of the Family Wall when embedded in a broader Anti-Bias Approach.

## After reading this chapter you should be able to

▸ begin developing a Family Wall project in an ECEC setting

▸ understand that the Family Wall is not a once-off activity, but should become a living tool in the setting

▸ recognise the value of the Family Wall for practitioners, children and families

▸ understanding its role in supporting children's identity and sense of belonging

▸ recognise the value of its use with babies, toddlers and pre-school children

▸ understand the importance of Irish research to support appropriate practice in ECEC in Ireland.

## Supporting each child's identity and belonging

**9.1**

This is my sister Kayla. She's sticking out her tongue. That's my granny Chris, my granny Langton, that's my mammy and daddy holding me when I was a baby.

(Practitioner, 2010)

The theme of Identity and Belonging is about children developing a positive sense of who they are, and a feeling that they are valued and respected as a part of a family and community.

(National Council for Curriculum and Assessment, 2009, p. 25)

Supporting each child's identity and belonging is one of the main aims of early childhood care and education, according to Síolta (Standard 14) and Aistear (Theme 2):

**9.2**

When children feel a sense of belonging and a sense of pride in their families, their peers, and their communities, they can be emotionally strong, self-assured and able to deal with challenges and difficulties. That creates an important foundation for their learning and development.

(National Council for Curriculum and Assessment, 2009, p. 25)

Introducing the theme of Identity and Belonging, the Early Childhood Curriculum Framework explains the importance of children's relationships with family members, other adults and children, friends and members of their community. All of these relationships play key roles in your finding out and becoming confident in who you are – your identity. Children feel they belong when these relationships with others are secure and are recognised in their everyday lives, e.g. in the ECEC setting.

## 9.3 Objectives of the Family Wall project:

- To support the identity and sense of belonging of every child in the ECEC setting
- To encourage parental participation and support open communication between parents from new communities, Traveller families, majority families, families with a disabled child or children, different family structures, families with gay/lesbian parents, etc.
- To create a focus of inclusion through ongoing engagement with the Family Wall
- To encourage open engagement and discussion on diversity issues amongst children, practitioners and parents
- To evaluate the Family Wall experience from within the Irish context.

As ECEC practitioners, we usually live with children for a particular time of the day – the time they spend with us in the setting. Understanding children's identity and belonging from a professional perspective requires curiosity, open-mindedness and a constant question in mind: who are you?

## Who are you?

A seemingly banal question, and yet it makes all the difference! Considering this question at encounters with every child, every day, will give you a professional stance that identifies you as a critically reflective practitioner – a concept we have introduced and discussed in more detail in Section Two, Chapter 5. Approaching each child and their family with an attitude of genuine curiosity is a way of showing that you are questioning your knowledge, rather than rushing to premature conclusions based on assumptions. *Wanting to find out* who this individual in front of you is – instead of assuming you already *know* – is, in very practical terms, what we explored from a more theoretical perspective in Chapter 6. This is theory about universal developmental stages being taken off its pedestal by a simple question! Besides, by showing an interest and approaching each child with a question in mind rather than an answer, you show a fundamental respect to the child's personality; you are dealing with Oisín and Jacinta, not the universal four-year-old boy or two-year-old girl.

Supporting children's identity and belonging is about the whole individual child, here, Omodele, Oisín, Jacinta, Leah, Michael and Paul. Each one of them is a child within a context of family and community. The child we encounter as part of a group in the setting doesn't leave her/his relationships and context at the door. They are always here, in the setting. The professional's task is to enable and empower children to connect their lives inside and outside the ECEC setting, and to actively initiate communication with and about the children's families and communities.

The Family Wall, as described in this chapter, is a practical tool to facilitate these connections and communications. However, as it is the case with all practical tools, you need to have a solid understanding of how to use it in the context of your professional practice.

## It's not the hammer, it's the carpenter...

This is where you, the critically reflective practitioner, come into the picture. Therefore, the Family Wall as described in this chapter is a project; it is neither a quick fix nor a once-off activity. It is also a tool for realising the four Goals of the Anti-Bias Approach. As you will hear from the practitioners involved in the project, it can change your entire way of working.

# The Family Wall – what is it and what are its aims?

The Family Wall is a project that involves introducing photos of the children's families to the setting. Used to initiate meaningful conversations about families, their uniqueness, differences and similarities, the Family Wall is a practical tool to make all children feel welcome, understood and valued in the setting. It provides a place for pictures of children's diverse family and community contexts. Thus, displaying the photos brought in by families, and by actively integrating them into the daily routines, the Family Wall can contribute to building respect for diversity amongst all children, families and staff involved in an ECEC setting.

Practitioners from ten different ECEC services across Ireland took part in a project to take children's family photos as a starting point for an exploration of the diversity of families in their settings. They encouraged children to talk about their families and friends and, by carefully listening to children, the practitioners themselves embarked on a reflective learning journey.

Photos and imagery are an integral part of any ECEC setting. You are likely to find photos of children or children's drawings on display in any early childhood setting across the country. So what is different about a collection of photos stuck to the wall? What's new? And why call it a project? First of all, this is about a different kind of imagery, one you are not so likely to find in many services. Second, the photos were only one part (the focal point, one might say) of a much broader, purposeful activity to connect the children's world outside and inside the setting, engage in meaningful conversations about the rich diversity of families, and to document and reflect upon practitioners observations and experiences during the project.

## The Family Wall as transformative practice: Learning together and making change happen

Introducing the Family Wall as a practical tool to engage in meaningful conversations about children's lives with their families is one way of putting the big concepts discussed earlier in this book (Section 2) to work for you, as it can open a door to **asking critical questions** and making them the starting point for changing your practice. The Family Wall project offers participants more immediate possibilities to enable more equitable and just experiences for all children. As practitioners report in their reflective journals, once you begin looking at children and families in a different way, with curiosity and an open mind, there is no turning back. A small step, but this is what **transformative practice** (Chapter 7) is about. Engaging with the project offered a platform for joint learning between practitioners, facilitators and researchers. It has provided **practice-based evidence** (Urban, 2010) for the effectiveness of a different approach, oriented by the Anti-Bias goals, and it showed Irish examples for how change can be achieved.

---

### 9.4 Participants of the Family Wall project

- Inagh Ark Community Centre, Ennis
- Childcare Services, Liscannor
- Community Centre, Athy
- Tir na nÓg, Athy
- The Haven, Ballina
- Traveller Preschool, Castlebar
- Little Acorns Children's Centre, Claremorris
- Doras Buí, Dublin
- Wallaroo Playschool, Cork
- Ashbourne House Accommodation Centre, Cork

---

(See the *Diversity and Equality* page on www.gillmacmillan.ie for a brief project outline.)

### *Documented experiences*

Working with imagery (see Chapter 15 in this section) can be a powerful tool to address issues of diversity and equality in your setting, and to support each child's identity and belonging. Using family pictures systematically to engage in conversations about – and with – children's families is even more powerful, because the pictures open a window into each child's reality. Unlike books and posters, Family Wall pictures are not 'representing' particular groups of children (see Chapter 14 in this section on imagery). For your children, these pictures are the real thing! Having the pictures of the children in your setting and their families present every day – or even the process of encouraging parents to bring in a photo of themselves with their child – will not just help you better understand the family background of your children, but will inevitably bring up surprising and sometimes critically important issues you might not otherwise have discovered in your service. The excerpts from practitioners' journals below illustrate some of the issues practitioners, children and families have encountered during the project.

## Introducing the Family Wall: No 'one size fits all'

There was no prescribed way of introducing the Family Wall to the different services listed in Box 9.4, and no 'one size fits all' solution for the actual design of the photos and the wall.

Practitioners were encouraged to develop their own Family Wall and to come up with solutions that worked best for them and their specific environment. Most services started by finding a dedicated wall space for the photos. They experimented with different formats and designs. While some Family Walls had their photos fixed to the wall, others used Velcro, which allowed the pictures to be taken down and carried around by the children.

---

### 9.5 A 3-D Family Wall?

Our boxes/cubes were all done this week and we introduced the children to them. All the children got excited when they saw the boxes. We showed Leah the picture of her older brother Michael, who attends playschool. She smiled happily and pointed to him on the box giving him kisses. Alicia saw the picture of herself as a baby saying 'baby, baby'. She turned the box over and saw the picture of Michael. Delighted she pointed – 'Michael, Michael' – and pointed out a picture of herself and then Tony, who was in the background, saying 'Tony, Tony'. Alicia turned the box around several times, looking, pointing and recognising the children who were on the box.

(Practitioner, 2010)

---

### *The Family Wall doesn't have to be a wall*

Family Walls come in all shapes and sizes – and they don't have to be walls at all! In one infants' room, photos were laminated and lowered from the ceiling on elastic string. Cardboard cubes with photos on each of the six sides were a great success too. Practitioners in a toddler room thought about how to display the photos in a way the children could best interact with them. After experimenting with different areas on the walls and corners, pins, Velcro and cellotape, they had a brilliant idea: they provided rectangular cardboard boxes, just big enough to hold a 5x7 photo and smaller photos on the ends if necessary.

On the day we arrived at the centre to interview the practitioners about their experience with the Family Wall, the children were having lunch. The practitioner asked them whether they would like to show their photo boxes. They surrounded us immediately, carrying their boxes and showing us their pictures of mum, dad and all the other important people in their family, including babies – and dogs, calves and goats! It was the most amazing and touching sight! We were handed the boxes by children who obviously enjoyed engaging in conversations with us, and our asking about the pictures and who was in them. Most of the children had very little understandable language, and yet we spent an hour talking and engaging with toddlers and their photo boxes.

The practitioners recalled how when they made the boxes the children began to play with them, putting them on top of each other and even throwing them about. They were afraid it wasn't going to work, but as the photos came in and were put on the boxes, the children began to treat them as precious objects. If, for example, a child was crying another child would toddle off to the shelf look for their box and bring it back to the crying child. They sat together chatting in baby language. In one case a child who was having a hard time settling in the mornings, settled when given her box and came out of her mother's arms.

It was a wonderful way of making the Family Wall pictures accessible, especially for very young children!

## Resistance, surprises and shock

As with any new initiative or project there may be reluctance to get engaged in 'yet another thing'. ECEC practitioners are bombarded with requests and requirements to improve quality of care and facilities. There is no question that providers want to improve their practice, but sometimes it seems like there is no time to get used to the latest innovation before another 'thing' comes along. So it happened that some practitioner in a service felt reluctant to take on another project. Besides, it was just more photos! Yet with encouragement, most practitioners got 'stuck in' and recorded surprising results.

---

### 9.6 Where do you come from?

One service provider encouraged her various rooms to incorporate the Family Wall. One room felt they had covered a lot about families and cultures already and they felt it wasn't necessary to do more. We encouraged them to have a go, and also to encourage parents to send in some information on the photo.

At that time they had a girl (4) in their room. They knew she spoke Spanish, and assumed she was from Spain. Once they began the process of collecting the photos (although like others, they had a few challenges getting all the photos in), the wall came alive.

To their surprise they discovered that the girl speaking Spanish wasn't Spanish at all! Her family came from Argentina. Her mother was the first to bring in the photo and information from the family indicating her desire to share information and to ensure inclusion for her child. This child had already been in the service for eight months. The practitioners themselves were shocked and once the Wall was in action they felt even more remiss. In our interview, they talked about not really realising the importance of talking about what was important to the children. They had introduced various cultures and various festivals, but they hadn't acknowledged what was important for the children in their room. The children showed them that 'talking about them' is what they wanted to do: to share their own lives. They felt they had not really embraced the identity of the child from Argentina nor had they engaged sufficiently with the parents. They found it an invaluable tool for engaging in conversation with the children and connecting with their families. They concluded that they would include the Family Wall for each year in the future.

## 9.7 Traveller Culture

A Traveller boy came to our service. He was a bit boisterous and the children were talking about how 'bold' he was. We were introduced to the Family Wall Project. Everyone brought in photos and in came the Traveller boys photos. He had horses in his photos. Wow was the response of the children. We discovered he was a wealth of information, he knew all the names of different horses. All of a sudden he moved from a negative position to a positive position in the setting. We realised that we hadn't tapped into his home knowledge. We were not recognising the qualities and knowledge of this Traveller child. We extended the family wall in a way as I changed the environment to ensure his interests were evident (variety of model horses and books on horses) and he could express himself.

(Practitioner, 2010)

## Language

Obviously, the Family Wall offers good opportunities for initiating conversations with children and families. Sometimes, it does a lot more for one child's language development:

## 9.8

At the preschool we have a little boy who attends two days per week. This little boy is nearly four and has very few words; he is waiting to be screened by a speech and language therapist, yet he can light up a room with his smile. He can make all the children laugh without speaking a word. While playing with him, he took my hand and brought me over to the Family Wall. At the Wall he pointed to his family photos and said 'Mummy, Daddy, Hon (Sean), O (Niall)'. I was speechless; this was the most Oisín had said in the past six months. I was gobsmacked, but it gave me an insight into how much Oisín can say. It also laid down the foundations for me to work with Oisín and try to build his language skills.

I spoke to Oisín's mum and she too was amazed with his response and agreed to send in more photos of friends, toys, etc.

I really feel that without the Family Wall I would never have gained the knowledge into how much Oisín can say and how much work is needed to help Oisín progress.

*Two months later the same practitioner notes in a follow-up entry in her journal:*

I spoke to Oisín's mum again about how Oisín values the Family Wall and how much speech and language he has when he speaks about his family. His mum is thrilled with the feedback.

(Practitioner, 2010)

## 9.9 The Family Wall and babies

**Jane** went over to the Family Wall and took down the picture of both her nannies. She pointed to one of her nannies and said 'Mom Og'. This is her first time saying her nanny's name. Alicia was very proud of herself smiling and laughing away that she had said her name.

**Leah** went over to the Family Wall and picked up the picture of her and her daddy. She pointed to daddy saying 'dad, dad', all excited laughing and smiling. Leah then put the picture back on the wall saying 'Bye bye', and continued to look at the other pictures on the wall.

**Evan** went over to the Family Wall, reached out for the picture of himself and his sister, and turned it around a number of times until he could see the picture the right way. He smiled and babbled away to the picture. He also reached up and got the picture of himself and his granddad, laughing and smiling at the picture.

(Practitioner, 2010)

Almost all practitioners in the project shared similar experiences. Having pictures of their own family in the room (often including siblings, dogs, grandparents, aunts and uncles, etc.) gives children a reason to talk about issues that really matter to them. While this is important for all children, for some it can make a crucial difference.

### English as a Second Language

In one service, a Polish boy (3) spent entire days in the centre without talking to anyone. The practitioners thought he was happy enough because he was playing. Then they introduced the Family Wall. Imagine their surprise when the Polish boy went to the Wall, stood in front of his pictures, pointed to the people in the pictures and started talking – in Polish!

This young boy finally had something to talk about in the centre, something he could relate to that was meaningful and made a difference for him. He could now connect to his mum and dad – and he was going to tell everybody how much that mattered to him! It also gave him a chance to talk during the day. Everyone had great fun with him as he regularly spoke to the other children in Polish about his pictures and because of the visual aspect and pointing, everyone could join in on the conversation despite the difference in language.

## Identity

Having real opportunities to talk and 'babble' about who you are and what and who matters most to you is a cornerstone for feeling confident about yourself. Knowing that it is OK to be who you are and that somebody is interested in you is an important part of developing your identity. This kind of chat is of course not limited to older children or to planned conversations with the practitioner during circle time.

Examples from some of the youngest children, even the babies and toddlers in the project illustrate how development of language and identity go hand in hand:

### 9.11

We use the photos in several ways for the babies. We had the Wall, which everyone looked at – parents, visitors, babes in arms and crawling babies. For the babies who couldn't yet crawl we also put the pictures on elasticated string in places where we lay them down. The babies reached up and pulled down the photos. They laughed and cooed and they kissed their mammies and daddies. We could see how valuable this was to the babies.

(Practitioner, 2010)

One of the practitioners who works with babies was amazed how babies responded to the Family Wall:

You know I can't believe it, we know the babies love to see their mammies and daddies when they arrive, and we believe once they are gone in the morning, the children settle and are happy with us. They are, of course, but when we introduced the Family Wall we couldn't believe the reaction of the babies. They kissed the photos of their mammies and daddies, they talked (in baby language) to the pictures, touching and hugging them. It gave us a different insight into our work and our understanding of the children's connections to home, their parents, pets and environment. The children were definitely happier, and so were we.

## Belonging and reassurance

Children have a right to experience being welcome and feeling a sense of belonging. Early childhood practitioners are obliged to ensure that each child feel that they belong both in the service and in connection with their world beyond the early childhood setting. For some children, the Family Wall pictures offer reassurance and comfort.

### 9.12 More baby examples:

**Ava** got unsettled and tired close to home-time today. She went over to the Family Wall and took down the photographs of her nanny, Buttons and her, and said who was in the photograph, continually saying 'Nanny coming soon', over and over and held the photograph the whole time. The photograph did provide her with reassurance and comfort that nanny was coming to pick her up soon.

**Omodele** reached up and grabbed the photograph of her and her brothers, laughing and smiling away at the photograph. She then started babbling away staying focused on the photograph for a long period of time, like she was in deep conversation with the people in the photograph.

**Kelley** picked out the photo of her and her brother and nanny babbling, pointing and also giving nanny in the picture kisses. She continued to return to this picture in particular regularly throughout the day, babbling, kissing, pointing and telling everybody what or who was in the picture.

(Practitioner, 2010)

## All kinds of families: Things can get awkward!

Families come in all shapes and sizes: single parents, two mums, mum and dad, two dads, step-parents – all of these and more are a reality in most early childhood settings. Different family constellations are certainly a reality for the children! Surprisingly, practitioners aren't always aware of the diversity of families in their setting, or of the specific situations and changes of particular families in their services. The Family Wall helped to identify some family situations the practitioners had not been aware of previously. Discovering that a child's family is not quite as you assume it to be can create awkward situations for practitioners. Engaging with these surprises is not always easy. In one service that offers support for single mothers, the introduction of the Family Wall triggered interesting developments. Asked to bring in family pictures, the mothers provided photos of themselves and their children. Some (separated) fathers, who picked up their children, became aware of this and asked to have their pictures put up on the wall as well. As a consequence, many children had photos of the two parts of their families – and an opportunity to talk about what it is like to live in two different houses with mum or dad. The practitioners thought this was a very positive development it gave them an opportunity to talk with the fathers and with the children about their fathers.

### 9.13 Challenges of the Family Wall

Here is another example of a situation that turned out to be difficult for the practitioner:

We have been asking the parents to bring in their family photos as our Family Wall is starting to come together. Today Magda [the practitioner] asked one of the children's grannies for a family photo, as they had sent in a photo of the child and her brother, and a photo of the two children with their dad.
 - Magda: We are just wondering, there are only photos of the two children and the children with their dad. Could we get a picture of the whole family, with mum as well?
 - Granny: Oh, they're not together anymore. They have split up.
 - Magda: Oh, I am sorry about that. I didn't know.
 - Granny: Not to worry, I will see what I can do.
This was an awkward situation, as we didn't know the parents had split up. So we just stuck up the photo of the little girl and her brother to get started.

(Practitioner, 2010)

**Discussion Point**

The practitioner who wrote this journal entry clearly felt uncomfortable being confronted with the separation of the parents and did not know how to deal with the information she got from the grandparent.

- How could she have addressed this more constructively?
- What would you have done?
- Discuss this with your learning group.

## Engaging parents

Parents and practitioners generally engage at the most fraught times of the day: dropping-off and picking-up times. ECEC practitioners recognise the importance of communication with parents, but often only get real interaction when they have something to 'fix'. Practitioners found that the Family Wall supported positive engagement.

### 9.14

One morning when we were sitting on the mat having our greeting time, a parent whose twin boys attend the service arrived with her children and their family photos. She sat on the mat and showed the children the photos. The mother explained to us all who was in the photos and their relationship to the children.

I feel this was a very kind gesture from the parent. It did put pressure on other parents to bring in their photos, because the other children asked their parents to come onto the mat and show their photos to their friends too. It was a great experience to have the parents involved and it gave me an opportunity to get to know the parents better.

(Practitioner, 2010)

## Extending the Family Wall

Supporting children's identity and belonging with the photos brings families alive in the setting and supports children in feeling good about themselves (Anti-Bias Goal 1; Síolta, Aistear). There are other benefits to the Wall too, because it also supports the development of empathy and comfort with difference (Anti-Bias Goal 2). It furthers the development of critical thinking among the children as they discuss differences between families, ask questions and come to conclusions supported by your engagement with any of the issues that arise.

The idea that the Family Wall is not just a once-off activity became clear to many of those involved. Practitioners saw the value of a permanent spot for the wall, which could be built upon when new events, stories and pictures came along. They also began to extend the wall linking to activities to counter stereotypes and prejudice.

## 9.15 All kinds of people

This week we introduced the children to a new book titled *All Kinds of People*, which deals with children who have different skin tones and other physical differences, i.e. glasses, braces, skinny, spotty, etc. Immediately, Alicia pointed to the Black girl on the cover asking, 'Look – who's that?' I explained to her that it was a Black girl, and she had a Black mam and dad, and that was why her skin was darker than ours, pointing to both mine and her hand, i.e. skin tone. She continued to point out the black boy on the page, and I explained it all again to her. Kelley pointed to the girl wearing glasses on another page asking, 'What? What?'. I again explained that the girl was wearing glasses and they made her eyes see better. Both girls were fascinated with the book, continually asking , 'What? What?'– girl with red hair, girl with braces, boy with no hair, etc. They were focused, and concentrated totally on the pictures and people/children in the book. Alicia did ask 'Where Dad?' when we were reading the book. We couldn't see any in the book. I plan to use this book and others as an introduction to the children into diversity and the wider world even at this early age.

(Practitioner, 2010)

In a toddler room in one service, all the photos of family were laminated and Velcroed down low on the wall with lovely cushions to sit on and chat about your family with a friend if you so wished. It was a higgledy-piggeldy mess, very alive and accessible. The children took their pictures and toddled off with them under their arms to tables nearby and laid them beside them when working on a jigsaw, looking at a book, etc. They were a great source of conversation and fun. The practitioner in this room decided to extend the Family Wall by providing laminated photos again Velcroed to the wall that challenged various stereotypes in society, for example images of women doing various jobs generally not ascribed to women, such as being a doctor, bus driver, etc. This is the type of activity that people often think is suited to older children. These images, with which the children could actively engage, were modelling alternative images, challenging stereotypes and informing children.

## Obstacles and how to overcome them

In any new ECEC activity, we generally find that there are obstacles that challenge the success of what you want to achieve with the children. Overleaf are some examples of challenges practitioners faced.

### 9.16

**Chloe** brought in her photos of her family including her grandparents and aunts.

**Michael** also brought in his photos today. The pictures showed Michael having great fun at a party. I spoke to Michael's dad on the same day, and explained in great detail all the aspects of the Family Wall and why it was so important to have photos of all his family. His father Paul just laughed and said 'I'm not sending in a bleedin' photograph of myself.'

**Alannah** brought in her family photos, which were lovely, but none of the photos had had pictures of her parents, just her siblings. I spoke to her father at home-time and explained why it was so important to have photos of all the children's parents on our Family Wall. The Dad just giggled and said 'Right.'

*Some time later…*

**Michael** brought in his photos at last. There is a lovely picture of him and his dad.

At first it was very difficult to get parents to bring in pictures and you feel like giving up. It was hard on some of the children who didn't have their photos up. One family just couldn't seem to get it together although they were very positive about it. So one day when they arrived I asked them if I could take a photo of them all together. They were delighted to do it and their family are now on the wall.

I would say don't give up on it, it's worth it for the children.

(Practitioner, 2010)

### 9.17 Unintended results!

Molly has fallen in love with Michael's brother on the photo on the Family Wall. Molly has never met Michael's brother, but kisses the picture every morning when she comes to school. It is so cute!

(Practitioner, 2010)

The Family Wall is wonderful way for children to stay connected to their loved ones during the day, to be proud of who they are (supporting their identity and sense of belonging) and to feel welcome, understood and valued in the setting.

## Summary

### The Family Wall as transformative practice: learning together and making change happen

Introducing the Family Wall as a practical tool to engage in meaningful conversations about children's lives with their families is one way of putting the big concepts discussed earlier in this book (Section 2) to work for you. It can open a door to **asking critical questions** and making them the starting point for changing your practice. The Family

Wall project offers participants more immediate possibilities to enable more equitable and just experiences for all children. As practitioners report in their reflective journals, once you begin looking at children and families in a different way, with curiosity and an open mind, there is no turning back. A small step, perhaps, but this is what **transformative practice** (Chapter 7) is about. Engaging with the project offered a platform for joint learning between practitioners, facilitators and researchers. It provided **practice-based evidence** (Urban, 2010) for the effectiveness of a different approach, as oriented by the Anti-Bias Goals, and it showed Irish examples for how change can be achieved.

## CHAPTER 10

# Dealing with Difficult Situations

'Oppression of the child is the most basic oppression.'

## Overview

The purpose of this piece is to discuss a very basic aspect of work in the early childhood sector from an equality and diversity perspective. Behaviour management of children is among the most common areas of difficulty reported by ECEC services. Yet the approach to discipline is a fundamental indicator of the respect the service has for the children and families in their care. Equality and diversity in early childhood must inform all areas of our work. The danger is that we get lovely new posters and jigsaws and don't change our practise. This chapter is based on my background of working with children and in ECEC. The quote above comes from my esteemed colleague, Joanie Barron, who has spoken of the oppression of the child as 'the most basic oppression', and of where and how we learn all about power.

### Behaviour Management: Taking a different approach

Below is a scenario of a challenging situation and a discussion piece that looks at how to truly engage with the principles of the UN Convention on the Rights of the Child and develop a culture and practise of respect for children.

Scenario 1: A family from Cameroon have just started in your service. One afternoon when the mother was collecting her daughter, the daughter refused to put her coat on. Her mother slapped her on her arm.

**What shapes our views on behaviour management:**
In a recent survey of in-service training needs in Cork (Cork City Childcare, 2008), behaviour management and issues of discipline were the topic for which most practitioners were seeking support. Each service has a different approach to the subject,

and our approach to discipline with children often comes from the core of *our own family culture*. Each adult working in or connected to the service has a deeply embedded personal view of the subject based on their own experience as children. As childcare professionals we must work

▸ through our own experience,
▸ through training and professional development, and
▸ work to develop clear policies within the childcare centre.

## The Pre-School Regulations:

By law, Irish childcare services must not inflict any form of corporal punishment on a pre-school child (Pre-School Regulations, 2006). The pre-school regulations go further, by requiring that a person carrying out a pre-school service ensure that no practise that is 'disrespectful, degrading, exploitive, intimidating, emotionally or physically harmful or neglectful [be] carried out in respect of any child' (Pre-School Regulations, 2006). It is also a requirement to have policies and procedures in place to support the staff to manage a child's behaviour and to assist the child to manage their own behaviour (Pre-School Regulations, 2006).

> **10.1 Consider this:**
>
> While we might be clear in our thinking about what 'physically harmful' means, take some time to explore what is meant by the other terms in the regulations, such as: disrespectful, degrading, exploitive or intimidating.
>
> How might you deal with the situation if you witnessed any of these behaviours in an ECEC setting?

## Missed opportunities:

While childcare workers don't slap children, other methods are commonly employed that discourage the creation of a child-centred environment. **Bold or naughty chairs or 'time out' spaces** are in evidence in many centres. Excluding children from the group is a common method of behaviour control. These methods are punishments and teach little about resolving conflict and developing self-managing behaviour. In best practise, workers see conflict as an opportunity to listen to the children, and support them to resolve the issue while honouring the feelings of each child involved. This model supports children to engage in the resolution of their conflict, increases communication skills and sees the child as a powerful participant in their own social world.

## A Children's-Rights-based approach:

An approach based on children's rights has developed from conflict resolution models developed in the 1960s. Many different ECEC philosophies such as High Scope Anti-Bias and Montessori share a conflict resolution model with small variations.

The first step in developing a children's rights approach to behaviour management in a childcare service is to develop a policy. As in all policy development, this starts with a conversation. The conversation is linked to the Anti-Bias Goals for Adults: **Start with yourself.**

Begin this process with the participation of the full staff team. Talk about the types of discipline the workers experienced as children. This conversation can be painful, but it helps workers to remember their own feelings as children. Staff members may feel that a slap never affected them. Exploring all attitudes around this issues is vital before you go forward.

Discuss how you would like to introduce a positive approach to behaviour management. Include simple changes such as **positive rather than negative language**, i.e. 'Let's walk' instead of 'Don't run'. Some workers may be worried that all the rules are being thrown out. Montessori has a great concept that we might borrow, called **'Freedom within limits'**. Boundaries are important to adults' and children's safety and well-being. Louise Derman-Sparks talks in terms of 'limit-setting' and 'learning to problem-solve'. She says that children 'must be free to ask questions, use their own ideas in problem solving, engage in real dialogue with adults, to make choices and have some say in daily school life' (Derman-Sparks, 1989).

The next stage in developing a children's rights approach to behaviour management with the ECEC team is to introduce the staff to a model for resolving conflict.

A sample model might be:

1. The first step is to get down to the level of the child.
2. Step two involves gathering information. Listen to the children. Don't assume you know what happened. Restate back to the children what you have heard, so that you are sure of the facts.
3. Step three is to ask the children involved for ideas on how the conflict can be overcome. Negotiate the solution.
4. Step four is to support the children in implementing their solution.

## Empowerment:

Empowerment is another great word from the 60s. Supporting children to learn how to work out conflict is an empowering act (Derman-Sparks, 1989). The time spent problem-solving to develop the child's sense of fairness supports the skills that underpin the achievement of the Anti-Bias Approach. For example, the listening skills developed support the child in developing an empathetic understanding of the other child's perspective, and encouraging the child to give their version of events supports the child's ability to speak up for themselves and others.

## Practise the new approach:

Get the staff team involved in role play, and practice the steps with the staff team. A useful scenario might be two children fighting about a toy they both want. A common solution to this might be to take the toy from the children and put it up high. The lesson learned from this is limited and not very positive. When the conflict resolution model is used, children quickly begin to negotiate solutions. Putting an emphasis on feelings helps to develop **the child's ability to regulate their own emotions.** So if one child calls another a hurtful name, the steps will be to listen to both children, check your information, ask the child how he/she felt to be called the name. With practise, **the child will be able to say how they feel.** In services using this model, children of three years will be able to share the likes of: 'I'm sad because you hurt my feelings'. You then explain to the other child that name-calling isn't used in the centre because name-calling hurts feelings. In this model, workers don't have to get cross, shout, add their own feelings into the picture or 'tease' the children. Children are supported in their emotional and cognitive development. What a gift to give a child at age three – *a life-long skill* many adults struggle with.

> ## 10.2 Learning Point
>
> Children have not always been treated well in Ireland. Corporal punishment in schools was only banned in the Irish Republic by regulation in 1982 and became a criminal offense in 1996. The Ryan Report into Industrial Schools from 1936 to recent times found that abuse was endemic and systematic.
>
> (Ryan Report, 2009)

## Supporting parents:

To return to the scenario above, the equality and diversity ethos of the centre is discussed from the point when parents first come to the centre to put their child's name down. It is very important to discuss the issue of discipline, with all families, especially with new community families. In the case of new community families be cognisant of the fact that all cultures have varying approaches to discipline and all families have individual view points.

The view we take in ECEC services is one based not on our own culture, but on the rights of the child; remember the pre-school regulations. ECEC services have a responsibility to ensure that all parents know that no hitting or any other physical punishment is allowed to happen in the centre. New community parents must be clear about what is expected of them, and this is especially important when there is a language barrier. Sometimes parents forget, act out of frustration and/or are under huge pressure, and sometimes parents disagree with our methods. Give the parent the chance to talk about how they feel or felt at the time of the incident. Speak tactfully and kindly to the parent again, and remind him/her of the service's ethos. Some parents of young children are only learning to be parents, and behaviour management is a skill that can be learnt. Excellent role models from among the ECEC centre staff, helpful talks at parents' evenings will support parents in their parenting. Respecting and valuing each child in our care is the most fundamental example of working within an equality and diversity and children's rights framework.

## Summary:

Our first and primary responsibility is to the child. To work from a children's rights perspective, we must look at all aspects of our practice to ensure their well-being. Having a children's rights approach to limit-setting and behaviour management underpins an equality and diversity ethos. The skills developed in problem-solving and conflict resolution are among the core skills for achieving the Anti-Bias Goals. Once we have established our approach within the centre, it is vital to share the approach with parents. This work takes time and will only take root as we develop fully as reflective practitioners and embrace the principles of the UNCRC.

### 10.3 Areas for critical reflection:

- How were you disciplined as a child?
- *Behaviour management* is a term used in the childcare regulations. Do you think the term is appropriate to describe the relationship between adults and children, or the professional task of ECEC practitioners? Discuss alternative terms.
- What would a children's-rights-based approach to behaviour in my centre look like?

**Practical activities to try out:**
- Practice following the steps through role play in resolving conflict situations.
- Write a children's-rights-based behavioural management policy.

## Meaningful engagement with parents

The second scenario was written in response to a number of issues similar to the scenario outlined below that have come up for providers in the past couple of years in relation to meaningful engagement with parents. To be clear, **misunderstandings between parents and childcare staff are common when culture is *not* a factor.** So it is no surprise that staff run into difficulties when facing parents from cultures other than their own. Working with parents is a vital part of the childcare practitioner's role. For this work to be effective it needs to have a focus on the well-being of the child.

**Scenario 2 – At a staff meeting, Nan tells her colleagues what happened when she introduced the service to two Nigerian parents. 'They were so rude. They would not look me in the eye when I was talking to them. They had no interest at all. I don't think they care. They just want somewhere to leave their child for a few hours'.**

### *Partnership with parents: Sharing the power*
Early childhood practitioners have the privilege of working with families. It is essential to the development and well-being of the children in our care that there be a real and meaningful partnership with parents. It is impossible to separate children from their parents and family context and it is harmful to their well-being to think in those terms. As practitioners, we hold the power when a family uses our service; we may not feel it to be true or be aware of it, but it is a fact. Parents are often not invited into playrooms, but are kept to the hall or the office. We have all the information about the programme, combined with a background in child development. We may use jargon or terms with which parents are unfamiliar. We also know all about our centre, how it works and we may have implicit expectations of families that use our service. MacNaughton and Hughes (2011) write about the difficulties that parents and practitioners have in finding time and space to collaborate effectively. To really work in partnership with parents, it is essential that this time and space be planned for. It is impossible to introduce an equality and diversity approach without the engagement of parents. Louise Derman-Sparks in her seminal book *Anti-Bias Curriculum* (1989) refers to the three components of work with parents – education, dialogue and involvement.

### *Genuine interest*
Meaningful engagement with families, and really sharing the childcare, starts with a genuine interest in each new family. Many services have a parents' handbook containing all the relevant information; some services have a checklist of things they need to ask new families, and of the information they need to give them. The handbook will contain a clear mission statement stating the inclusive nature of the centre's programme. It is really important to go through the information with the parents when the child starts and to give the parents the information to take home to read. Of course practitioners need to be aware of language and literacy issues parents may be facing, and to support the parents where possible. The enrolment or admission form must be equitable (Derman-Sparks and Olsen Edwards, 2010) and should contain inclusive terms like 'family' instead of 'mother and father'. Along with giving information the practitioner must also listen and gather information about the family. Information is shared to empower parents with

the knowledge needed to get the best from the service, and even more importantly, to help the service best meet the needs of the child.

## Culturally safe

Teresa Rosegrant (1993), an American kindergarten teacher and early childhood specialist, says that we need to go further once we have gathered information about a family. Each year, she finds out the cultural background of the children in the class, or what countries they have lived in, and gathers information, stories, images and children's books in the relevant language to use in her classroom. Rosegrant will only celebrate the festivals and holidays that the families of her current children celebrate. She believes that making the classroom a culturally safe environment is as important as physical and psychological safety (Bredekamp and Rosegrant, 1993).

---

### 10.4

Building on the work of 'éist', the 2011–2012 National Pre-school Education Initiative for Children from Ethnic Minorities (Equality and Diversity) is addressing training needs of the sector in this area. As a result of this project, we will have recorded examples of high-quality Diversity and Equality practice in Ireland.

---

## Inclusive of all parents

Families come in all arrangements, and all are welcome. When parents no longer live together, clear information is even more important. Letters home are sent to both home addresses, and verbal information is repeated for both parents. The definition of family should be wide and inclusive. If, for example, grandparents share the primary care it is appropriate to include them in the information. It is also vital that we only ask for the information we need to know in order to meet the child's needs; we don't need to know which of the mothers in a two-mother family is the birth mother, just as we don't need to know if parents are married or not. The information received about a family is of course always kept in the strictest confidence and never shared with the wider community.

## Building communities

Once a family is using the service there needs to be an opportunity for parents to learn something about the programme and the practise. Organising parents' evenings is the way many centres share this information. These evenings are also an opportunity for parents to meet each other and for friendships to develop. ECEC settings have a role in building communities. I had an opportunity to witness this in Cork a few years back, on the second morning in a new ECEC centre built on a new housing estate was open. Parents were talking to neighbours for the first time, and offering each other lifts to work. Giving parents the opportunity to connect can stop the isolation that many parents of young children feel. This helps to ensure that children grow up in a supportive community. To achieve this, the atmosphere in the ECEC centre must be welcoming; the staff had the foresight to put a comfortable sofa in the entrance area.

## A welcome morning

The practitioner's role is to know every parent's name, and to introduce parents to each other. Some centres have a welcome morning for parents in the second week of term. Including new parents by asking them to do a task, like make the tea with a more established parent can break down barriers and help to make people feel included. One of the best ways we can serve the children in our centres is to help their families connect with and support each other (Derman- Sparks and Olsen Edwards, 2010).

## What did you do today?

Young children usually give their parents very little information about what goes on in the service. Practitioners need to inform parents about the programme, because equality of access to information is essential in inclusive practise.

When talking about the programme it is important to give clear, accessible information. Here again the information exchange is two-way. Parents are encouraged to ask questions and criticism is received with openness and reflection (Derman-Sparks and Olsen Edwards, 2010). Some centres find a notice board about the programme helpful. This is kept updated with news of what the children are working on and how the parents can extend the interest at home. Other services send newsletters home keeping the channels of communication open, keeping in mind literacy and language issues. Forming a caring pre-school community where all children can learn and thrive means forging a working relationship based on what families wish for their children and the practitioners believe is important for children (Derman-Sparks and Olsen Edwards, 2010). These hopes and beliefs will only come together once a relationship of trust is established.

## Being positive

When services truly work in partnership with parents, they only view the families in a positive light. In one centre in Cork, the staff talk about their families with such respect, care and positive regard that you would just love to send your child there. Staff never engage in gossip or make negative generalisations about families such as, 'you know what to expect from the families around here'. Parents and children are met with genuine regard and every opportunity is taken to engage with the family. This centre has not got to this point by accident; it involved a lot of work and focus. The more frequently you can chat with a family even for a brief time, the more your relationship will grow, the deeper the connection and the more genuine the partnership with parents (Derman-Sparks and Olsen Edwards, 2010).

## 10.5 Areas for critical reflection:

- Have you heard negative comments in services where you have been on placement or worked?
- What would you do to support a respectful ethos in a service?
- Use the critically reflective questions in the Diversity and Equality Guidelines for Childcare Providers (OMC, 2006).

## Nan and her new parents

To get back to the scenario at the top with Nan and the two Nigerian parents, there is a lot going on in this exchange. Eye contact is an area of huge cultural difference. In one culture it is disrespectful to make eye contact; in another it is rude not to. Nan is unaware that cultural differences may be at root of her issue with the new parents. In many cultures a teacher is someone to be respected and obeyed. Nan needs to look at how welcoming she was with the parents and how at ease she made them feel. How welcoming was the centre? How would the family have known just by looking that a Nigerian child would be welcome there? It would be interesting to know how the other staff responded to Nan's outburst. You would hope that a more experienced worker would explain the cultural differences and arrange for the staff to be informed about culturally different ways of communication and of showing respect. In time, staff will also share with the new family the cultural norms in Ireland – which may vary widely between different groups in Irish society – so that their ways of expression are not misunderstood.

## Summary

Working from an equality and diversity standpoint means always **looking for opportunities to share power**. In ECEC, we can achieve this by being child-centred in our approach to children, and being family-centred in our approach to those who provide their primary care.

## 10.6 Areas for critical reflection:

- How do we communicate with parents?
- How do we welcome parents?
- Would the admissions form stand up to equality-proofing?
- When do we provide opportunities for parents to meet?

**Practical activities to try out:**
- Put together a parents' handbook.
- Develop a newsletter template to regularly update parents attending the centre.
- Revisit your mission statement.

## CHAPTER 11

# Persona Dolls

Babette Brown (2001, p. 76) bases her work on the adage 'People will forget what you said. People will forget what you did. But people will never forget how you made them feel'.

'Did a new boy start in pre-school? He has been talking about his new friend, Sean, all evening.'

> (Parent's question following a first visit from
> Persona Doll Sean to the pre-school, 2009).

'Ann, will you ring Sean's and Kathleen's mammies and see if they can come today?'

> (Request from pre-school child for the Persona Dolls, 2010)

## Overview

In this chapter I will introduce Persona Dolls and share my experience of using the dolls in an Irish context. I will also explain what they are, how to use them and why you might use them. Then I will discuss the benefits of using the dolls, linking them to the Anti-Bias Goals and Síolta (2006) and Aistear (2009).

## After reading this chapter you should be able to:

▸ Understand what Persona Dolls are and how they can be used to reflect children's individual and group identities.
▸ Understand the importance of introducing children to social and cultural diversity in an Irish context.
▸ Identify how using the dolls is linked to the four Anti-Bias Goals (OMC, 2006), Síolta (2006) and Aistear (2009).
▸ Understand how the Persona Doll storytelling sessions help children to develop empathy and respect for people who are different to them and also to discover the ways in which they are similar.
▸ Identify the benefits of using Persona Dolls for parents and practitioners.

## Introduction: Meeting the needs of all children

In 2002 while working in St Catherine's Segregated Preschool for Travellers in Mayo, I became very interested in working with diversity and equality issues. This was primarily due to the prejudice and discrimination I witnessed against the Traveller community. I began to work with the Anti-Bias Approach following a pilot training project by '*éist*' from Pavee Point in 2000. I found working with the Approach very beneficial to the children, and as I progressed with the Anti-Bias implementation, I enhanced the work using Persona Dolls.

All of the children in St Catherine's were Travellers; in 2002 Traveller preschools were segregated. These preschools have been phased out and Traveller children since 2010 can avail of the free preschool year in integrated services.

I knew that when the children left the pre-school, they would be in a mixed setting. I wanted to support the children to have a strong sense of their own identity and to also have some understanding of other people's lives and feelings. I wanted to achieve this in a way that reflected the realities of people's lives.

Persona Dolls are one of the tools I use to bring diversity alive for the children. We are all different, including both the minority and majority communities. In our case the Persona Dolls were primarily about the Traveller community. I say that because your choice of doll is determined by the needs of the children. We focused first on the Traveller children and since Traveller children were largely isolated in the community and in the segregated provision I then brought their awareness to the diversity in the broader community by introducing new community and majority population dolls.

Once I began using the dolls, I realised how powerful they were. Persona Dolls have been used in many countries in tandem with the Anti-Bias philosophy, and their success has been well documented (Brown, 2001; Wagner, 2008).

Before you embark in using the dolls, you need to have undertaken Diversity and Equality training, which focuses on anti-discrimination and the Anti-Bias Approach in an Irish context. Having a strong background in diversity issues, and becoming critically reflective is vital for engaging in Personal Doll work correctly.

### What are Persona Dolls?

Persona Dolls are very special dolls. They have their own personas – characters with a name, family, likes and dislikes. Just like the children in the setting, the dolls have a name, a family, a home, likes and dislikes. As the practitioner you build the identity of the doll with the support of the parents or other staff so that the children can identify with the persona. No two families are the same, and in order to avoid stereotyping, it's important that the information for each doll's persona is accurate and not fantastical.

Below are two examples of personas that I used recently in a mixed setting. Afua was developed with the help of one of our Cameroonian parents, and Sean was developed with the help of parents and centre staff.

I chose to develop these two personas because they represented the lives of some of the children in the setting accurately, both from the majority and minority. I wanted to introduce the children to the social diversity present in the centre and the wider community, to present positive images of Black children and their families and to help the children discover all the things they have in common as well as the ways they were different. I wanted to use the dolls to support children's individual and group identities and to give all children a sense of belonging in the service. Another aim was to support the children to have empathy and to become comfortable with difference (Goals 1 and 2 of the Anti-Bias Approach). I wanted to be proactive, and hoped that because the children had developed a relationship with the dolls and cared about what happened to them that we could use the dolls to tackle difficult issues that might arise. Working with the dolls in this way can give the children strategies and language to deal with these issues (Goals 3 and 4 of the Anti-Bias Approach).

## What type of doll should you use?

Any doll can be used as a Persona Doll as long as they meet the following criteria. It's important that the dolls look real and that they accurately portray skin colour and physical features. I'm sure we have all seen dolls in shops with white features that have just been painted brown to represent a Black child. When purchasing a doll to use as a Persona Doll, ask yourself if it looks like someone you know from the relevant group. Consider hair, skin colour, facial characteristics and body shape. Another important characteristic I discovered through using the dolls is size; my first Persona Dolls were only a foot high and had to sit on my shoulder to talk to me. My new dolls were purchased from a UK website, www.persona-doll-training.org. They are soft, child-sized dolls that sit comfortably on my lap and can wear real clothes and shoes that can be changed regularly to suit the weather and the current fashion trends. Like the children, the dolls get their coats and gloves and boots out for the cold weather and wear shorts in the summer. This helps to make the dolls more real for the children, so real, in fact, that recently, one child said while holding Sean, 'He's getting bigger Ann, isn't he?' My dolls have acquired an extensive wardrobe thanks to the parents who have kindly donated old clothes and shoes for use with the dolls.

In building a collection of Persona Dolls, also think about the cultural, ethnic, economic backgrounds, ability and family status – the identities of the children in your setting. You will need a variety of dolls and personas that accurately represent the children in your setting and some dolls with other differences so that children can identify with them and the stories that they tell.

Developing the Persona Doll's family's socio-economic status, for example, is very relevant in today's economic climate, as many parents have become unemployed because of the economic downturn. Each doll needs a persona that reflects some of the children in your group, but a doll should not wholly represent any individual child. Always change the name, sex, etc. The whole point of Persona Doll stories is that you discuss issues that are coming up for the children without focusing on any one child.

Look at the family makeup of the children in your setting. Are there children who live in a one-parent family, live with a stepfamily, have two mums or dads, live with grandparents or are fostered or adopted? All children need to see their family makeup reflected positively in the setting, and Persona Dolls are a flexible tool for doing just that.

When developing your Persona Dolls, consider:

▶ gender
▶ physical characteristics
▶ cultural and ethnic backgrounds
▶ socio-economic groups
▶ family makeup.

### Introducing Afua
▶ Afua was born in Ireland and her mum and dad were born in Ghana. She will be four years old on 14 December. Afua is her Ghanaian name. In Ghana names are given based on the day you were born. Afua was born on a Friday, and all girls born on Friday are called Afua. The child will also be called after a relative, papa, mama or nana to honour them. So Afua might also be called 'Nana' by her parents. Children are often given Christian names too when they go to school, like Mary. The girls may also have 'Ewura' added to their name, which means 'lady'.
▶ Afua is living in Ireland with her parents. Her parents moved to Ireland because they were afraid that they might be hurt if they stayed in Ghana. Afua lives in Mayo and has a big brother called Nana. Afua and her brother have black skin like her mummy and daddy.
▶ Afua has never been to Ghana and has been living in Ireland all her life. Her granny lives in Ghana, and Afua has cousins, uncles and aunties in Ghana too. She likes chips, sausages, roast potatoes, turkey, rice, yoghurt and pizza. Afua also likes Ghanaian food like plantain and fufu, which is made from cassava and plantain. Plantain is like a banana but not as sweet; bananas are usually eaten raw while plantain is usually cooked before you eat it. Cassava, okra soup and yam flour are other basic foods.
▶ Afua cannot speak any Ghanaian languages; she speaks English.

- Afua has another name that she was given when she was baptised: Mary. Afua's mum and dad are Christians and when they were in Ghana, they attended the Catholic Church, which is the same as the Catholic Church in Ireland and that is why she was given the name Mary.
- Afua sits at the table with her mum, dad and brother together to have meals.
- Afua likes dancing to all kinds of music.

(This information was given to me from the parent.)

### *Introducing Sean:*
When introducing the dolls, I like to start with a boy doll to ensure that the boys engage with him, and also to challenge stereotypes; many children may never have seen male dolls before, and may think that all dolls are female. This persona was developed as a team effort to represent the lives of some of the children in the setting accurately. Sean was also used to challenge gender stereotypes. For example, Sean came to visit the children wearing his new pink jacket, his best friend is Kathleen and they love to play together in the home corner.

- Sean is nearly four years old. His birthday is 10 November .
- He has brown hair and green eyes.
- He has just started in pre-school.
- He has a baby sister called Jessica.
- He lives with his mammy and daddy and baby Jessica on a farm just outside the town of Claremorris.
- His dad is a farmer and drives a Massey Ferguson tractor.
- His favourite food is the bacon and cabbage that his mammy makes.
- Sean loves playing with his toys. He has a play tractor and he pretends he's a farmer baling hay like his dad.
- He helps his mummy with the shopping and gets things for her when she's tired.
- Sean's favourite days are when he goes farming with his daddy, and Christmas, when Santa comes.

## What is the purpose of using Persona Dolls?
The dolls and their stories are used to help children think about diversity issues, including what is fair and unfair. In this way we aim to prevent children from learning prejudiced attitudes, and to help unlearn any of the negative messages they might have already picked up. This is very important work, as Murray (2004/2011) explains:

> As professional adults sharing children's lives, we have a major influence on how children evaluate difference and relate to others. Because all children are affected

by prejudice and discrimination, this can impede their educational progress if left unchallenged. As educators, we can work actively to prevent the development of negative attitudes and promote understanding and respect among young children (p. 13)

The dolls represent the diversity in the setting and in the wider community, like the people the children are meeting or seeing in the community. We are not just talking about cultural diversity, but different family makeup, disabilities, gender and different socio-economic groups. The dolls are not left down for children to play with in the setting, but are kept in a special place in the room, or they come and visit.

Like the Anti-Bias Approach, the dolls and the issues they raise will not and should not be the same in every setting, as the dolls you choose and the issues you discuss will depend on the individual children in the setting and the issues brought up by the children.

## Using Persona Dolls and the Goals of the Anti-Bias Approach:

The Anti-Bias Approach has four Goals for both adults and children that build on each other (See Section 2, Chapter 4). Working with the Anti-Bias Goals influences how you develop your stories for the dolls. If you have a clear focus on the Anti-Bias Goals, you use them constructively to support and build on identity and empathy development, critical reflection and empowerment for all children.

### 11.1 Anti-Bias Goals

**Anti-Bias Goals for Children**

- **Goal 1: To support children's identity (individual and group) and their sense of belonging:**
  By introducing dolls that accurately reflect the children in your group, the children see themselves and the group they belong to reflected positively in the setting.

- **Goal 2: To foster children's empathy and support them to be comfortable with difference:**
  By using the dolls to reflect the children in our group, you are already working on Goal 2. The dolls are a brilliant way of introducing and helping children become comfortable with people who are different to them.

- **Goal 3: To encourage each child to critically think about diversity and bias:**
  As the children develop relationships and begin to care about what happens to them, they want to help solve the problems that the dolls are experiencing. The dolls support children to think about what's fair and unfair, and gives them new language to name feelings.

- **Goal 4: To empower children to stand up for themselves and others in difficult situations:**
  Through problem-solving, the children develop strategies to deal with times when they or others are treated unfairly.

As with all Anti-Bias work, adults cannot work with Persona Dolls without first looking at themselves, being aware of their own prejudices and stereotypes. Using Persona Dolls can also help practitioners work on the Goals for adults.

**Anti-Bias Goals for adults**
- **Goal 1: To be conscious of one's own culture, attitudes and values and how they influence practice:**
  When developing personas for the dolls, it's important to be aware of the stereotypes, prejudices and biases that we have, and we all have them. We need to acknowledge and counter them through discussion and education, and what better way than working in partnership with parents and other people from groups who are different to us to develop the dolls' personas. In this way we can ensure that we do not make assumptions about children's background, ethnicities or family and do not introduce dolls of different ethnicities, background, abilities, etc., in an inaccurate or stereotypical way.
- **Goal 2: To be comfortable with difference, have empathy and engage effectively with families.** Are we comfortable with the diversity of parents/staff in the service? Are we willing to listen to each child's and family's life stories, and to ask for their help in developing personas and stories for the dolls? The dolls help practitioners to develop empathy and understanding about what it's like to be a Traveller, asylum seeker or child with a disability, and from talking with parents, they gain more confidence and begin to work more effectively with families.
- **Goal 3: To think critically about diversity, bias and discrimination.** Working with the dolls help practitioners to recognise 'teachable moments' in the service and use the dolls to work on them with children.
- **Goal 4: To engage confidently in dialogue about diversity, bias and discrimination.** Work to challenge individual and institutional forms of prejudice and discrimination. From working with the dolls we are more aware of prejudice and discrimination faced by children and their families in the service and will have more confidence and want to challenge biased behaviour.

## 11.2 Persona Doll Work: Links to Síolta and Aistear

We now have Síolta (2006) the Quality Framework and Aistear (2009) the Curriculum Framework guiding best practice in Early Childhood Education and Care in Ireland. Using Persona Dolls, practitioners can ensure that they are adhering to these frameworks in their settings.

### Síolta
Working with Persona Dolls helps practitioners adhere to many Síolta Standards, especially Standard 3: Parents and Families, and Standard 14: Identity and Belonging.

### Aistear:
Using Persona Dolls effectively in your service ensures that you are meeting many of the learning goals and aims of all of the Aistear Themes. For example:

- **Exploring and thinking:** using the dolls to help the children solve problems links directly to Aim 2: Learning Goals 4–6.
- **Well-being:** using the dolls to critically think through the issues links to Aim 1: Learning Goals 1, 2 and 5; to Aim 3: Learning Goals 4 and 6; and to Aim 4: Learning Goals 5 and 6.
- **Communicating:** encouraging all the children to participate and to discuss the issues raised by playing with the dolls links to Aim 2: Learning Goals 4–6.
- **Identity and Belonging:** introducing dolls that represent all of the children in the setting positively and accurately links to Aim 1: Learning Goals 1–6; Aim 2: Learning Goals 1–6; Aim 3: Learning Goals 1–6; and to Aim 4: Learning Goals 1–6.

## Introducing the Persona Doll to the children

The dolls visit the children in the service at least once a week. The children get used to this, look forward to it, and if the doll misses a week the children will ask for them. Although the children know that they are dolls (and sometimes will say when you first introduce them, 'He's a teddy') through sharing experiences they become friends and begin to believe in and empathise with the dolls and their stories.

When they visit, they usually sit on my lap and whisper in my ear what they want me to tell the children. The doll does not speak and the practitioner acts as interpreter and tells the children what the doll has come to tell them. When the dolls were introduced first, the children asked why they didn't talk. I explained that he speaks to me and later in the year when the children were holding the dolls themselves, I saw them putting their ears down to listen to the dolls and answering the doll like I do.

We start off by telling a short story of the doll's life as a way to explore experiences that are similar and different to the children's. I usually start with happy stories, and let the children become familiar with the doll and develop a relationship with it. Stories can come from experiences that the children have had or are going to have in the future, or an incident that has happened in the setting. When the doll tells her story or problem, keep it short, so the children won't lose interest. She then invites the children to respond and using appropriate questions, for example: What would you do? How do you think she feels? Can you help? The children are encouraged to 'think critically' (see Section 2: Chapter 3) and independently, and to express their ideas. The children love to give advice to the doll and talk about similar experiences and feelings that they may have had. This is more important than coming up with perfect solutions. The story is then brought to an end, with the doll thanking the children for being so helpful and kind. The doll tells the children they will try out some of the solutions and when they visit next they will tell them how things worked out.

Once the children have developed a relationship with the dolls, they begin to empathise with them and care about what happens to them. They learn that discrimination hurts, and see the unfairness of the situations in the stories, so the children want to help and are motivated to come up with solutions. Problem-solving helps children feel good about themselves and will encourage them stand up for themselves and others in the face of bias (Anti-Bias: Goal 4).

Make sure to record the doll's introduction and the stories the dolls share with the children so that you remember what you have already told children. This is essential, as the children will pick up on inaccuracies and inconsistencies. You need to take the time to practice using the dolls before you introduce them to the children, including how you hold, listen to and talk to the dolls, so that you are relaxed and comfortable. It is particularly important that you know the doll's persona very well; in fact you need to appear to have a relationship with the dolls, and to treat them like friends that you care about who come to visit the centre. I recommend that you prepare a Persona Doll file for each doll that is made available to share with practitioners and parents.

After each session, it is important to reflect back on what happened during the session. Consider the following questions:

▸ Did all the children have the opportunity to participate?
▸ Were the children encouraged to discuss and supported to express their feelings?
▸ Did the children do most of the talking?
▸ Did you listen carefully and respond to their contributions?
▸ Were the questions you asked open-ended? Did they encourage the children to think critically about the issues and express their ideas?
▸ Were all the children encouraged to give advice and share similar experiences?
▸ Was the session too short or too long?
▸ Did you achieve what you hoped from the session? Did the children learn what you hoped they would?
▸ Did the children ask questions that you couldn't answer or that made you uncomfortable?

## 11.3 Building Empathy

Before the pre-school children move on to primary school, we bring them on an outing. Our children were very excited about going to Pots of Fun, an indoor activity centre, and were telling the Persona Dolls Sean and Kathleen about it. One child asked if Sean and Kathleen could come with us on the outing. We asked the dolls if they would like to come and they said yes, so on the morning of the trip the dolls accompanied the children on the bus to Pots of Fun.

While in Pots of Fun, the children took care of the dolls, helping them take off their shoes and taking them to see all the fun things to do. Sean, it seemed, like some of the children, was afraid to go on the big slide, so one of the children said 'Sean can come with me'. The children held the dolls while they went on the slides and enjoyed all the activities. When the dolls were 'tired', a parent took care of the dolls.

## Why use Persona Dolls?

> Research confirms that children are influenced by prevailing attitudes in society and their own attitudes develop from a very young age.
>
> (Milner, 1983 and Connolly, 2002)

Persona Dolls are a fantastic resource for children to see themselves and others accurately and positively reflected in the setting. The dolls help children learn about diversity and to help them feel comfortable with it.

---

### 11.4

Anti-Bias for Children Goal 1:
To support children's identity (individual and group) and their sense of belonging.
Anti-Bias for Children Goal 2:
To foster children's empathy and support them to be comfortable with difference.
(See Section 2, Chapter 3: Approaches, which introduces the Anti-Bias Goals. See also Aistear Theme: Identity and Belonging, Aim 1: Learning Goals 1–6, Aim 2: Learning Goals 1–6.)

---

Persona Dolls are a flexible alternative to children's books about diversity, which, as they tend to be published in the US and the UK, rarely reflect the Irish context accurately.

---

### 11.5 Supporting Identity

I will never forget the joy on one child's face when I introduced a black persona doll called Mary into the setting. As I was telling the children about the doll's life, one child kept repeating over and over again 'Just like me, Just like me!' and jumping up and down with delight.
Or the Traveller boy who was sitting on the edge of the group when I began to introduce Kathleen (the Traveller doll), but as I was talking about the doll's life, started to move closer and closer to me and asking questions about the doll. By the end of the session he was sitting beside Kathleen holding her hand. This example highlights the importance of every child being visible in the setting and reminds me of a quote from a Traveller child in Murray (2004):

> Pictures, jigsaws and books would show that Travellers really exist in the world, and people won't call you names then.
>
> (Traveller child, age 7)

---

The dolls help practitioners discuss issues around stereotyping, unfairness in the setting without focusing on any particular child.

## 11.6 Persona Dolls supporting Anti-Bias Approach and Aistear

**Anti-Bias Goal for Children 3:**
**To encourage children to think critically about diversity and bias**

- **Aistear Theme: Identity and Belonging**
  Aim 1: Learning Goals 1, 2, and 3.
  Aim 3: Learning Goals 1, 2, 3, 4, 5, 6.
- **Aistear Theme: Exploring and Thinking:**
  Aim 2: Learning Goals 4–6.
  Aim 4: Learning Goals 2–5.
- **Aistear Theme: Well-being**
  Aim 1: Learning Goals 1, 2, 4 and 5.
  Aim 3: Learning Goals 4 and 6.
  Aim 4: Learning Goals 5 and 6.

## Building Empathy

One of the most powerful reasons to use Persona Dolls is that they support the development of empathy for *all* people.

## 11.7 Jargon Buster: Empathy

**Empathy** is defined as: the ability to understand others feelings by experiencing the same emotion oneself.

(Epstine, 2009)

The following story is an example of how the dolls help children to support the development of empathy.

Gerrard Pio is a Traveller doll and Temitope is a refugee doll from Cameroon. I introduced these dolls when refugee children were enrolled in the Traveller pre-school. I was concerned when I noticed that the Traveller children did not want to hold hands with the Black children during outside time, an issue that is reported regularly from preschool workers.

This is how the session went:

'Gerrard Pio has come to visit us today, and he has brought his friend again. He wants to know if you can remember his friend's name. Temitope, that's right. Gerrard Pio wants to ask your help with a problem they have.

Some of the boys and girls in Temitope and Gerrard Pio's pre-school wouldn't hold Temitope's hand at playtime in the yard. Gerrard Pio wants to know how you think Temitope felt when that happened. He also wants to know if you ever felt like that.'

'Owen wouldn't let me play with the trailer and I was sad', said one child.

I asked them to show me their sad faces, which they did.

'What could Temitope do if the children won't hold her hand to play Farmer in the Dell?'

One of the boys piped up, 'Beat them?' 'Hit them?'

We discussed our morning agreement where we said that we would be kind to each other, and that we don't hit anyone in pre-school.

'Who could Temitope talk to?' asked the practitioner.

'She could tell teacher.'

'Temitope wants to know what she could say to the child who won't hold her hand.'

One child said, 'I'm sad.'

'Yes, she could tell the child that it hurts her feelings when she won't hold her hand.'

Gerrard Pio asked if this had happened to any of the children, and they said 'No.' Temitope thanked the children for helping, and said that she will tell the child who won't hold her hand that it hurts her feelings. She will also talk to her teacher and tell her what is happening, and report back to the children next week.

Over the next few weeks when holding hands to play ring games or engaging in activities, I would remind the children about Gerrard Pio's story and how Temitope felt. The children would chime in with the story as well. I would then suggest we all hold hands. We didn't have a problem with hand-holding after that.

### Benefits for my child: Parents' experience of Persona Dolls

From a personal point of view, adopting this approach brought many benefits to my child and the other children such as:

▶ It provides information on a particular topic or about a particular person without the person feeling awkward or singled out.

▶ It helps to improve integration, as children are able to understand and accept each other regardless of nationality, colour, background, family structure or ability.

▶ Talking about a particular child from a different background, ethnicity, ability or family structure brings with it a sense of importance and builds the confidence of a child who would otherwise may have felt different (in a negative way) to his or her peers.

▶ Educating others about the different backgrounds, ethnicities, family structures and abilities, including values and attitudes, by using the Persona Doll boosts children's morale and confidence. It helps children to communicate and socialise freely.

(Parent 1)

▶ It is a way of broadening the mind and increasing the knowledge of those who are narrow minded when it comes to how to relate to people who are new to their communities or foreign people in general'.

(Parent 2)

*Benefits for staff:*
Implementing the Anti-Bias approach in your setting is not about carrying out once-off planned activities, but observing children's play, listening to their conversations and talking to parents so that you are aware of the issues that are coming up for your group of children. This means using your teachable moments to develop your curriculum.

---

**11.8 Jargon Buster: Teachable moment**

A **teachable moment** occurs when a child makes a comment or asks a question that raises an issue for the wider class. You then have an opportunity to use this moment to give accurate information or tackle the question or problem that has come up. For example, girls in the home corner tell a little boy who is playing with a doll that 'boys can't play with dolls'.

---

Persona doll stories come from teachable moments and conversations with parents. Instead of being unsure about what to say or do when a child makes an unfair comment or calls names, you can use the dolls to talk to the children about the problem. In my case, using the dolls helped me to raise difficult issues with the children that I would have previously felt uncomfortable about and ultimately ignored.

## Health warning for beginners!
The dolls can be used to implement an Anti-Bias Approach and work on all four Goals of the Anti-Bias Approach for Children and Adults. Persona Dolls should not be used without first attending Diversity and Equality Training and Persona Doll training (see www.pavee.ie/edenn for more information). These dolls are a very powerful resource and if used incorrectly can reinforce prejudices and stereotypes for children. Children also ask very direct questions, so you need to be prepared and have appropriate and accurate

answers about even difficult topics as your discomfort with a subject can be transferred to the children. Remember that working with Persona Dolls is not a game, but a structured way to open up discussion about diversity in a safe way. It is also about addressing issues that the children are raising or are uncomfortable with in a child-friendly way, so you need to be prepared.

## Summary

The aim of this chapter was to introduce practitioners to Persona Dolls and to show how these dolls are a very powerful resource when used appropriately by a skilled practitioner trained in Diversity and Equality. I have been using the dolls for many years and what always hits me when I introduce the doll is the children's ability to empathise with it, and how much they care about what happens to the doll. Having accurate information is crucial to nurturing children's individual and group identity. When you get it right, it is a joy to see the children grow in confidence and self-esteem. As early childhood practitioners, we have a very important role to play in young children's lives and Persona Dolls help us carry out this role of empowering children and helping to create a better and more just world for all children.

### 11.9 Reflective questions

Discuss the possible benefits of using Persona Dolls for working on diversity and equality issues with children.

- Have you observed situations in a setting where you think you might use the dolls?
- What are the difficulties/barriers you might experience when using the Persona Dolls with children?

## CHAPTER 12

# Embracing All Languages in the ECEC Setting

I once had a four-year-old girl in the playschool. I didn't know for sure where she came from exactly, nor was I familiar with her home language. I couldn't understand what she was saying when she tried to communicate in her language. Unless she pointed, I didn't understand. I thought she just needed time to adapt, but looking back now, she was isolated from other children and stayed close to me. She became quiet and rarely spoke, just carried on with activities quietly. I thought she was happy! I don't think I ever had a full conversation with her mum. It was very difficult. I know I felt awkward about not being able to discuss things and share information. I didn't know how to do things better at the time.

(Patsy Baissangourov, 2011)

## Overview

This chapter will support your understanding of the advantages and challenges for multilingual children, their peers and adults in the ECEC setting. The experiences of parents, early childhood practitioners and trainers offer strategies you may employ when children are learning English or Irish as an additional language. Reflective questions will help guide you to find ways of working in the setting for recognising and embracing family languages. Consideration is also given to involving parents both in the home and the setting. A study carried out in Donegal gives insights into personal experiences from early childhood practitioners and parents of multilingual children. We will also share learning and experiences from our work with children and families other trainers and learners.

### After reading this chapter you should be able to:
▶ develop an awareness of the advantages of children acquiring two languages
▶ communicate effectively with children with additional languages using verbal and non-verbal methods

▸ provide play opportunities for children with additional languages to build positive peer interactions

▸ involve parents of multilingual children through supports for home and in the setting

▸ identify the child's rights to an equal voice, choice and access in relation to the UNCRC and Childcare Regulations

▸ understand the challenges a child with additional languages may face in accessing the curriculum.

## The good fortune of having multiple languages

**Multilingualism** is the ability to communicate in two or more languages with equal or similar fluency. A **receptive multilingual** is considered to be someone who understands a second language without being necessarily able to speak or write it. In our home, my seven- and four-year-old children hear their dad speak Russian on a daily basis. Although they understand what he is saying, the children always respond in English. When visiting family in Russia they spoke a few key words such as 'please', 'good morning' and the names of some foods. The children talk about an occasion when out at shops with their Russian grandparents. 'Baboo didn't know what I was saying and she didn't get me the sweets I wanted so I pointed to them. Then she understood what I meant. ('Baboo' is a pet name for *babushka*, grandmother.) When I asked my son why he didn't use the Russian word for sweets, he said he was 'too shy'. Although children may know words in their second language, they may not be confident or able to use these to communicate verbally. Such children are considered to be receptive multilinguals. The foundations of the second language they are acquiring at this early age will assist them later in life to develop the ability to speak Russian. Their capacity for learning subsequent languages will also be increased (Baker and Prys Jones, 1998).

The younger the child is, the easier it is to develop fluency in a second language. Unless the child is multilingual at an early age, the language is not part of the learner's primary cognitive development. It is a learned language, just like we learn Irish in school. The key is to support the child's first language in ECEC and at home.

Multilingual children have the ability to change from one language to the other quickly and process both languages. This process is known as 'code-switching' and requires more complex thinking strategies than the mastery of just one language. For example, young children learn to determine the meaning of vocabulary along with knowledge and understanding of how to put these words into grammatically correct sentences. Children acquiring two languages are putting extra effort into their thinking skills and code-switching. According to Flood (2010), if children are multilingual, it will have a positive effect on their cognitive development, such as attention, reasoning and concept formation. Having seen it from a parent's perspective, I feel that children gain in their thinking and learning skills by the consistent exposure to two languages from an early age.

## Recognising and embracing the family languages in the setting

Some children in multilingual families will have only one dominant language, which is likely to be the spoken language of the main caregiver at home. Giving children opportunities to use and extend their home language will consolidate and extend their language and literacy understanding. It is also essential for their cognitive development. Abandonment of the child's home language, according to Siraj-Blatchford and Clarke (2000), could have serious consequences for the child's second-language-learning and self-esteem. ECEC practitioners will benefit from understanding that maintaining the first language as well as learning English is essential. Therefore, before the practitioner tries to help the new child to learn English, they are advised to have a familiarity, celebration and engagement with the child's home language.

---

### 12.1 Discuss

1. What are the benefits of children being bilingual?
2. How would you find out about the languages children speak at home?

---

Let's return for a moment to the quote at the beginning of the chapter about my experience of working with a child whose first language is not English, and outline how I would now change my approach:

> To engage more effectively with the child's mum, I would show that I am comfortable using gestures and eye contact, and would be openly friendly. My lack of skills to engage with her made me fearful, which prevented me from being openly friendly. I would now say, 'Come on in', with wide-open hand gestures. I would use visuals, point to maps to find out where the child and family were from. I would also have pictures of the playschool routine and encourage the mum to say the word in their home language. I would write this down and practice saying it with the mum's help. Once I know which language the child uses, I can find out if there is someone locally to help me translate. I may discover that the mum has some English, and like the child in Russia, might not be confident in verbalising it. Partnership with the parent will give me the information I need to support the child's language and communication better.

## 12.2 Links

- Anti-Bias Goals:
  Goal 1 for adults:
  To be conscious of one's own culture, attitudes and values and how they influence practice.
  Goal 2 for adults:
  To be comfortable with difference, have empathy and engage effectively with families.
  Goal 1 for children:
  To support children's identity (individual and group) and their sense of belonging.
- Aistear Themes: Identity and Belonging.
  Aim 1: Learning goals 1–6. Aim 2: Learning goals 1 and 4. Aim 3: Learning goals 1 and 3.
  Aim 4: Learning goals 2 and 5.
  Síolta Standard:
  14: Identity and Belonging. Components 14.2 and 14.3.

The language spoken by the child and their family is part of who that child is, how they interact and express themselves in the world. In order to work with Goal 1 the practitioner must find ways to engage effectively with the child. Also by doing so in a sensitive and caring manner will build towards a good sense of self for the child within the setting.

- Aistear Theme: Communicating. Aim 2: Learning Goal 6

## 12.3 Discuss

1. What could the lack of recognition of the home language in the ECEC setting mean for children?
2. How can you support children to value their first language at home and in the ECEC setting?
3. How can you support parents in understanding the importance of maintaining their child's first language at home and in the ECEC setting?

## Challenges facing children with additional languages

The demographic changes in Ireland over the past decade have seen ECEC practitioners coming into contact with children with a different language to that used in the setting (generally English, but sometimes Irish). The quote at the beginning of this chapter demonstrates the concern and challenge facing practitioners and children.

It is common to find that practitioner's positive concern leads them to focusing only on the acquisition of the English language, which is also often informed and supported by parents anxious to see their children fit in. There are, however, some problems with this approach.

Maintenance of a child's first language is more likely to help than to hinder learning English and the child's cognitive engagement. When the home language is not valued or supported it can lead to children having doubts about themselves and their families. What this means is that children can reject their home language and think of their parents/grandparent as being deficient in some way because they speak a language other than English. Parents are often compromised in this type of situation because they want their children to adjust to their new surroundings and country, but they also want their children to maintain their language and cultural background. The celebration of all home languages by the early childhood practitioners will contribute and enhance the promotion of language development in the setting.

Other children in the setting don't always understand why they cannot communicate with the child. Children have been heard to say things like, 'he talks funny', 'why does she talk like that?' and 'they mustn't have a tongue' referring to children who are in the 'silent phase' – see below.

Children can lose confidence and self-esteem and feel undervalued and rejected by peers if their home language is not acknowledged or valued in the setting. The consequence of non-recognition can lead to children not participating at their level of development.

## 12.4 Links

- Aistear Theme Well-being:
  Aim 1: Learning goals 3 and 6.
  Aim 4: Learning goal 1.

## 12.5 Discuss

- Consider ways that you can ensure that all children's first languages be valued and supported by peers and adults in the setting.
- Describe some activities using children's home languages that you could include in planning in order to promote play experiences with peers.

A small-scale study carried out in Donegal preschools (Baissangourov, 2008) examined the perceptions of ECEC practitioners on the challenges facing children with **English as an additional language (EAL)**. Attention also focused on their knowledge of support strategies for EAL. One practitioner reported that she generally could not understand what children with no English were saying. The practitioner couldn't determine whether the child was looking for something, asking a question or making a statement. In this case, the ECEC practitioner focused on trying to understand the child through verbal communication and did not reveal any alternative skills, such a using images for communication. It is evident from the study (2008) that specific training is required in order to develop a variety of strategies to enhance practitioner skills, which go beyond cultural awareness and include practical support to communicate effectively with multilingual children.

In my experience as a Diversity and Equality trainer, practitioners tend to hold the view that children have 'the language of play' and that the language barrier isn't an issue. On the contrary, as shown above; barriers can and do exist for the child. Communication helps people to make connections with others, and although using the same language may heighten communication and the comfort of all involved, it is not the only way to engage with children.

A colleague working in a naíonra preschool (Irish-speaking ECEC service) highlights the need for non-verbal gestures and body language during the settling-in stage, such as bending to the child's level, eye contact, warm smiles and facial expressions, pointing to an item or place, taking the child by the hand to show them something, or getting the children to show you. The child has English, but is being supported in an Irish-speaking environment to learn Irish. According to this practitioner, the positive relationship and connection made between the adult and child is crucial to laying the foundations for participation in the setting. Building this sense of trust and respect comes *before* rushing to encourage verbalisation of the language of the setting. Similar strategies can be used for children learning English as an additional language.

## 12.6 Discuss

- Why is the relationship with the practitioner so important in settling in the child with additional languages?
- Can you list methods or resources you would use to communicate with children who do not speak the language of the setting?

## Strategies for supporting children to acquire a second language

According to Tabors and Snow (1994) children acquiring a second language often go through a stage of observing and listening, known as the **'silent phase'**. At this time, children will be processing what they hear in the setting and surroundings before being in a position to verbalise the language.

> The silent phase is a natural part of the language learning process [...] the child takes time to become familiar with the words and rules of the new language, and to observe and take in information about the new environment.
>
> When learning a language, the child develops listening skills before speaking skills.
>
> (NCCA, EAL Guidelines, 2006)

## 12.7 Links:

- Aistear Theme Communicating:
  Aim 1: Learning goal 1, 2, 3, 4, 5 and 6.

## 12.8 Learning Point

Can you think of non verbal ways to communicate with children who do not have the language of the setting?

### *Children have a voice*

The National Children's Strategy (2000), consistent with the UNCRC (1989), states that children have a voice in matters that affect them. One of the main adjustments to the revised Preschool Regulations (2006) is that they place a duty on practitioners to ensure that each child's learning, development and well-being is facilitated within the daily life of the service. As a result, according to the Síolta Research Digests (2007) this puts a duty on practitioners to ensure that these rights are met to enable every child to exercise choice, use initiative and participate in the childcare setting. Children learning an additional language must be supported in achieving this right.

## 12.9 Links

- Childcare Act: Revised Preschool Regulations (2006): Article 5.
- CECDE (2006) Síolta: The National Quality Framework for Early Childhood Education.
- National Children's Strategy (2000–2010): Principles
- UN Convention on the Rights of the Child (1989): Articles 2, 7, 8, 12 and 29.
- Equal Status Act (2000): Prohibits discrimination in all public and private services, not to discriminate in terms of admission, access, terms or conditions and expulsion.

## 12.10 Links

In your learner group access and research the following documents;

- OMC (2006) Diversity and Equality Guidelines for Childcare Providers.
- Childcare Act: Revised Preschool Regulations (2006); Article 5. Including Appendix B the whole child perspective
- CECDE (2006) Síolta: The National Quality Framework for Early Childhood Education.
- Look for information in these documents that highlights the equality rights of children.
- List what each document says about the rights children have in your service.
- Give specific examples of what you can do in your service to ensure that children with additional languages have their rights met.

## 12.11 Links

- Anti-Bias Goals 1 and 2 for children

Language differences should not be a barrier to sensitive and quality interactions between the practitioner and children. Learners attending training in Equality and Diversity in ECEC (2010) report in their learner journals the methods they use to support interactions.

> I used key words from the child's home language, which were useful in helping the child settle in. Words and phrases like 'hello', 'how are you?', 'coat', and 'toilet', 'outside', 'snack', 'juice' and names of different activities.
>
> (Learner journal, 2010)

> I found role play a good way of involving children who didn't speak any English. Each day we included a role play without words, but using puppets and props – more like mime. I did one first with the other practitioner and the children followed, understanding that we weren't using words, just actions. Later in the year when children were more familiar hearing English, we introduced a few words and eventually it became more child-led. Some days the Polish children would use a little English or Polish during their role play.
>
> (Learner journal, 2010)

## 12.12 Links:

- Aistear Theme Communicating:
  Aim 4: Learning goals 2–6.

Tapors (1997) suggests strategies for responding to the child in the various stages of learning an additional language.

## 12.13 Support strategies:

- **Start with what the child knows:** use a few words in child's home language. ('Come, eat') to allow for low-level communication.
- **Start slowly:** allow the child to become familiar with the setting before approaching them with questions and directives in English.
- **'Scaffold' communication:** combine words with gesture, action or a directed gaze.

- **Provide safe havens:** allow the child to regain energy and focus by providing spaces and activities in which the child can participate with few, if any, expectations for verbal communication.
- **Get help from the English-speaking children:** show the child's peers ways to communicate and ask questions in order to encourage interaction and provide additional language models.
- **Expand and extend:** as the child moves towards fluid use of the language, start with what the child already knows and go from there. If the child says 'car', reply 'that is a red car'.
- **Provide familiar imagery,** i.e. Family Wall (see Chapter 9).

Adapted from Tabors (1997).

There were two Latvian children in the setting. When organising small group activities for children, I sometimes invited the two together to give them a chance to use their language freely with each other. I also made sure to invite them individually to other small groups where their own language was not spoken. In these groups it was more important that I be present to role model non-verbal interactions. I asked the parents of the Latvian children to bring in music CDs, which we added to our music games collection. One of the parents came in and read stories in Latvian. We translated the story after she read it to all the children. The Latvian children had a strong sense of belonging. Their language and identity were embraced and celebrated. Having a different language was seen as a great thing in our setting and the children recognised that.

(Learner journal, 2010)

### 12.14 Links

- Anti-Bias Goals 1 and 2 for adults, goal 1 for children
- Aistear Themes Identity and Belonging:
  Aim 1: Learning goals 1–6. Aim 2: Learning goals 1, 2 and 4. Aim 3: Learning goals 3 and 4. Aim 4: Learning goals 2, 3 and 5.
  Communicating:
  Aim 2: Learning goal 6. Aim 3: Learning goal 2.
- Síolta Standards:
  14: Identity and Belonging. Components 14.2 and 14.3.
  3: Parents and Families. Component 3.1.

## Identity and self-esteem

Children will know if their home language is valued by the practitioner and parent. They will also benefit from encouragement and praise at all attempt when communicating in

English regardless of accuracy. Baker (2007) emphasises that parents' attitudes and encouragement are extremely important in the child's second-language development. Praise will assist their language development, but just as importantly, it will help their self-esteem in using the second language. Baker (2007) also believed that parents should not worry about accurate grammar or vocabulary, or the child mixing the two languages. Instead they should ensure that the child's experience of learning the second language is enjoyable.

## 12.15 Links

- Anti-Bias Goal 2 for adults; goals 1 and 2 for children.

# Giving professional support

There are strategies that ECEC practitioners can carry out to ensure that they are supporting both the child and the parent. We list some suggestions below. Discuss what other options you might have.

## 12.16 Discuss

You are expecting children from Spain and Slovakia to join your preschool in September. On enrolment day, you meet the parents from Spain, who have a little English. You have not yet met the family from Slovakia as their friend enquired and pre-enrolled for the parents. As leader, describe how you will prepare in advance for the enrolment of these children in the service.

- How will you communicate with the parents prior to opening in September?
- What strategies will you use for providing information, completing forms and building a relationship with the parents?
- Consider how each child might feel on the first day of arrival in the setting. What difficulties might they face?
- What will you do to plan for each child's settling-in period?
- What strategies might you employ to ensure each child's individual and group identity is celebrated?
- On that first day, what do you think may contribute to each child's sense of well-being and belonging in the setting?
- How will you prepare and support the staff team?

(See Diversity and Equality Guidelines, 2006)

▸   Know the name of the child's first language. Know what country they come from (not just the continent).

▸ Always learn to pronounce the child's name correctly. This encourages parents not to change their child's name to an English version. Learn the parents' names too.

▸ Use labels with words and pictures in key areas of the room, such as sand area, water area, block area, home corner area, toilets, etc.

▸ Use repetitive phrases.

▸ Learn some key words in the child's own language, such as 'hello', 'good-bye', 'welcome', 'snack time', etc., to acknowledge and respect the child's home language.

▸ Have a selection of pictures to assist the child communicating, such as a visual plan of the day, various pictures of activities such as greeting time, circle time, story time, snack time, outside time, etc. The child can follow visually what is taking place during the day and can also demonstrate to you what they want to do by pointing at the plan.

▸ Use the Family Wall to support recognition of the child's language and their self-esteem.

▸ Bring music from the child's world into the setting.

▸ Sing and use lots of rhymes for all sorts of activities.

▸ State the words for the child in English and use the same key words and phrases, but do not force a child to speak the new language.

▸ Observe the child and record your observations.

▸ When a child does use the English word, praise and encourage the child.

▸ Encourage parents to stay in the setting so they can explain the routine to the child.

▸ Remember that body language is important, including eye contact, gestures and facial expressions, but be aware of variations between cultures, such as the use of eye contact. Remove any pressure to speak.

▸ Always encourage and support the use of the child's home language.

▸ Remember that most children acquiring a second language will go through the 'silent phase' and this can last anything up to two years.

▸ Children will acquire English as they play, so play with them.

(This list was compiled from a selection of research, including Baker, 2007; Crutchley, 2000; Siraj-Blatchford and Clarke, 2000; Tabors, 1997; Diversity and Equality Guidelines for Childcare Providers, 2006.)

## 12.17 Areas for critical reflection:

- Why might people feel that they are not being heard?
- Are people being silenced (i.e. feeling unable to speak openly) by the ways both practitioners and parents communicate?
- How do you find out if parents feel that they are not welcome or included?
- How can we improve understandings of both the home and school situations for both parents and practitioners?
- Outline what you think could be done to address this situation.

# Summary

Abandonment of the child's home language can give a message that the child and his/her family are undervalued, leading to a low self-esteem. This may in turn affect the child's confidence and motivation to participate in the setting at their level of development. This is why it is vital for practitioners to ensure they value all children's home languages. The role of the practitioner is to find ways of communicating effectively with both parents and child to ensure equality of access and participation in the service. The child has a right to have their views and needs heard and understood, so that these can be met on equal par with their peers. By supporting interactions between the children who are learning English and their peers in the setting, practitioners will help to promote a sense of well-being and belonging for the child.

## 12.18 Links

- Anti-Bias Goals 1, 2 and 3 for children.
- Síolta Standards
  3: Parents and Families. Components 3.1–3.4.
  14: Identity and Belonging. Components 14.1–14.3.
- Aistear Themes
  Identity and Belonging: Aim 2, Goals 1–6 .
  Communication: Aim 2, Goal 6.

CHAPTER 13

# Working with the Anti-Bias Approach

Perhaps even more central to adult learning than elaborating established meaning schemes is the process of reflecting back on prior learning to determine whether what we have learned is justified under present circumstances. This is a crucial learning process egregiously ignored by learning theorists.

(Jack Mezirow)

One can easily get caught with work. I realised it is good to step out and question the work I am carrying out and see if any changes can be made.

(Orla Fitzpatrick)

## Overview by Mathias Urban

Theory and practice are two sides of the same coin. That one isn't possible without the other is particularly important to understand for working in a context of diversity and for implementing an Anti-Bias Approach in ECEC. In the first chapters of this book we have explored the concept of becoming **critically reflective** as a fundamental aspect of becoming and being an early childhood professional. In this chapter, we present a very personal perspective on what that might mean for your day-to-day engagement with children, families and communities. Orla Fitzpatrick, who works in Ruan Children's Centre, Co. Clare, has attended the '*éist*' Anti-Bias in ECEC training. In this chapter she shares with us her reflections which she shows **how knowledge, action and critical reflection come together** and enable her to change her practice with children and families confidently.

The chapter follows Orla's journey closely. As editors we have structured it into several sections in order to emphasise themes and topics we find particularly important in the context of this book. Her story starts with a brief description of the setting in Co. Clare. It then moves on to discuss Orla's experiences and reflections on the '*éist*' Anti-Bias training. The next sections focus on specific areas of day-to-day practice in the setting. Working within an Anti-Bias framework permeates every aspect of ECEC practice. This is illustrated in the section on **environment** and **activities**. As we have explored in the earlier chapters of this book, children are members of families and communities; they don't lose their ties with them when they enter our setting. Becoming a critically reflective ECEC practitioner, therefore, extends your reflections and your practice to include all children and their context. Orla shows this in the section on **exploring the community**. What does realising the Anti-Bias Goals look like in practice? **Use your voice** to illustrate this with regard to Anti-Bias Goal 4 for Adults and Children – work to challenge individual and institutional forms of prejudice and discrimination, and empower children to stand up for themselves and others. Before you move on to the concluding section of the journal, we should perhaps give you a warning: once you get into an Anti-Bias mindset, there is no turning back. Speaking out against discrimination certainly doesn't stop at the preschool door. In Orla's case, it affects her engagement with her family and community.

We present Orla's thoughts and reflections in her own voice, and link her reflections to the Anti-Bias Goals for Adults and Children.

Reading Orla's notes and reflections in this chapter should enable you to

▶    better understand how to develop your critical personal reflection.
▶    identify the connection between reflection, asking critical questions and changing your practice.
▶    link your own experiences and critical reflection to the Anti-Bias Goals for Adults and Children.
▶    see how keeping a personal journal can become a practical tool for reflective practitioners.

## Introduction: Orla's journal

I obtained my degree in Social Studies from Sligo IT, where I studied from 2003 to 2007. For the past four years I have been working in an early childhood setting in North Clare. The Children's Centre that I work in is in Ruan, a small village seven kilometres from Ennis, Co. Clare. Ruan has three pubs, a church, a community hall school and GAA. We started the playschool with four children in the community hall in 1993. Before that there was no early childhood facility in the area.

We cater for up to 30 children now. These children come from a range of backgrounds, some from urban settings, some rural, some have special requirements; some are from the Traveller community. Some children now travel long distances to our service. We have three places for children with special requirements. Having an inclusive service has built a culture amongst the children in our service of acceptance of diversity. This carries from playgroup into the primary school. The children are encouraged to ask questions about diversity, and we believe that through our work, our children are open to difference between people. We also run an after-school service for children up to 13 years.

---

### 13.1 Anti-Bias Goal 2

**For Adults**
To be comfortable with difference, have empathy and engage effectively with families

**For Children**
To foster children's empathy and support them to become comfortable with difference

---

## Becoming critically reflective

I began my *'éist'* equality and diversity training in September 2009 in Ennis, Co. Clare. I went on the course because I wanted to learn about issues of diversity and equality, and to share this information with my fellow workers. I also wanted to be able to deal with issues of discrimination, and with my own biases and prejudices. But I wasn't really sure what to expect when I first began the course. After the first session my eyes were opened to the world of equality and diversity.

There were three women from Nigeria on the course with me, and a woman from the Traveller community. Initially I did not know what to expect but it could not have worked out better. We exchanged stories and experiences and I realised that my way is not the only way. They shared stories of discrimination and bias. As the course went on we began to gain confidence to stand up to various incidents of discrimination. I became so much more open-minded. I began to observe newspaper articles, TV and the media in general and began to critically evaluate what was being said. During the course I began to cut out newspaper articles that were discriminatory towards minority groups and I continue to do so now.

I feel I am much more proactive now in how I deal with prejudice, bias and even discrimination in my workplace. To be honest it also affected my life socially and I am amazed how much I learned!

---

### 13.2 Anti-Bias Goals for adults:

1. To be conscious of one's own culture, attitudes and values and how they influence practice
2. To be comfortable with difference, have empathy and engage effectively with families
3. To critically think about diversity, bias and discrimination
4. To confidently engage in dialogue around issues of diversity and discrimination. Work to challenge individual and institutional forms of prejudice and discrimination.

During our first week we talked about the importance of names, how it is so important to spell and pronounce them correctly. Our name is such an important part of our identity – something I just didn't think about before. Now I am the worst at calling children the wrong name. I am aware of this, but at times I do slip up. Only last week I was calling a new girl in our summer camp the wrong name. I was wondering why she was looking at me so strangely!! With every new child in our service we ask the correct spelling and pronunciation of the child's name and of the parents'/guardians' name. This has become very important for me and I see the value in it for the children and the family.

## 13.3 Anti-Bias Goals 1 and 3

**Goal 1 For adults**
To be conscious of one's own culture, attitudes and values and how they influence practice

**Goal 1 for children**
To support children's identity and sense of belonging

**Goal 3 for adults**
To think critically about diversity, bias and discrimination

**Goal 3 for children**
To encourage each child to think critically about bias

The training has changed my outlook on life completely. Before this training, I thought that equality was treating everyone the same, which it is *not*. Equality means that the needs of every child and their family, every individual within a community are treated in terms of their access, participation and outcomes. Equality looks at representing cultural and personal identity within a society, and that all individuals are encouraged to participate in any society to the best of their ability.

During the course of the module I met an ECEC practitioner working in a service and she remarked that a FETAC Level 5 qualification would be suitable for a manager of a childcare setting. I was so annoyed that I decided that I would challenge this statement constructively. I found this inner confidence and I know it came as a result of completing this module. It got me thinking; are childcare workers valued enough for the work that we carry out in society? I think my awareness about all areas of inequality has been raised.

I now feel that as workers in early childhood settings we have a responsibility to address comments, prejudices, discrimination and racist attacks. We have the power to instil in our young the importance of respecting everyone in our society; to empower our young to use their voice and to challenge those who are disrespectful to minority groups.

In order for this work to be carried out, practices and policies in early childhood settings need to be reviewed. This is when the Anti-Bias Approach comes into play. It is vital that childcare practitioners have the opportunity to do this work and in turn it will empower young children. I am convinced that working with this approach will help young children in their future in how they will interact and treat people.

---

## 13.4 Anti-Bias Goals 4

**For adults**
To confidently engage in dialogue around issues of diversity and discrimination
Work to challenge individual and institutional forms of prejudice and discrimination

**For children**
To empower children to stand up for themselves and others

---

This course helped me to think critically about bias, discrimination and so on and it has helped me to 'unlearn discrimination in all its forms' (Murray and O'Doherty, 2001, p. 14).

As the weeks passed I found myself constantly thinking of how we could make changes in my setting to suit *all* of the needs of *all* our children. I was beginning to question the work that I was carrying out and how it could benefit all children in my setting.

## Environment and activities

In my setting, every area is now accessible to *every* child. We work to make sure every child feels valued and part of the setting. Some of these areas and activities include:

### Pictures

We are always taking pictures of the children while they are playing, carrying out activities or when we are out on day trips. Recording the work of the children with pictures has changed how we work in the setting.

### Supporting communication

We have a boy, Eoin, who was born with Down's syndrome, and we have put a little book together for him with pictures of all the activities that he enjoys. He often takes it and shows his book to people when they come into the playgroup. This has been very important for Eoin, and it supports his sense of belonging in the setting.

To further Eoin's inclusion, we took pictures of toys, games, etc., that Eoin liked to play with. We put the pictures on pieces of Velcro and Eoin could then choose what he wanted to play with by pulling the pictures off the board and going to get the toy or showing what he wanted to do to the adult.

## Cooking

We have also made up a book of pictures of and comments by the children making and icing buns. The children love recognising themselves and seeing themselves in the setting.

## Trips

This year we went on a trip to the fire station, and we took lots of pictures of the children at the station. The following day we put a collage of their pictures down low on the wall to show everyone all the fun that we had the day before. On that day I found so many of the children sitting down on the ground talking to one another about the fun that they had and talking about what they had seen and liked most from the fire station. It was lovely to see.

We broadened the activity out by asking the children to draw on a blank piece of paper what they most enjoyed from their trip to the station and we wrote it underneath along with comments that they made. The children loved showing their parents what they had drawn.

The following day we put the pictures on our laptop and we put them on a slide show and we showed the pictures to the children. You should have heard the stories and laughter that came from the children. They loved seeing themselves on the computer.

We realised that when you think outside the box – bring the children out of the setting, bring their lives into the setting and then capture their views – the setting becomes more like a home and a lived-in playschool.

## Dress-up area

Our dress-up area covers all occupations! One of our mums was on holidays and brought us back dresses and shoes from Spain. Our dress-up area is diverse, which all the children love. Boys can wear dresses, girls dress up as builders – anything goes, although we have one dad who is not too happy when he sees his son wearing a pink spotty dress! But through discussion we worked that out.

The boys wear nail varnish along with the girls, and the boys like it more than the girls. I think gender is a huge area in the childcare. Everything is encouraged and offered to all the children.

## Lámh

We have Lámh signs up on our wall as this is what one of the children in our setting uses to communicate. Placing the signs up on the wall gives everyone the opportunity to communicate with the child in our setting. The children in after-school are interested in learning how to use Lámh and know some of the signs.

(www.lamh.org)

## More activities

I have carried out some activities with the children in playgroup focusing directly on diversity. Some of these include drawing out 'body maps'. All the children lay down on pieces of blank paper and we drew around their body shape. They painted or collaged in their clothes and their faces. We hung their representation of their bodies up on the wall. We had great fun discussing all of our bodies' shapes. We discussed different sizes, as some of us were taller, smaller, some had bigger hands than others; some of us had darker skin colour, etc. We then followed it up by drawing our body shapes on the wall outside with chalk. These exercises were very successful; they were fun, but they also asked the children to discuss difference in a positive and constructive way, recognising all our diversity.

## Exploring the community

Another exercise we did on the training was all about our community, so we went on an outing to our own village. We visited the shop, post office, church, graveyard and other places of historical interest. We took pictures of our trip and made a poster of how our day went.

The older children drew a map of the village and of the places we had visited. The aim of the activity was to build up an image of the community that they live in.

I encouraged the children to talk about about issues and services in their area and we interviewed a local man about the area. I wanted to support the children to really think critically about the areas they lived in. You could sense how proud the children are of their community.

We extended this activity by asking the children about the things and services that they liked in their community, what else they would like in the community, and one thing they would change about their community if they could. We also asked some of the parents for their input into our activity. We spoke about how accessible our community is for people in wheelchairs, we looked at the signposts in our area and we discussed how people could read the sign if they did not speak English. We looked at what new services should be in our community. We noted that there was a lack of dustbins, only one bus stop located in the village, and we found that the bus stop location is not the most central for all of the people in the community, and there was a lack of parking facilities for disabled drivers.

We spoke about the different types of houses that we saw while we were on our field trip, and we spoke about the different types of houses that we all live in. We went into the local shop and I asked the children what kinds of foods they had in their houses. We found out that each of us had different food and the same food in our cupboards in our houses. We talked about the fact that some of the children live in an estate and some children do not.

Talking about difference with the children and getting the children to think critically about difference was a great exercise. My aim was to get across the point that being different is okay. In fact this exercise was much more than that, as it brought our whole community into the setting. It was very meaningful to us and to the children. We continued to make up posters with pictures from our trip with the comments from the children and the map. I found the children stopping and looking at themselves and chatting about the trip and what they saw and learned for weeks. A lot of parents came and looked at our posters. One of the girls started to cry when her dad came to pick her up while we were out on the trip – he had to go back home until it was over!

---

### 13.5 Discuss

- How familiar are you with the situations described by Orla?
- How are Orla's examples linked to the Anti-Bias goals for adults and children?
- What other connections could there be between the examples, the thoughts and reflections and the Anti-Bias goals for adults and children?
- Do you have similar or different experiences?
- How you can use a personal journal to support your critical reflection? (You might want to re-read Chapter 5 for ideas.)

---

## Challenges

Working in an early childhood setting, you meet challenges daily. You discuss with children daily what is ok and not ok, and what is nice and not so nice. We always encourage the children to use their voices to tell other children what they want, or what they did not like about what someone said or did to them. We always get the children to think whether they would like it if the same were done to them. We discuss openly how being mean or slapping other children is not the way to behave or get what you want. It is about educating children to be proactive and to use their voice to stand up for themselves if faced with difficult situations.

One day in playgroup, we heard one of the boys, Michael, telling his friend who was upset because another little boy would not let him play in the game, 'Use your voice and tell James that you do not like it because he won't let you play with him.' It was great to hear a child supporting another child. The little boy did use his voice, and he was able to play in the game.

In after-school there is a girl, Karen, who was recently diagnosed with diabetes. It was a stressful time for Karen and for her family. Karen had been absent for some time. When she came back one of the children chanted, 'Karen has got diabetes, Karen is diabetes girl, ha ha'. Karen was really upset. The chanting was interesting, because the child didn't know what diabetes was; he was confused about what the word 'diabetes' meant. We discussed, sensitively, the hurt that was caused with both children, and then we looked up what it meant to have diabetes. Now we all have a greater understanding of what diabetes means.

In our after-school setting we have a boy from the Traveller community. Patrick is in school and I often help him with his homework. Patrick's homework is different to the rest of his classmates and at times he gets teased about this. On one occasion someone asked him 'Why do you have different homework to us?' and 'Why are you helping Patrick with his homework? This is an awkward situation because I have to be sensitive to Patrick and also make sure the teasing is not also linked to his identity as a Traveller. We discussed getting help in a general way. I also asked if anyone ever had to ask for help before with homework or any other issue, and the children agreed they had. I tried to get an understanding across that we all ask for help, and that it is okay to ask for help. I also discussed it with both children individually.

Through these experiences I have learned the importance of giving children honest and accurate information; not to hide things, and to deal with them openly and clearly; not to be afraid of saying the wrong thing, but engaging the children in sorting out the issue.

## Speaking out and taking action – not only in the preschool

Attending the '*éist*' Anti-Bias training made me aware of my own biases and prejudices. We investigated our own ideas about diversity during the training sessions. This training has influenced my family life and also my friends. My two friends Moira and Ann are nurses and they encounter incidents of discrimination on a daily basis. Since I completed the course, they have been asking me how I would deal with these incidents. They feel more aware and see the importance of treating all patients equally in their work and not being irritated because people are different. I have another friend who will not go into a taxi at night time if there is a Black man driving the taxi. I am aware of this prejudice, and we discuss questions such as where she got this fear.

A family member had an incident in his workplace involving discrimination. Because he has been hearing me talking about the training, he was shocked when an incident occurred in his work. Normally he would keep his head down and ignore awkward situations, but he stood up for a worker who was Black and was being verbally abused by a fellow worker. It is about being courageous and speaking out against people who are being unfair towards minority groups – and having the confidence to do so! I do know it's not always possible to do that, especially in potentially violent situations, but at least having the awareness and knowing is an important starting point.

## Concluding thoughts

I have come on some journey on this course, and it has had its ups and downs. After week three, I hit rock bottom when we discussed proofing our environment (see Chapter 14). I realised how much work I had to carry out, and I thought, 'Will I ever be able to do this?' I spoke to my two tutors and I must say they were brilliant. After speaking to them I realised that baby steps are what's needed. Taking small steps is OK; we can't change the entire world in one day. That was one of the hardest but most valuable lessons from this course. It helped me to move forward and implement changes in my workplace and also in my social life that I have to say are very positive.

I have found that I have become much more confident in approaching people when I see them being unfair to other people. I approached a local pub owner asking her why she would not allow Travellers into her pub. It is a real problem in the area that pubs display signs saying 'private party' when there's rumour that Travellers are in the area.

I also approached a friend when she was giving out about some members of the Traveller community at Mass one Sunday.

I feel as early childhood professionals we have a responsibility to respond to negative comments, prejudice and discrimination. We have to live our values both inside and outside the setting. We can instil in our young people the importance of respecting everyone in our society and empower them to use their voice and stand up for those who are hurt. It is vital that this approach be taught to early childhood workers.

Through attending this module I have become more of a critical thinker. I will continue on with this work in both my professional and personal life!

## Summary

This chapter builds on what you have read about critical reflection in the second section of this book. It shows how your professional knowledge (which will increase constantly through education, experience and professional development), your day-to-day practice and your critical thinking about your practice and its social context are all linked together. They are, in fact, inseparable. This is illustrated by the reflections and thoughts collected by Orla, which we have linked to the Anti-Bias Goals for Adults and Children. While being a very personal account, the chapter is also an illustration of how reflective writing can support you on your journey towards becoming a critical reflective practitioner.

## CHAPTER 14

# Developing an Inclusive Space: Proofing the ECEC Environment

We really have no reflection of our children. How come we never thought of that!? It is so simple and makes so much sense.

(Learner, 2011)

## Overview

In this chapter we explore the issue of proofing the physical environment for diversity in the ECEC setting. We look at why it is important to represent each child and family in the materials and imagery used in the setting. We also address the consequences of the non-recognition of each child. Enhancing children's well-being, and in particular, supporting their identity and sense of belonging is a right supported by the UN Convention of the Rights of the Child. The chapter reflects the voices of learners and practitioners engaged in that representation and its consequences, both positive and negative. As you read the chapter, we encourage you to engage with the discussion points. The chapter concludes with a description of how to 'proof' the ECEC environment.

### After reading this chapter you should

▶ be aware of the importance of providing an inclusive environment for all children in the setting
▶ know how to assess materials and equipment in the setting
▶ know how to assess the ECEC environment for changes that may be needed
▶ be able to set up an environment that supports all children in developing a sense of self and belonging

## Introduction: Proofing the ECEC environment

The physical environment where children are educated and cared for includes the imagery, activities, equipment and materials used, in addition to the layout of the space and its aesthetics (beauty). People are the essential ingredient in creating the atmosphere of the ECEC setting, and that includes the physical environment. In this chapter we look at the importance of how to assess and proof the ECEC environment for diversity and the inclusion of all children and families.

## 14.1 Jargon Buster: Proofing

'Proofing the environment' means assessing all the materials and equipment in the environment to ensure that they are appropriate to the make-up of the current group of children and families in the setting. It also means checking to see if the imagery supports the identity of each child both individual and group in the environment. Proofing is a way of ensuring that the environment meets the needs of the children and families attending the setting. It also means that stereotyping, bias or gaps in the images and play materials can be identified and action taken.

The environment we live in includes not only our home but the full variety of settings we enter on a regular basis. That includes our workspace, along with the outside environment, and the local community, whether that is in the city centre, suburbs or the countryside. The spaces we live in and interact with influence how we will create spaces, and in this case, ECEC spaces. Our relationship and interactions with space begins in our own home environment, learned through the values and beliefs of family: how, for example, spaces should look and be maintained; what one considers to be beautiful or representative; all of this depends on an individual's background, culture, exposure to various influences, and of course, personal taste.

In this chapter we are primarily discussing the importance of having an ECEC environment that represents all children. This will require some creativity, and in some cases 'thinking outside the box'. We may often reproduce what we are familiar with ourselves and the way we like things to look. Our perception of what children like to see and be surrounded by in the setting also influences our choices. Drawing on the Anti-Bias Goals for Adults, and Chapters 5 and 6 on personal reflection and approaches to diversity will raise your awareness and support you in creating an inclusive environment for all children.

## First impressions

When we enter a new environment, people tend to be a little apprehensive, yet their apprehension is often tinged with excitement as they look forward to the new experience. Early childhood settings are no exception to this. When families enter the setting, what will be important to them? They will want to feel welcomed and they will want to see happy and cheerful staff and children. Parents will want to know that their child will be appreciated and cared for in the setting. How do they find that out? First impressions are the beginning of that process for all parents. If your child is from a minority community, first impressions are even more important. All parents have concerns for their children's well-being. If your community has been subjected to prejudice or discrimination, you will want to be assured that your child will be safe in the setting, the place where you choose to leave your child. Would you leave your child in a place where they might not be valued or supported? The atmosphere of acceptance begins with the ECEC provider. The physical environment will contribute to that atmosphere and reassure parents that their child will have a sense of belonging in this setting. Derman-Sparks and Olsen Edward (2010) say that ensuring that each family feel welcome and comfortable creates a crucial foundation for a mutually respectful relationship. It is an essential first step in an Anti-Bias setting. One element of creating such an atmosphere is having an inclusive physical environment.

## Identity and belonging

A sense of belonging is integral to, and inseparable from, many important aspects of identity, as well as to numerous other dimension of children's, needs, rights and development. Ensuring a sense of belonging requires that all individuals – adults and children, providers and users of services – feel that they are respected and recognised, both for their uniqueness as individuals and for the qualities they share with their community, and with all other humans.

(Woodhead, 2008, p. 6)

---

**14.2 Identity and belonging**

One day, a young Traveller child came home from preschool very animated and said 'Mammy, I was in school today!' The child's mother was baffled by the comment, and asked the practitioner did she know what her daughter meant.

The practitioner explained that she had just put out a new jigsaws that represented Traveller life on a halting site. She told the mother that the child cried out, 'Look, I'm here, I'm here!' when she had made the jigsaw.

(Of a four-year-old child, from Máirín Kenny)

---

Identity is who we are. We are all different, but we each come from a particular ethnic group and socio-economic status, we have a gender, abilities or disabilities, skin colour, religion, etc. We all want to feel liked, recognised, accepted and supported in our identity. We certainly don't want to hide it. We want to belong. The UN Convention on the Rights of the Child (UNCRC) supports the concept of identity by stating in Article 8 that each child has a right to their identity. The Convention also explicitly states that each child has a right to non-discrimination and the right to their voice being respected for their views and feelings (Article 12). A rights-based approach to ECEC supports the implementation of the UNCRC and in essence, the importance of supporting a child's identity and sense of belonging. Woodhead (2008) talks about the dynamic of inclusion and exclusion being learned early in life; children's early identification with their families, their gender and religion go hand in hand with feelings of difference. While for some children, this experience is one of being different in a negative way (I am not the norm), for other children this difference is all to often expressed in terms of superiority (being better than other children), and overt and hostility. Even if there is no *obviously* different child in the setting, children learn that who they are is the 'norm', and this can give them a false notion of superiority (Derman-Sparks et al, 2006).

Building a positive sense of self and having a sense of belonging is vital for a child's well-being, and their active participation in the setting. Children's sense of self can be distorted and undermined if they and/or their communities are not recognised or respected, and they can experience prejudice and discrimination. Creating an inclusive and respectful environment can support children and can also counter negativity for children.

## Why is the physical environment important?

Imagery used in the setting gives messages to adults and children whether we are aware of it or not. Powerful messages about with is valued or not are also given by what is *not* depicted – what is absent from the environment. Positive, visible depictions of diversity are vital to reassure and show respect for all children and families in the setting. If you display imagery that represents each child in the setting, it supports the child's developing identity, both individual and group, and their sense of belonging (Anti-Bias Goal 1 for Children, Síolta Standard 14 and Aistear Theme Identity and Belonging).

**Imagery** is broader than what is depicted on the walls in the individual rooms of a service. It includes all visual information and messages available across the whole service: toys, art materials, books, dolls, dramatic play, musical instruments and linguistic representation.

Society has produced a whole landscape of imagery, which is generally dominated by images of the majority, and in fact, the middle-class majority.

In terms of the messages the imagery in your setting gives, consider *what types of messages you want to give children*. Then ask yourself *whether the imagery in the setting reflects the ethos, mission and values you're trying to convey*. If you are working from an Anti-Bias perspective, you will want to support children's positive attitudinal development, critical reflection about diversity and social justice issues, and to counter the learning of stereotypes about human diversity.

## 14.3 Gender stereotyping

Two girls were playing together. One girl went to play with Thomas the Train, but was stopped by the other girl who said, 'Don't play with that. They're boys' toys.'

(Learner, 2009)

Messages that children receive about difference in society are both overt and covert. **Overt messages** are picked up from visuals including the media radio and TV and explicit comments from adults on diversity such as: 'We don't mix with their kind' (mother picking up her white three-year-old; the child was chatting with his Black friend. Ireland, 2011). **Covert messages** come from omissions in the imagery or an imbalance of kinds of images in the service, meaning that some children attending are not represented in the books, dolls, visuals on the wall, etc.

## 14.4

A four-year-old white girl living in the north of Scotland, where very few Black people live, was visited by her aunt and a black Nigerian man friend. When she saw the black man she said, 'Are you a boxer?' When he said he wasn't, she said, 'Well, you must have been in prison then.' This demonstrates that she had learnt these attitudes from somewhere, but it was only the presence of the Black man that revealed what she was thinking. If he had not visited, her family might never have known what she had learnt.

(Jane Lane)

## 14.5

A little girl aged four was in the back of the car, and her mam was driving. She pointed out the window at a small group of Black men walking along the footpath. 'Look at those bad guys,' she said.

Her mam said, 'Who? Where?' 'There – those black guys. All those are the bad guys.'

(From mother to practitioner shocked at her child's comment, Ireland, 2010)

### Remember

▸   Omitting some groups (e.g. Travellers, Black people) from imagery in the setting is as powerful as depicting other groups (e.g. white children), because only one 'way of being' is supported.

▸   Omissions send messages about who is valued and who is not valued. When all the images in the books are of white, settled, able-bodied people, or heterosexual, two-parent family units, what does that say to Black, Traveller or disabled children, or those with a lone parent or same-sex parents?

▶ Omissions don't support the positive identity development of all children.

▶ Omissions may give children who *are* represented a sense that their way is the only way, or the 'norm'.

---

### 14.6 Are you 'colour blind'?

In a rural community, one Black child was living with his white mother. His black father was living in another country. There were no other black children or adults in the community. This child was very settled in the ECEC service. The service had no depictions in books, imagery or material of Black children. The staff never thought it was important or relevant. Following Diversity and Equality training, the staff introduced new materials into the setting. They were shocked at this child's reaction. He was delighted to see images that represented him and he expressed that openly in the setting. It had never occurred to the staff to get materials that depicted people like him. They simply accepted him and did not 'notice' his colour. This is called being 'colour blind'.

This child did not express concern that these images were absent, and he was happy in the setting. The reality is, however, that he did notice his colour, that he was different from the other children, and there was an absence of other children of colour in his life and community. It was only by introducing the imagery that the service discovered his awareness and the need and importance of representing this child in terms of his identity. Providing appropriate materials affirmed this child's identity, he felt recognised and his sense of belonging was enhanced.

(Diversity and Equality Trainer, 2009)

---

A rich diversity of images provides a creative space for children to observe positive images of all cultures. It also provides opportunities to discuss the images with children as issues arise, such as: 'Why is there no daddy in your family picture?' or 'You have two mammies'. Images can also help to counter negative stereotypes, such as: 'Girls can't be doctors, only boys can.'

## Being recognised

In the first instance, images should depict the children and families who are immediately in the setting, as in the Family Wall. When you are satisfied that all the children are appropriately represented, then extend the visual representations by bringing in images from the broader community. This imagery can include rural and urban examples. Finally, the imagery can embrace depictions of life further afield (global diversity). As a practitioner, you will need to judge what is useful for the children and what is beyond their comprehension. Be clear about *why* you want to introduce particular imagery and what its subsequent benefit to the children might be.

## 14.7 Consider this

Material that only depicts children from countries in Africa as living in poverty is an inaccurate depiction of all children from African countries. But it also misrepresents Black children from or living in Ireland. If you use such material to enhance children's understanding of global inequality, it is important to counter it with accurate information about Black people living in other circumstances.

(Practitioner and Trainer 2010)

Reflect back on Chapter 2 on the diversity and inequality in society. Ask yourself again who and what is valued in society, and how societal prejudice can negatively affect people's lives. In providing a rich, diverse environment for children, they can embrace diversity and be supported in developing a positive attitude to diversity. The setting serves as a basis for raising issues and initiating conversations, giving accurate information, countering stereotypes and enriching both majority and minority children's lives. Being recognised by peers, staff, other adults and the community confers self-esteem and belonging on children. The consequences of a lack of recognition and belonging are grave: 'children may feel worthless and incompetent' (Woodhead, 2008, p. 5).

## 14.8 Discuss

Sometimes we are not aware of the messages children are getting from imagery in the setting, until we hear a child's comment or question.

A four-year-old in his first year in primary school asked his mum for more lunch for his Black friend in his class. This was as a result of his introduction to the Trócaire box collections.

He told his mam that 'they are starving', even though he had been in the preschool with the same child for two years.

(Practitioner, 2009)

A Nigerian child expressed concern to her parents about returning to live or visit Nigeria. They said that 'everyone was starving' and were concerned for their grandparents that they might die from hunger.

- What messages are the children getting from the use of the Trócaire box in relation to Black children and countries in Africa?
- What could the teacher/practitioner have done to enhance the child's knowledge?
- In this case, the imagery did not reflect the Black child's own world or experiences of living in Ireland.
- Accurate information must be given to children regarding poverty, various countries in Africa and skin colour. This will support the children's understanding of global diversity and will also support the Black child's reality of living in Ireland.

## How can a rich, diverse environment support children and parents?

Images, materials and active engagement in the environment can:

▸ counter the prevailing bias in society.
▸ support adults to prompt discussion with children about specific issues or to address incidents or challenge issues.
▸ highlight our many similarities.
▸ support families and their children to feel recognised for who they are.
▸ ensure that children see themselves and feel like they are part of the group.
▸ support self-esteem, acknowledgement and mutual respect.
▸ confirm the idea that difference is accepted and can help children to be more comfortable talking about or interacting with children who are different.
▸ help to promote an ethos of respect for 'minority ways' in the setting.
▸ support families to feel that their child will be protected and treated fairly.

## A whole-service approach

Providing diverse images and materials is only the first step; they are not worth much without the commitment and honest engagement of all staff.

> We have to believe in the approach for it to really work and flourish. I see this in my workplace. Every so often I proof the environment to ensure that the books and materials, etc., are appropriate and can support the children's sense of belonging and sense of self. Every time I do this proofing, I find materials that contradict the message we are trying to promote. My team knows the basic theory behind the Anti-Bias Approach, but as yet only a few of them have embraced it. Using reflective practice helps them to explore why we use the material we do, and why we challenge prejudice.
>
> (Anti-Bias trained Practitioner, 2009)

---

### 14.9 Discuss

A practitioner in a setting has begun to build a Family Wall (see Chapter 9) with the families in her room in the ECEC centre. There are several Travellers attending the service. In this case the Family Wall was put up in the hall outside the door of the setting. When the pictures went up on the wall, all the families were gathering and chatting looking at the photos. The manager witnessing this asked the practitioner to take the Traveller pictures down as she didn't want people to think there were too many Travellers attending the service, as otherwise settled people wouldn't enrol in the service.

(Practitioner in the service, Ireland, 2007)

• Can you identify what is going on here?
• What would you do in this situation?

# How to proof the environment: Getting Started

> We had to conclude that many family types were not represented and minority ethnic groups were invisible in our book corner!
>
> (Learner, following the proofing of their book corner, 2009)

## What is tokenism?

Representation of minority groups should be accurate and spread out in the environment. Just having one black doll in the setting to represent different Black children misses the point. Black children and families are not all the same. They come from different countries, including Ireland, and look different, too; they have different skin tones, hair types, etc. Representations of any particular group should include various depictions so that children from those groups can identify with them .

Equally, having exotic or stereotypical versions of the culture being represented is also problematic. For example, one old-fashioned wagon to depict Traveller culture or costumes to represent children from different countries across whole continents are not enough. Representations should cover the daily lives of the children. Almost no one goes around in their national costume on a daily basis, so representation needs to be less 'touristic' and more realistic if we are to support children's identity and belonging.

---

### 14.10 Discuss

- Do the books depicting children from Kenya represent children from Nigeria?

---

## Proofing your early childhood environment

To get started, go into the service where you work or are on teaching practice. Ask as appropriate for permission to carry out the proofing exercise. To do the exercise you will need to choose one child, and based on the information relevant to this child, carry out the exercise.

---

### 14.11 Practitioner proofing example:

I have chosen a boy called Henry. His dad works abroad and he lives with his mam and his brother and sister in a small housing estate. Henry wears glasses. I don't know what religion they practice. He misses his dad.

---

*Step 1.*
Choose one child in your early childhood service. Think about that child in terms of:

▶   gender
▶   family structure
▶   ethnicity
▶   religion
▶   physical appearance
▶   special learning needs or disability

Also think about:
▶   where they live
▶   the culture and community to which they belong
▶   the language spoken in the child's home
▶   any other aspect of that child's identity

Write down all of this information *without identifying the child*.

*Step 2.*
Walk through every room in your setting with this child in mind. Look at the images on the walls, all the materials used in the different activity areas, including home corner, art and crafts, music, children's books, dramatic play, jigsaws, etc. Consider:

▶   where and how this child *is* represented
▶   where and how this child *is not* represented

Again, write down all of your observations.

*Step 3.*
Discuss these observations with the early childhood team as appropriate, comparing the information about the child and your observations. Reflect on how the physical environment looks now and what can be done to make improvements.

*Step 4.*
Identify any changes you can make to the early childhood environment that will benefit this child and materials or images that will reflect this child in a positive way. Suggest changes to reflect the child's background, language, family or community that will:

▶   support that child's individual and group identity
▶   encourage a sense of belonging

## 14.12 Links

- Anti-Bias Approach: Goal 1
- Síolta Standard 14
- Aistear Theme 2
- Diversity and Equality Guidelines for Childcare Providers: Section 2

In doing this exercise you do not have to pick the most 'obvious' child, because this exercise is for *all* children in the setting. It is important to repeat this process many times within the setting.

# Questions to guide practitioners

Remember to Check:

▸ Is this child's identity (ethnic group/community) under-represented in the learning environment?
▸ Can you find pictures or characters in the books available that this child will be able to identify with?
▸ Is this child's identity group reflected in a fair, non-tokenistic way? Are the images you see around you meaningful and relevant for this child?
▸ Will this child see himself/herself or his/her cultural background reflected in the surrounding images?
▸ Are there sufficient art materials for children to create images with different skin tones?
▸ Are there play props in the home corner to represent the child's home culture (cooking utensils, dress-up clothes)?
▸ Is there a need for more images that are accurate, positive and relevant with which this individual child can identify?

## When assessing children's books
▸ Look for stereotypes (see Chapter 3).
▸ Look for tokenism.
▸ Examine the characters and their roles for bias.
▸ Check the storyline for bias.
▸ Check the language for bias.
▸ Are cultural differences visible?
▸ Are the images negative, dated, tokenistic or stereotyped?
▸ Is disability represented?
▸ Is it sexist?

▶    Is there ageism?
▶    Is the imagery accurate and relevant?

## Summary

In the early childhood context, we have an opportunity to create an environment that reflects all children in a meaningful way. All children draw conclusions about themselves and others on the basis of the information available to them. Children need to be exposed to positive images of their identity to feel affirmed, valued and proud of who they are. Imagery and positive interaction with that imagery will support children's identity and help to build positive self-esteem. Where children see only negative images of who they are, their identity can be undermined. Omissions send strong messages to children too. These messages can be internalised and may have negative results. Accurate representation is only one element of building a child's self-identity. Services engaging actively with identity, belonging, respect and recognition can counter negativity for some families and support each child to value themselves, others and contribute to the ECEC setting and beyond to promote diversity in society.

### 14.13 Get active

Take some time to look at images in the media for how various groups in society are depicted and referred to.

### 14.14 Discuss

- How might a child feel when he/she sees him/herself reflected in the images and materials in the setting?
- How might a child feel when he/she does not see him/herself reflected in the images and materials setting?
- How might a child feel when he/she or his/her community or culture is represented in an unfair (e.g. negative or inaccurate) way?
- How can we encourage services to make changes to their environments in a way that will actively support identity and belonging for each child and reflect the Anti-Bias Approach?

## CHAPTER 15

# Travellers and Roma in Ireland Today

Well, maybe you can tell him (the Minister for Education) that when you're a Traveller, you're a Traveller, you can't change it. You might as well tell anyone you know that you're a Traveller and that they are not Travellers. They will probably understand and listen to you and still be your friend, people who are good and sensible.

(Interview with eight-year-old Traveller girl regarding her education, 2008. Pavee Point, unpublished.)

## Overview

I have worked with the Traveller community for more than 20 years, initially working directly with Traveller children and families with Barnardos and then working as an advocate for the appropriate inclusion of Traveller and Roma children in the education system with Pavee Point. It has been a long journey weaving through policy twists and turns, some of which have been of benefit to Travellers and Roma, and some of which have continued to undermine Traveller culture and Roma inclusion. In this chapter I will draw on that experience by providing some information on the Traveller and Roma communities and address the complex issue of being a Traveller or Roma in Ireland while negotiating a society that doesn't value Traveller or Roma identity and life style.

### After reading this chapter you should be able to:

▸ gain an understanding of the Traveller and Roma communities in Irish society.
▸ understand how policy can affect the lives of Traveller and Roma children and families.
▸ understand how long-standing oppression can jeopardise the health and well-being of a community.
▸ support the identity and sense of belonging of Traveller and Roma children in ECEC.

▸ begin the process of understanding how particular thinking habits regarding Travellers and Roma can lead to unfair treatment.
▸ recognise that Traveller and Roma families are not all the same.

# Introduction: Two worlds

Up until 2010, most Traveller children attended Traveller-specific ECEC provision. Some Traveller parents made a personal choice for their children to attend integrated services. With the introduction of the Early Childhood Care and Education (ECCE, 2010) and the Community Childcare Subvention (CCS, 2010) schemes, all Traveller and Roma children have access to integrated pre-school for one year like all other families. This means that Traveller and Roma children come in contact with the settled/majority culture and community earlier than they did before, when integration began at primary school. It also means that parents and children have to find their way in an unfamiliar system within ECEC provision. Practitioners in turn also have to begin the process of understanding and communicating with Traveller and Roma families and in supporting their children's identity and belonging. It can be challenging to find common ground, to be trusting and to feel comfortable in an unfamiliar situation.

'Travellers inhabit two worlds, the hostile settled world and their own Traveller world' (Kenny and Binchy, 2009, p. 123). They are recognised as among the most marginalised communities in Europe and in Ireland and Mac Gréil's (2011) findings on prejudice in early twenty-first-century Ireland suggests that 'the overall position of Travellers is very serious and will not improve without a new initiatives from the State at the national and local levels'.

## Who are the Travellers?

> Being a Traveller is the feeling of belonging to a group of people. Knowing through thick or thin, they are there for you. Having the supports of family systems. Having an identity.
>
> (Michael McDonagh, 1991)

Irish Travellers are a small indigenous ethnic group with a nomadic tradition whose presence in Irish society was first officially recorded in the twelfth century. A serialised RTÉ programme, *Blood of the Travellers* (2011), has proved through genome research that biologically, Travellers have been a separate population for at least a thousand years. Travellers have a long shared history with common cultural characteristics and traditions, evident in the organisation of family, language, social and economic life (Murray, 2002). Not much of Traveller life is recorded in history. However, traditionally Travellers provided services such as repairing buckets and other metalwork (hence 'tinkers') and other implements, as well as bringing news and in particular musical entertainment to local rural communities. They also worked as seasonal farm labourers, generally camping in extended family groups on the roadside. There are traditional spots all around the country where families halted; now most are covered by motorways. With modernisation Travellers moved toward the cities and developed a new Traveller economy working with cars, collecting scrap, working in markets, selling carpets, landscaping. With urbanisation, Traveller children began to attend school more regularly and today, all Traveller children enrol in primary school, and most transfer to secondary school, though many leave education early. The extended family is as important as the immediate family to the Traveller community, and living together and sharing a sense of 'peoplehood' (awareness of the underlying unity that makes the individual a part of a people) is emphasised within the community. The extended family is the embodiment of community for the Travellers and Roma, rather than a particular geographical location. While family is also considered important to the settled population, their notion of community is generally associated with a geographical location.

In the past decade Traveller nomadic lifestyle has been constrained through legislation (Housing Miscellaneous Act, 2002 (Trespass Law)). This law has caused considerable hardship for Traveller families and has forced many families into standard housing which inhibits their practice of living with extended family. The constraint on nomadic practice means that some Travellers are shifting towards settled-style economic activities and accommodation. This is 'not necessarily freely chosen' (Kenny and Binchy, 2009, p. 118), but is a type of forced assimilation (see Chapter 7), which is driven by official State policy. This constraint has led to isolation and loneliness for many Travellers, which in turn has had an effect on Travellers' well-being and has, in some cases, led to serious mental health concerns (Kelleher et al, 2010).

---

### 15.1 Links

**The Housing (Miscellaneous Provisions) Act 2002**

The legislation makes it a criminal offence to trespass on and occupy public or private property. This offence is punishable by immediate eviction; a month is jail and/or a 3000 euro fine and the confiscation of property.

When the legislation came into operation the state promised it would not be used against Travellers living on the roadside and awaiting accommodation. Instead it was to be used in instances of large-scale illegal encampments. This has not been the case.

(See www.irishstatutebook.ie/2002/en/act/pub/0009/index.html)

---

## Roma in Ireland: Lives and Policies

**Roma** is an umbrella term that refers to the international Roma community, which is made up of diverse groups throughout the world. The global population of Roma is estimated to be 10–12 million with 8 million domiciled in the EU. Like Travellers, Roma are *not* a homogeneous group and, similarly, their nomadic traditions have been constrained. Nomadism was not permitted under Communist law in Eastern Europe and, as a consequence, Roma are largely sedentary. Some Roma are **peripatetic nomads**, which means that they travel in order to practise their trades and skills where they can (Pavee Point, 2009). Roma do not share a particular homeland, but akin to Travellers, the Roma are a minority ethnic group and share a common ancestry of origin, history, culture and language.

In common with the Traveller community, the extended family is central to Roma values and culture. With the opening up of the EU, Roma families have emigrated to Ireland and Europe seeking a better life and, in some cases, fleeing persecution in their home countries. There are an estimated 3,000–5,000 Roma legally resident in Ireland who have come from EU countries such as Romania, Slovakia, the Czech Republic, Poland and Bulgaria (Pavee Point, 2009).

International organisations including the UN, the EU, the OECD, Amnesty International, UNICEF, the Fundamental Rights Agency and others are highly critical of the treatment of Roma in Europe, as they are of the treatment of Travellers in Ireland. Historically, Roma have been subject to sterilization, slavery, genocide (500,000 Roma were killed during the Holocaust) and exile. They continue to be subjected to segregation and assimilationist policies in education in many European countries. Mac Gréil (2011, p. 144) raised concerns about the level of negative attitudes towards the 'Romanians' in Ireland today, and warns of 'the seeds of discrimination against this ethnic category' present in his research findings.

Over the past decade, Roma who have come as asylum seekers and those who have the right to work and access welfare have been able to integrate fairly well in Ireland. Being able to work legally reduces vulnerability and may reduce stigmatisation, too.

Two national policies have adversely restricted the immigration of Roma from Bulgaria and Romania. Following their accession to the EU, Ireland (and nine other EU member states) introduced laws that targeted immigrants from Bulgaria and Romania. These laws restrict these citizens in accessing work and social welfare services in Ireland and include:

▸    The Irish Naturalisation and Immigration Service (INIS, 2007) Exemption Order
▸    The Habitual Residence Condition Act (HRC, 2009).

Many Roma families from Romania and Bulgaria have limited or no education, and arrive in Ireland ill-informed, believing they can access employment. Unable to work or receive social welfare benefits, they can find themselves living in appalling conditions in overcrowded and inadequate accommodation. With little or no English, virtually no education and evident prejudice in Irish society, Roma families and their children often find themselves in a very vulnerable position. Unfortunately, this has resulted in some Roma from Romania and Bulgaria begging to survive. It is important to note that many Roma frown on the practice of begging and many are forced to do so in difficult circumstances. As Mac Gréil (2011, p. 26) points out, 'generalisations about negative behaviour and traits are often given legs by careless talk', as there has been much talk about organised begging and exploitation within the Roma community in Ireland, though to date there is no foundation for such accusations. However, there is some evidence of Roma exploitation and, in particular, of women and children through organised begging in the United Kingdom (BBC documentary, 2011).

### 15.2 Links

**Moving to another EU member state**

The Roma are aware of their general right to leave their country, but less aware of the specific, and often complex, array of rights and obligations concerning the establishment of residence for EU citizens in another Member State. Poverty caused by unemployment, discrimination and racism is the main factor pushing Roma to leave their countries of origin. The Roma face difficulties in finding jobs in the formal labour market of their destination country because they face stereotyping and discrimination. The Roma face difficulties registering their residence in their new country of residence. As a consequence, they may face difficulties in accessing national health systems, public housing, social assistance and labour market integration measures.

(FRA, 2010)

### *Roma and Travellers: The connection*

The Roma and Traveller communities have much in common, including the importance of extended family, beliefs and values associated with family culture and traditions. Irish Travellers and Roma are not linked by origin; the Roma originate in India, whereas Travellers are indigenous to Ireland. Yet in more recent Europe policy discourse, 'Roma' is used as an umbrella term understood to include Irish Travellers. This however can be problematic for Irish Travellers because it can assume a hierarchy (i.e., Travellers being seen as a sub-group of the Roma population) and can in some circumstances lead to the further non-recognition and exclusion of Travellers at European and national level policy discussions. Pavee Point recommends that new strategic plans for Roma and Travellers in Ireland encompass both communities, who share a common experience of marginalisation, oppression, social exclusion and discrimination.

## Discrimination and marginalisation

In a report on his mission to assess the human rights situation in Ireland, Thomas Hammarberg, Council of Europe Commissioner for Human Rights, stated that:

> Travellers have been subjected to discrimination and racism in the fields of education, employment, housing, healthcare, media reporting and participation in decision-making.

And further stated that he:

> ...considers it essential that Travellers are effectively protected against discrimination and racism under national and international law.
>
> (Council of Europe, 2007)
>
> The European Commission has also reported that Roma in Europe face prejudice, intolerance, discrimination and social exclusion in their daily lives. They are marginalised and live in very poor socio-economic conditions.
>
> (COM, 2011)

The EU Fundamental Rights Agency (2011) has catalogued the multiple discrimination and disadvantage experienced by Roma, including difficulties when they migrate to another EU Member State. Roma experience problems with border/visa officials, including demands for bribes by corrupt officials when leaving and/or returning to their countries of origin.

Traveller marginalisation and oppression has been documented in Ireland by many, including Micheál Mac Gréil (2010/2011) and in Europe through the UNICERD, UNCRC and the Fundamental Rights Agency (see Chapter 4).

> Recognition of cultural identity is essential to personal and social self-worth.
>
> (Kenny, 2011, p. 7)

How you are viewed as a community by the State and by individuals in society affects your well-being and engagement with society. Historically, the state has had an ambivalent relationship with the Traveller community and with the concept of nomadism. The community has been viewed not as an ethnic community, but as a subculture of poverty with a deficient lifestyle. Travellers have been named pejoratively by the state in various state reports including the Report of the Commission on Itinerancy (1963). In 1995 in the Report of the Task Force on the Traveller Community, Traveller culture and their group title was finally appropriately recognised. More recently, Travellers have had the term 'settled Travellers' imposed on them by the State when they are living in local authority housing, despite the fact that being a Traveller is not defined by active nomadism alone. Travellers' name of choice for all members of their community is 'Traveller' (see Chapter 3).

In 2000, Irish Travellers were recognised in the UK as a minority ethnic group. The Irish Equality Authority (www.equality.ie) and the Human Rights Commission (www.ihrc.ie) have pressed for the recognition of Traveller ethnicity in Ireland. The UN Human Rights Committee (2011), the Council of Europe Commissioner for Human Rights (2008) and the UN Committee on the Rights of the Child (2006) have requested that the State address this matter. The Committee for the Elimination of Racial Discrimination (CERD) (see Chapter 4) has also urged the State to engage in dialogue with the Traveller community.

## A step in the right direction

> Recognising Travellers as an ethnic group would be very symbolic. It would be emotional; it would mean that we are something of substance and not some misfits.
>
> (Pavee Point, 2011)

At Ireland's hearing for the UN Universal Periodic Review of Human Rights on 6 October 2011, Alan Shatter, Minister for Justice and Equality, announced that the government was 'seriously considering' conferring recognition of Travellers as an ethnic minority group. Pavee Point, along with other Traveller organisations, welcomed this decision (Pavee Point, 2011). Ireland will report to the UN Universal Periodic Review in March 2012.

### What do you think about Roma and Travellers, and what do Travellers and Roma think of us?

In my experience of working with and training ECEC practitioners and other educators, negative attitudes about Travellers and Roma prevail, including stereotyping, prejudice and even racist comments. People tend to be polite at first, but once the discussion opens up, many contentious issues arise. This can be useful as the issues can then be deconstructed and myths or untruths addressed, such as the notion that Travellers don't pay rent or electricity bills on halting sites – they do. It can also offer an opportunity to explore how oppression, negative stereotyping and social prejudice can affect settled/Traveller/Roma relations.

Be aware that questions about a community's lifestyle and traditions can be disrespectful, voyeuristic and inappropriate, and lead to homogenising Travellers and Roma. It is not necessary to know about cultural practices, such as the custom of early marriage, to work well with Traveller/Roma children in early childhood. Questions that degenerate into negative comments or thoughts are not helpful in honouring and respecting Traveller and Roma families' human rights when they come to avail of an early childhood service.

Coxhead (2007) in his book *The Last Bastion of Racism: Gypsies, Travellers and Policing* describes how people seem to feel they have licence to say whatever they like about Travellers and Roma, even though they might think twice before expressing negative views while discussing other minority groups. It is also important to recognise that some people have had negative experiences with individual Travellers or Roma that also need to be addressed. However, like all communities, Travellers and Roma are diverse and made up of individuals, families and clans. Most Travellers and Roma want the best for their families, to maintain their lifestyle and have good relations with the majority population.

## Working with Traveller and Roma Families and Children

> You always need to be open and try to find out why parents are not engaging with the service or communicating their issues. If you have been oppressed and discriminated against in society it is hard to trust the dominant group. Building trust is everything; it helps you as a practitioner to ensure that the marginalised child in society has a voice and space in your service.
>
> (Irish Practitioner, DECET, 2011)

Have you ever imagined what it might feel like to be marginalised or to live on the edge of society? To hear or feel from others that you are somehow worth less than them, not welcome, excluded, called names? Think for a moment of how that might make you feel.

If you are aware of human rights, and in particular children's rights (see Chapter 4), you are on the road to understanding how being oppressed in society might affect an individual or community (see Chapter 2). That understanding will give you insight into and recognition of the need for respect and appropriate inclusion. In this chapter, you have been offered some background information on Travellers and Roma and some policies that affect their lifestyles and ability to work in Ireland. Gathering information on the community you are working with will help your understanding, and reading information from advocacy organisations and the EU that promote the human rights of Travellers and Roma will also support your knowledge base (www.pavee.ie). Ultimately, talking to families is the best way to find out about their needs, although this, too, may have its challenges.

## 15.3 Discuss

**Supporting Traveller and Roma identity and belonging in ECEC**

Not all parents will want their children identified as Travellers in the service provision. Many Traveller and Roma parents have had a negative experience in education and this has influenced their relationship with the system.

This can be confusing for practitioners and they may choose to operate out of a ethnicity-blind perspective (see Chapter 2), in other words they ignore the differences thinking this is the best way for the children to settle in.

- What do you think might be going on for the family who says 'treat my child the same as the other children'?
- How might you address the situation?
- What do you know about supporting children's identity and belonging?
- What do you know about treating children equally in ECEC? Do you understand it to mean treating children all same? (See Chapters 2 and 7.)
- Do you believe it is important to support all children's identity and sense of belonging?
- What can you do to honour and respect Traveller/Roma identity in such a situation? (See Chapters 9 and 12.)
- What might you do to support Traveller pride?

Sometimes people ask why Travellers or Roma won't attend meetings, or why they are cautious about talking with you, or even hostile. Traveller and Roma families know how difficult it is to live in an often hostile 'settled world' and maintain their traditions and lifestyle. They have to support their children to survive and may operate in ways you don't understand in order to protect and prepare their children for life beyond their own communities. This may appear to you as rejection of their culture in favour of settled culture. Don't assume that because a parent doesn't want to give out information about their lifestyle that they are rejecting their culture and want their children assimilated.

Traveller and Roma have a right to privacy just like anybody else. In supporting children's identity and belonging, of course, you may need particular information. Consider finding imaginative ways to explain to reluctant parents why you might need information to support their child.

> Sometimes, for instance, Traveller families don't want their children's Traveller identity known in the setting. Taking the time to explore and support their understanding of why and how to support a child's identity is useful. Sometimes this takes a lot of time and reassurance because Traveller parents are afraid their child will be singled out and discriminated against in the setting.
>
> (Irish practitioner, DECET, 2011)

This may take some time, particularly with Roma parents who may not speak English well. Don't assume that parents don't want to share any information. In my experience, parents want to do the best for their children and benefit from receiving information that supports their understanding of ECEC practice.

## 15.4 Discuss

- Settled people often say they don't trust Travellers/Roma. Do you think that Travellers/Roma trust settled people?
- Why might Travellers/Roma not feel comfortable with 'settled' people?

When trying to find common ground between Travellers and Roma, ECEC practitioners are faced with the challenge of recognising and honouring their different ways of being and living their lives. The two groups may not agree with each other, perhaps based on preconceived ideas about each other. So how can they move forward in partnership?

## 15.5 Discuss

- Is there something about Travellers/Roma that makes you feel uncomfortable?
- Do you think that the Traveller/Roma lifestyle is lacking and should change?
- Do you think all Travellers/Roma are all the same and behave in the same way?
- Do you think the settled way of life is a better way to live life, and that Travellers/Roma should change to fit into ECEC and society?
- Do you think Traveller/Roma have a valuable contribution to make to their children, the ECEC system and in education?

## Settling into ECEC

When Traveller/Roma children enter the formal world of ECEC, they may find out for the first time that the way they do things, dress, speak and play is different. They might even begin to recognise that their family is perceived as different and perhaps 'not as good as' other families. This may not be overt, but children pick up on the values and norms in ECEC that are different to those of home. We know that messages are conveyed both consciously and unconsciously, and that children know when their way of behaving, of being, is not accepted. Traditionally, Traveller/Roma children have been fully part of adult Traveller/Roma society, speaking readily and frankly with adult company. Space for work, home and children is not segregated in Traveller/Roma culture, and gender roles were clearly defined. From the earliest age, children are integrated into the family work unit, learning skills by apprenticeships in home-making, childminding and the economic domains (Murray, 2002, p. 58). This way of being in their culture is less about the individual but more about a collective;

> In literature on ethnic identity practices, the focus is on boundary (us/them) issues; there is little discussion of the primacy of collective over individual identity in cultural groups such as Travellers.
>
> (Kenny et al, 2009, p. 9)

As a result, Traveller/Roma children bring a knowledge base to the setting that may not be recognised or valued. For example, Traveller children may know a lot about communicating with adults, homemaking, working with horses, cars and trading. Recognition of what children bring to the setting supports children's sense of identity and belonging. Traveller and Roma children may find the ECEC setting bewildering, and the practitioner may also be uncertain and view a child's behaviour as inappropriate. We know that children also learn negative views about difference very early (Connolly et al, 2002; Mac Naughton, 2006).

Therefore, we need to support children's understanding of difference in a proactive way. Traveller and Roma children need to acquire positive social identities and self-esteem. They also need their peers to respect them, and vice versa. Finding ways of making the unfamiliar familiar, and building real bridges between ECEC and the home culture will help to shape both the views of the Traveller and Roma children and the settled children. Getting the message that you are either inferior or superior is not healthy for either group of children.

## Summary

Extended family and community are valuable to Travellers and Roma. While some Travellers and Roma may have had negative experiences in the education system, parents continue to be interested in education for their children. How parents understand ECEC will differ from parent to parent, from family grouping to family grouping. The communities are the most marginalised in Ireland and Europe, and while they share much in common, their origins are different. Human rights organisations and watchdog bodies regularly challenge governments to ensure that Travellers and Roma are respected and treated with equality, but much work remains to be done. Travellers and Roma are not a homogeneous group and it is risky to make assumptions that they are all the same. We all carry prejudices and hence we have to challenge our own views in order to bridge the cultural gap between ECEC and the home. Traveller and Roma children, like all children, need to be affirmed, have friends and enjoy the ECEC setting. Expanding your point of view, challenging your own assumptions, and engaging Traveller and Roma parents with honour and respect is a step in the right direction.

# SECTION FOUR

SECTION FOUR

# A Roadmap to Equality

*Caminante. No hay camino, se hace camino al andar.*

Traveller, there is no path. The road is made by walking.
From the poem 'Caminante' by Antonio Machado

## Overview

We begin this chapter by remembering the journey through this book, and through the history of the struggle for more just and equitable experiences for *all* children in Ireland. This chapter revisits the stations on the road to equality – some of which you have explored in more detail already – before taking a look forward. We ask if there can be a roadmap to equality. We begin by looking at the recommendations that came out of the initial '*éist*' consultation a decade ago and at subsequent recommendations from Irish policy documents that emphasise the need to mainstream the anti-discriminatory diversity and equality approach developed by '*éist*'. Findings from recent European research (CoRe) and shared views of ECEC practitioners in ten countries (DECET) complement the picture. The chapter concludes with an outline of four dimensions, or compass points, to a roadmap to equality: leadership, advocacy, resourcing and research.

## Introduction: Why a 'roadmap'?

As we conclude this book about an Irish perspective on Diversity and Equality in early childhood, it is worthwhile to remind ourselves where we started this journey. By 'journey' we first mean the route we have offered you through the often difficult, sometimes treacherous and sometimes pleasurable terrain of Diversity and Equality in ECEC. In keeping with the analogy of a journey, we also want to remind you that the struggle to achieve more just and equitable experiences for all children in this country and in ECEC has been going on for years. You, as a reader of this book and as a practitioner or student and future practitioner working with children, families and communities, have a choice to become part of it. The journey is far from over.

Diversity has always been at the heart of Irish society, and there have always been champions of human rights and social movements that carried the struggle for human rights and social justice. There have been plenty of policy developments, within the early childhood sector and beyond, that have lead to important frameworks, legislation and guidelines that shape and orient our approach to Diversity and Equality in early childhood. You have already familiarised yourself with the most important of these policy frameworks.

Research and professional experience show how children learn about difference in positive or negative ways from an early age, and how important it is to engage proactively with Diversity and Equality in everyday ECEC practice.

As we have explored, there is also a professional framework that helps us to orient our practice with children and families. The Anti-Bias Approach offers clear Goals for Adults and Children that are not prescriptive, but rather, ask you to engage critically with the Goals and with your experiences in ECEC and in the wider society. How the Anti-Bias Goals inform practice makes a difference for children and families has been illustrated by the selection of voices from the sector.

We know that Diversity and Equality matters in early childhood, and we have legislation and policies in place and we have clear goals to orient our practice. So why do we need a roadmap? Because the different parts of the picture – the terrain of the journey – are still disjointed. The words are there, but they need to be turned into actions!

We need to keep in mind, however, that no map, however detailed, will do the journeying for us. It will be the steps we take and our actions that will make the road to a more equal society. As Spanish poet Antonio Machado has put it beautifully in his poem – we make the road by walking!

## Recommendations from previous reports and documents

Any roadmap that we can outline in this book has to build on recommendations for policy and practice made by previous reports and policy documents. We aren't starting from scratch. Fortunately, we can draw on a broad consensus that a comprehensive approach to Diversity and Equality is necessary to ECEC in Ireland. We summarise key points from existing recommendations below. Building on the experiences made in the Irish ECEC sector, we then suggest some necessary next steps.

### What did 'éist' recommend?

We began this book by looking at the analysis of Irish ECEC provided by the 'éist' report as a result of a consultation process with the sector a decade ago (Murray and O'Doherty, 2001). The report concluded that the Anti-Bias Approach was best suited to meet the needs of all children attending early childhood education and care services in Ireland. In order to realise a comprehensive Anti-bias approach in professional preparation and practice, the report developed a set of recommendations for policy, training and providers. So, what did '*éist*' recommend?

▸ A national approach to diversity education for early years grounded in Anti-Bias principles should be acknowledged, resourced, developed and implemented without delay
▸ Policy, training and ECEC practice should be informed by Articles 2, 29 and 30 of the UN Convention on the Rights of the Child, which relate to quality of provision, equality, human rights and respect for diversity
▸ All services for children need to put equality policies in place that protect children against discrimination
▸ Recommendations for diversity education made by government reports must be implemented
▸ Funding must be made available to enable trainers and providers to implement an Anti-Bias Approach in ECEC
▸ All service providers working with children should have anti-racism training embedded in their pre-service and in-service courses.

(Murray and O'Doherty, 2001, p. 78)

## 16.1 Discuss

The recommendations listed above were made in 2001.
• How far do you think Ireland has come towards realising these recommendations, which were then seen as both necessary and achievable?
• Are these recommendations still relevant today?
• If so, how can they be realised?

These recommendations give a general orientation from which the '*éist*' report draws more specific recommendations for government, training (including accreditation and certification) and ECEC providers and organisations.

'*éist*' identified government responsibilities in the following areas:

▸ development of coordinated national policies that incorporate diversity and anti-racism principles
▸ raising public awareness
▸ initiating research to identify the nature and extend of racist and discriminatory incidents and how these are handled in ECEC
▸ inclusion of the Anti-Bias Approach in curriculum development

▸ implementation of recommendations made by the Task Force on the Traveller community

▸ amendment of Pre-School Regulations to ensure diversity and equality policies and practices are included as inspection criteria

▸ compulsory Diversity and Equality training for preschool and early years services inspectors.

'*éist*' identified the following responsibilities for training institutions (including accreditation and certification bodies):

▸ the mandatory adoption of the Anti-Bias Approach in their diversity and equality training, integrated throughout the curriculum as well as in specialised diversity and equality modules

▸ training institutions and accreditation/certification bodies to develop written statements (policies) regarding respect for diversity and equality

▸ commitment to diversity, equality and anti-racism principles to be evident in all early childhood courses as a prerequisite for validation, accreditation or certification.

'*éist*' identified responsibilities for ECEC providers and voluntary organisations in following areas:

▸ develop written diversity, equality and anti-racism policy, together with a framework for implementation

▸ ensure extensive Anti-Bias in-service training and continuous professional development for practitioners

▸ develop and put in place support systems and resources for practitioners to work with the Anti-Bias Approach

▸ develop criteria to evaluate and proof equality, diversity and anti-racist policies and practices in ECEC settings.

## Recommendations from Irish policy documents

The decade from 1998 saw the development of a number of important policy documents in rapid succession (see Chapter Four). The 1998 report of the National Forum for Early Childhood Education (Coolahan, 1998) identified key challenges for the ECEC sector including provision of 'variable' quality, lack of childcare places and concerns about the qualification of staff. Based on this report, the Department of Education and Science in 1999 published the White Paper *Ready to Learn*, which for the first time outlined a political strategy to develop the ECEC sector. Quality of provision, the qualifications of staff, and programmes that meet the needs of individual children are brought together in one picture for the first time:

... early childhood intervention is effective when it provides high quality, intensive and clearly articulated programme, delivered by highly skilled and carefully trained personnel in contexts of small group and individual instruction and which are planned to specifically to address individual, identified needs.

(Department of Education and Science, 1999, p. 84)

The White Paper also laid the foundations for the establishment in 2002 of the Centre for Early Childhood Education and Development (CECDE) and the development of Síolta (CECDE, 2006).

Other important documents from that period include the National Childcare Strategy (Department of Justice Equality and Law Reform, 1999) and the National Children's Strategy, which outlined the vision of

... an Ireland where children are respected as young citizens with a valued contribution to make and a voice of their own; where all children are cherished and supported by family and wider society; where they enjoy a fulfilling childhood and realise their potential.

(Department of Health and Children, 2000)

## 16.2

The Early Childhood Care and Education Sector values:

- childhood in its own right.
- the rights of children, who are active agents in their own growth and development.
- parents, guardians and family as the child's primary source of well-being.
- professional development as central to good practice.
- the role of the practitioner as the facilitator of enhanced well-being and development of the child.
- diversity by acknowledging and promoting each child's and each adult's individual, personal and cultural identity.
- equality of access and participation in services.
- a positive approach to Irish language and culture.
- the right of children to protection from any form of abuse, neglect and discrimination.
- the right of children, families and childcare staff to confidentiality, balanced with the interests of the child and the right of all to protection from harm.
- experiences and activities which support learning and allow children to actively explore, to experience, to make choices and decisions and to share in the learning process.
- play as the natural, constructive mode of children's interactions with their peers, adults and environment.

(Department of Justice Equality and Law Reform, 2002)

*A model framework for the profession*

A key document was published by the Department of Justice and Law Reform in 2002: the *Model Framework for Education, Training and Professional Development in the Early Childhood Care and Education Sector*. In this document, the professionalisation of the early childhood workforce in Ireland is grounded in a set of 'core value statements'. They include a commitment to diversity and equality.

*'éist'* has informed the development of the model framework. Explaining in more detail what the commitment to diversity and equality entails, the model framework builds directly on the work of *'éist'* and emphasises the importance of professional development and critical thinking.

---

**16.3**

**Diversity**

Diversity can be described as differences between people in terms of disability, skin colour, culture, ethnicity, race, religion, language, gender and other background factors. ECEC practitioners' respect for difference applies to curriculum design and delivery, selection of materials and equipment, staff training and development, all interaction within the setting, and all written documentation. Every child attending an early childhood setting should be able to feel a sense of belonging and should be encouraged to recognise and value his or her personal and cultural identity throughout the activities and interactions. Children are not all the same. Adults play an important role in shaping children's attitudes, by providing accurate explanations and information, by challenging prejudice and discrimination and as role models. The learning environment should depict positive images that reflect a range of backgrounds, cultures and minority groups, in realistic, non-stereotypical, everyday contexts.

**Equality of access and participation**

Equality of access and participation as a value asserts that early childhood services need to be inclusive. There should be no barriers to access and participation in ECEC services for any child on any grounds. Equal participation includes planning and monitoring of programme activities and ensures that all children receive adequate support to participate fully. Policies should be equality proofed at the planning stage and implementation procedures monitored on a continuing basis to ensure equitable practice.

**Professional development as central to good practice**

Education and training is valued as a means to ensure quality practice, and as a mechanism and measure of ongoing professional development. ECEC practitioners need to seek out and keep up to date with new approaches, theories and thinking, as the profession continually develops both nationally and internationally.

(Model Framework for Education, Training and Professional Development in the Early Childhood Care and Education Sector, Department of Justice Equality and Law Reform, 2002)

## 16.4 Discuss

- With your group of learners, identify the key terms in the model framework's explanation of Diversity and Equality values for the early childhood workforce.
- Where in this book have you already encountered them?
- Discuss their relevance for you and your (future) professional practice in ECEC.

### *Recommendations of the National Economic and Social Forum (NESF)*

In 2005, the NESF published a detailed review of early childhood policies. The report makes reference to the anti-discriminatory approach to diversity developed by '*éist*'. Its recommendations are explicit:

> A useful model from which to draw is the '*éist*' programme developed by Pavee Point under the EOCP, which is designed as a vehicle to promote anti-discriminatory practice and respond appropriately and inclusively to the needs of young children. This programme should become part of more mainstream provision. Opportunities to involve Traveller interests also need to be reflected in the structures that are established to manage the delivery of ECCE services in the future.
>
> (NESF, 2005, p. 70)

> The '*éist*' programme developed by Pavee Point should be used as a model for reflecting diversity in early years settings.
>
> (NESF, 2005, p. xiii)

## Recommendations from international studies

European studies and policy documents have long reached a broad consensus about which factors influence the quality of services for young children, and what is needed to improve them. These factors include:

▸ staff-to-child ratio
▸ group size
▸ working conditions and pay
▸ continuity of employment / low staff turnover

In addition, researchers agree on the need for

▸ adequate public investment in ECEC (1% of a country's GDP)
▸ an increased level of qualification (at least 60% graduates at degree level/ISCED 5)

Documents that have contributed to this consensus include:

▸   the Quality targets in services for young children (European Commission Network on Childcare and Other Measures to Reconcile Employment and Family Responsibilities, 1996)
▸   the EPPE study (Sylva, Melhuish, Sammons, Siraj-Blatchford and Taggart, 2004)
▸   the OECD Starting Strong reports I and II (OECD, 2001, 2006)
▸   the Children in Europe policy paper *Young children and their services* (Children in Europe, 2008)
▸   the UNICEF *Report Card 8* (UNICEF Innocenti Research Centre, 2008)
▸   the NESSE report on early childhood policies in Europe (Penn, 2009)
▸   the EURYDICE report on early childhood and inequality (Eurydice, 2009)
▸   the CoRe report (Urban, Vandenbroeck, Van Laere, Lazzari and Peeters, 2011)

### *Recommendations based on recent European policy documents*
There are a number of recent European policy documents that emphasise how 'high-quality' early childhood education and care for all children contributes to achieving crucial policy goals for Europe and its member states. Among them are the 2009 report *Early Childhood Education and Care in Europe: Tackling Social and Cultural Inequalities* (Eurydice, 2009) and the EU communication on early childhood education and care published by the European Commission in February 2011, *Early Childhood Education and Care: Providing all our children with the best start for the world of tomorrow* (European Commission, 2011). This latter policy paper is particularly important for our roadmap, as it makes an explicit connection between diversity and the need for critical reflection and systemic professionalisation of the workforce.

### *Recommendations based on the findings of the CoRe study*
The policy conclusions in the EU Communication are strongly supported by findings from a recent European research project. The CoRe project conducted a comprehensive literature review in several European languages, a survey in 15 countries and seven in-depth case studies to explore understandings of competence, quality and professionalism and how the three are connected (Urban, et al., 2011). The project concludes that not only the practitioners have to be competent in ECEC, but also the institutions and ECEC systems they work in:

> '... competence unfolds in four dimensions, at every layer of the ECEC system:
> 1.   Individual level
> 2.   Institutional and team level
> 3.   Inter-Institutional level
> 4.   Level of Governance'

(Urban, et al, 2011, p. 33)

The study suggests that these elements, brought together in a coherent framework, constitute a **competent system** (p. 33). You have already seen an overview over the competences identified by CoRe in Chapter 5, when we discussed critical reflection.

Important for the roadmap is that one of the competences identified by CoRe is about knowledge, practice and values of diversity, Anti-Bias Approach and anti-discriminatory practice: 'Knowledge of working in contexts of diversity (Anti-Bias Approaches, intercultural dialogue, identity …)' (p. 38) and 'Knowledge of diversity in all its forms and anti-discriminatory practices' (p. 44).

### *Diversity and Equality competences recommended by DECET*

The European DECET network has developed a range of resources for practitioners and trainers working in contexts of diversity and equality. In 2011, the DECET working group on professionalism in early childhood published a brochure that explored practitioners' experiences in ten countries and is closely linked to the work of the CoRe project. They asked if there are specific competences needed for working towards respect for diversity and towards equality for all children. Below are some suggestions for professional competences in the context of diversity and social inclusion in ECEC:

---

### 16.5 Working towards social change

For me, as an educator, it is important to sensitise the broader community to the rights and needs of families living in disadvantaged communities. To mobilise communities about human rights, and address human rights with a view to solving problems. Simultaneously we need to do so with respect for the privacy of each family, and only if the family agrees.

(Practitioner, Serbia)

Professionals working with diversity need to have an awareness of the power and privilege of the dominant group and the difficulties faced by some minority groups in society. You should understand that there is a knock-on effect on opportunities and experience.

(Practitioner, Ireland)

#### Open communication and dialogue

I take the initiative and always try to communicate with parents in a way that is understandable. Starting out, I look for the best way to make contact with parents. This can require a lot of creativity while communicating. It is not something found in books; you just have to do it. It doesn't matter if the language you use is not perfect.

(Practitioner, Belgium)

If I work with families in which the parents are divorced, it's necessary to work and talk with both parents in order to respond to the needs of the child. I maintain a certain balance between personal engagement and maintaining a personal distance, and I avoid gossiping or making negative comments about the other parent or any other parent.

(Practitioner, France)

**Critical reflection: exploring complex issues from various angles**

It's useful for practitioners to have some knowledge of asylum seeker and refugee status in Ireland, having empathy for and being aware of the stresses and difficulties facing families in a new culture and language – also, being sensitive about the family's distance from their extended family is important for working with people with respect.

(Practitioner, Ireland)

I would accept same-sex parents, but I'm afraid that my own traditions and upbringing would affect my behaviour. We would have to talk a lot as a team in order to share feelings and biases and explore how we all feel about same-sex parents.

(Practitioner, Serbia)

**Learning from disagreements**

Sometimes staff members don't want to discuss diversity for fear of showing some personal prejudice. They feel such a discussion may jeopardise their position in the job or cause other staff to be critical of them.

(Practitioner, Ireland)

In order to promote fathers' and male carers' participation in a female-dominated ECEC environment, we need practitioners who are willing to preserve their sense of humour, practitioners who are thick-skinned enough to accept when their efforts might not be successful.

(Practitioner, Scotland)

**Constructing new knowledge with children, parents and colleagues**

I realised I was not recognising the qualities and knowledge of the Traveller child [in our setting]. His experiences were not present in the setting. Then we did the Family Wall, and the other children saw his horses and he began to name the various types of horses and share his knowledge. I changed the environment to ensure his interests were evident and he could express himself.

(Practitioner, Ireland)

Most importantly, I'm aware in the work with all parents and children that I don't know all the answers. I know that I need to build the most appropriate practice in collaboration with parents and children so it respects different perspectives.

(Practitioner, England)

(All quotes from practitioners from DECET, 2011)

## A roadmap to equality?

We have come a long way from the findings and recommendation of the initial '*éist*' report. Much has been incorporated in policy documents and legislation. There can be no doubt, the *language* of Diversity and Equality has made it into the frameworks for professional preparation, training and practice in ECEC in Ireland, including Síolta and Aistear and the Diversity and Equality Guidelines for Childcare Providers. The problem is obvious: the challenge for our roadmap is not a lack of appropriate language or policies, but a lack of implementation!

So, if we were to give a policy recommendation at the end of this book, it would be similar to the one given to a European conference on early childhood policies in Budapest in February 2011:

**Implement existing policy recommendations!**

(See http://tempus.tpf.hu/ecec on 'staff competences' for this and other recommendations.)

But what exactly would implementation mean for the Irish early childhood sector today? A study of the *Conceptualisation of Diversity and Equality in Early Childhood Care and Education* (Murray, 2006) identified four areas where action can and should be taken. They form, we suggest, the compass points for our map:

1. **Leadership:** There is a need for political leadership, but the early childhood sector has a role to play as well. Early childhood practitioners, trainers, lecturers and researchers need to speak out and get organised. EDENN and the Cork-based Association of Childcare Professionals (ACP) represent steps in the right direction.

   The sector has not yet fully embraced the recommendations for a mandatory comprehensive approach to Diversity and Equality, or engaged proactively with anti-discriminatory practices like the Anti-Bias Approach in ECEC. However, the '*éist*' module is now available as an elective at FETAC levels 5 and 6, and trainers have also been trained as part of the '*éist*' project. The Diversity and Equality training has been accredited by NUI Maynooth. The 2011–2012 Pre-school Education Initiative for Children from Ethnic Minority Groups is an excellent example of leadership and dialogic learning initiated from within the sector to build on and disseminate the work of '*éist*' with the support of the Department of Education.

   Consistent leadership is now required. To ensure a consistent approach to implementation, a crucial next step will be to ensure that all trainers delivering the elective module (i.e. at VECs and colleges) avail of the '*éist*' training of trainers.

2. **Advocacy:** While the language of Diversity and Equality can be found throughout the Irish ECEC sector, Anti-Bias and anti-discriminatory practices are hardly mentioned in policies and documents. An organised, professional, Irish early childhood sector needs to be more articulate – and explicit – about addressing prejudice and discrimination from an early age. While we all have a responsibility to speak out, we see a particular task for education and training providers, namely,

to understand how prejudice, discrimination and racism works, and how we can engage in Anti-Bias practices. This task needs to be embedded in the content of pre- and in-service education and training; otherwise, we won't be able to move beyond multicultural practices that may have a value, but carry the risk of being superficial or tokenistic.

3. **Resourcing:** There is a wealth of experience from Irish ECEC practitioners, and plenty of excellent examples and material that needs to be made accessible to the sector. The 'voices from the sector' part of this book gives some examples, but more is needed. Resourcing also refers to appropriate working conditions – not least paid time for all staff for planning and critical reflection.

4. **Research and Evaluation:** We expect practitioners to become reflective, and we encourage them to ask critical questions constantly in order to transform their everyday practice with children, families and communities. But how do we as a profession work to make a difference in society, learn from these everyday reflections? How are we asking critical questions at all levels of the ECEC system? Research has an important role to play here, and so has systematic evaluation. We need research with (as opposed to on) practitioners, children, families and communities and evaluation of learning processes rather than assessment of predetermined outcomes. As mentioned above, the 2011–2012 Pre-school Education Initiative for Children from Minority Groups and its evaluation illustrates what this can look like.

> It is not enough to depend on the next generation; adults themselves must take part in change.
>
> (Margaret Mead, cited in Schwartz, 1976, p. 13)

## Summary

This chapter ties together the different elements of our exploration of an Irish perspective on diversity and equality in early childhood education and care. It links the experiences and recommendations that came out of the initial '*éist*' project to Irish and international policy developments and research. The chapter argues that much has been achieved in terms of policy developments and inclusive language. Much less in terms of embracing a proactive anti-discriminatory approach in ECEC practice, training and professional development. While there are pockets of excellent policy and practice, in general the parts are still disjointed. This is why we need a roadmap to equality in early childhood education and care. We conclude the chapter with an outline of what we argue are the compass points of this map: leadership, advocacy, resourcing and research. As with a real map, those points give orientation. It is upon us to take the necessary steps.

The road is made by walking.

# References and Further Reading

## INTRODUCTION TO BOOK

### References

Centre for Early Childhood Development and Education (2006). *Síolta* http://www.siolta.ie/about.php, accessed 1 March 2008.

Connolly, P. (1998). *Racism, gender identities and young children: social relations in a multi-ethnic inner-city primary school*. London: Routledge.

DECET (2011). Diversity and Social Inclusion. *Exploring competences for professional practice in early childhood education and care*. Brussels: DECET.

Derman-Sparks, L. (1989). *Anti-Bias Curriculum: Tools for empowering young children*. Washington, D.C.: National Association for the Education of Young Children.

European Commission (2011). *Early Childhood Education and Care: Providing all our children with the best start for the world of tomorrow*. Brussels: European Commission.

Eurydice (2009). *Early Childhood Education and Care in Europe: Tackling social and cultural inequalities*. Brussels: European Commission.

Immigrant Council of Ireland (2011). *Taking Racism Seriously: Migrants' experiences of violence, harassment and anti-social behaviour in the Dublin area*. Dublin: Immigrant Council of Ireland.

MacNaughton, G. (2003). *Shaping Early Childhood: Learners, curriculum and contexts*. Berkshire: Open University Press.

Murray, C. (2010). *Ar an mBealach/On the way: Diversity and equality training for early childhood trainers*. Dublin: Pavee Point.

Murray, C. (ed.) (2001). 'Respect: Education without prejudice – a challenge for early years workers in Ireland'. Proceedings of a conference in October 1998. Dublin: Pavee Point.

Murray, C. and O'Doherty, A. (2001). *'éist': Respecting diversity in early childhood care, education and training*. Dublin: Pavee Point.

National Council for Curriculum and Assessment (2009). *Aistear/Creatchuraclam na luath-óige: The early childhood curriculum framework principles and themes*. Dublin: National Council for Curriculum and Assessment.

Office of the Minister for Children (2006). *Diversity and Equality Guidelines for Childcare Providers*. Dublin: The Stationery Office.

Urban, M., Vandenbroeck, M., Van Laere, K., Lazzari, A. and Peeters, J. (2011). *Competence Requirements in Early Childhood Education and Care. Final report*. London and Brussels: European Commission Directorate General for Education and Culture.

Van Ausdale, D. and Feagin, J. R. (2001). *The First R: How children learn race and racism*. Lanham: Rowman and Littlefield Publishers Inc.

# INTRODUCTION TO SECTION ONE

## References

Clark, M. and Drudy, S. (2006). 'Teaching for diversity, social justice and global awareness', *European Journal of Teacher Education*, 29(3), 371–386.

Cockrell, D. and Middleton, J.N. (1999). 'Coming to terms with "diversity and multiculturalism" in teacher education: Learning about our students, changing our practice', *Teaching and Teacher Education*, 15(4), 351–366.

Dufrene, P. (1991). 'Resistance to multicultural art education: strategies for multicultural faculty working in predominantly white teacher education programs'. ERIC, Document preproduction Service No. ED 347 113. www.eric.ed.gov, accessed 7 September 2010.

Lenski, S., Crawford, K. and Crumpler, T. (2005). 'Preparing pre-service teachers in a diverse world'. http://pdfs.scarecroweducation.com /SC/T_A/SCT_ATE_fall2005.pdf, accessed 7 September 2010.

Haritos, C. (2004). 'Understanding teaching through the minds of teacher candidates: a curious blend of realism and idealism', *Teaching and Teacher Education*, 20(6), 637–654.

# INTRODUCTION TO SECTION TWO

## References

Dahlberg, G. and Moss, P. (2005). *Ethics and Politics in Early Childhood Education*. London; New York: Routledge Farmer.

# INTRODUCTION TO SECTION THREE

## References

Derman-Sparks, L. (1989). *Anti-Bias Curriculum: Tools for empowering young children*. Washington, D.C.: National Association for the Education of Young Children.

Murray, C. and O'Doherty, A. (2001). *'éist': Respecting diversity in early childhood care, education and training*. Dublin: Pavee Point

Urban, M. and Dalli, C. (2011). 'A profession speaking – and thinking – for itself', in L. Miller, C. Dalli and M. Urban (eds), *Early Childhood Grows Up: Towards a critical ecology of the profession*. Dordrecht and London: Springer, 157–176.

# CHAPTER ONE

## Further reading

Donnelly, J. (2002). *The Great Irish Potato Famine*. Stroud, UK: Sutton Publishing.

Moving Here Migration Histories: http://www.movinghere.org.uk/galleries/histories/irish/settling/racism_prejudice_1.htm.

## References

Crowley, N. (2006). *An Ambition for Equality*. Dublin: Irish Academic Press.

Cowley, U. (2001). *The Men Who Built Britain: A History of the Irish Navvy*. Dublin: Wolfhound Press

Central Statistics Office (2006). *2006 Census Report*. Dublin: CSO

Donnelly, J. (2011). *The Irish Famine*. http://www.bbc.co.uk/history/british/victorians/famine_01.shtml, accessed 15 June 2011.

Equality Authority (2009). *Discrimination in Recruitment: Evidence from a field experiment*. Dublin: Equality Authority.

Fanning, B. (2002). *Racism and Social Change in the Republic of Ireland*. Manchester: Manchester University Press.

Fundamental Rights Agency (2009). *European Union Agency for Fundamental Rights Annual*. Vienna: FRA.

Farrell, F. and Watt, P. (eds) (2001). *Responding to Racism*. Dublin: Veritas.

Hickman, M. & Walter, B. (1997). *Discrimination and the Irish Community in Britain*. London: Council for Racial Equality Report.

Ignatiev, N. (1995). *How the Irish Became White*. New York: Routledge.

Keane, J. B. (1976). *Self-portrait*. Dublin: Mercier Press.

Kelly, A. (2011). 'Anti-Israeli mood rife in Ireland says new survey findings'. http://www.irishcentral.com/news/Anti-Israeli-mood-rife-in-Ireland-says-new-survey-findings—122794539.html#ixzz1aHYHTPO0, accessed 8 June 2011.

Immigrant Council of Ireland (2011). *Taking Racism Seriously: Migrants' experiences of violence, harassment and anti-social behaviour in the Dublin area*. Dublin: Immigrant Council of Ireland.

Lentin, A. F. (2004). *Racism and Anti-Racism in Europe*. London: Pluto Press.

Lynch, C. (2008). *ENAR Shadow Report: Racism in Ireland*, Brussels: ENAR.

McGahern, J. (2009). 'Life as it is and life as it ought to be' in *Love of the World: Essays*. London: Faber and Faber.

Mac Gréil, M. (2011). *Pluralism and Diversity in Ireland*. Dublin: The Columba Press.

Mc Veigh, R. (1992). 'The Specificity of Irish Racism', *Race and Class*, 33(4) 31–45.

Marreco, A. (1967). *The Rebel Countess: the life and times of Constance Markievicz*. London: Weidenfeld & Nicholson.

Moore, C. (2000). *One voice: My life in song*. London: Hodder and Stoughton.

Murray, C., Cooke, M. and O'Doherty, A. (2004/2011). *Ar an mBealach: Diversity and equality training of trainers manual*. Dublin: Pavee Point.

National Consultative Committee on Racism and Interculturalism (NCCRI). *The Muslim Community In Ireland. Challenging Some Myths & Misinformation*. http://www.nccri.ie/pdf/ChallengingMyths-Muslims.pdf, accessed 10 October 2011.

O'Keeffe, G. (2003). *The Irish in Britain: Injustices of recognition?* http://hal.archives-ouvertes.fr/docs/00/61/27/20/PDF/The_Irish_in_Britain-Injustices_of_ Recognition_.pdf, accessed 10 October 2011.

Pavee Point, (2011). 'DNA Study: Travellers a distinct ethnicity group' Pavee Point [website] <http://www.pavee.ie> accessed 10 October 2011.

Politico (1970). *Pogrom: Limerick 1904*. http://politico.ie/index.php?option=com_content&view=article&id=6238:pogrom-limerick-1904&catid=234:nusight-politics&Itemid=761, accessed 10 October 2011.

Rolston, B. and Shannon, M. (2002). *Encounters: How racism came to Ireland*. Dublin: Colour Books Ltd.

Russel, H., Quinn, E., King, O'Rianin, R., & Mc Ginnity, F. (2008). *The Experience of discrimination in Ireland: evidence from self report data in making equality count*. Dublin: Equality Authority.

Smyth, J. (2011). 'Emigration to Britain up 25% to almost 14,000, data reveals', *Irish Times*. http://www.irishtimes.com/newspaper/frontpage/2011/0614/1224298865280.html, accessed 15 June 2011.

Smyth, J. (2011). 'Safe havens', *Irish Times Magazine*, 18 June 2011.

Sullivan, A. M. (1894). *The Story of Ireland: A Narrative of Irish history, from the earliest ages to the insurrection of 1867*. Dublin: M. H. Gill & Son. E-book available from forgottenbooks.org.

Sweeney, E. (2010). *Down, Down, Deeper & Down: Ireland in the 70s and 80s*. Dublin: Gill & Macmillan.

University College Dublin (2010). *All-Ireland Traveller Health Study: Our Geels*. Dublin: University College Dublin.

Walter, B. (1998). *Outsiders inside: Whiteness, place and Irish women*. London: Routledge.

Margaret Ward (1997). *Hanna Sheehy Skeffington: A Life*. Cork: Cork University Press.

Wikipedia (2011). 'Constance Markievicz'. http://en.wikipedia.org/wiki/Constance_Markievicz, accessed 10 October 2011.

## CHAPTER TWO

### References

Allport, G. W. (1954). *The Nature of Prejudice*. Boston: Beacon.

Baker, J., Lynch, K., Cantillon, S. and Walsh, J. (2004). *Equality from Theory to Action*. Hampshire: Palgrave MacMillan.

Community Workers Union (2008). *Equality Proofing*. London: Community Workers Union.

Connolly, P., Smith, A. and Kelly, B. (2002). *Too Young to Notice*. Belfast: Community Relations Council.

Lane, J. (2008). *Young Children and Racial Justice*. London: National Children's Bureau.

Lynch, K. and Lodge, A. (1999). *Equality in Education*. Dublin: Gill and Macmillan Ltd.

Lentin, R. and McVeigh, R. (eds) (2002). *Racism and Anti-racism*. Belfast: Beyond the Pale.

Mac Gréil, M. (1997). *Prejudice in Ireland Revisited*. Kildare: The Survey and Research Unit. Dept. of Social Studies, NUI Maynooth.

Mac Gréil, M. (2011). *Pluralism and Diversity in Ireland*. Dublin: Columba Press.

MacNaughton, G. and Hughes, P. (2011). *Parents and Professionals in Early Childhood Settings*. Maidenhead: Open University Press.

McDonald, H. (2008). 'Ireland's immigrants return home as slump sharpens fear of racism', *Observer*. http://www.guardian.co.uk/world/2008/may/04/ireland.immigration, accessed 4 May 2008.

Murray, C., Cooke, M. and O'Doherty, A. (2004/2011) *Ar an mBealach: Diversity and equality training of trainers manual*. Dublin: Pavee Point.

Milner, D. (1983). *Children and Race Ten Years On*. London: Ward Lock Educational.

National Economic and Social Forum (1996). *Equality Proofing Issues*. National Economic and Social Forum: Dublin.

OMC (2006). *Diversity and Equality Guidelines for Childcare Providers*. Dublin: OMC.

Platform Against Racism (1997). *Information Pack*. Dublin: Platform Against Racism.

O'Brien, E. (2009). 'The Country Girl' in Quinn, J. (2009). *The Curious Mind*. Dublin: Veritas.

Van, D. and Feagin, J. R. (2001) *The First R: how children learn race and racism*. Maryland, USA: Rowman and Littlefield Publishers Inc.

## CHAPTER THREE

### References

Allport, G. W. (1954). *The Nature of Prejudice*. Boston: Beacon.

Benedict, R. (1935). *Patterns in Culture*. London: Routledge & Kegan Paul, cited in Mac Gréil (2011). *Pluralism and diversity in Ireland*. Dublin: The Columba Press.

Crickley, A. (1998). *Racism in Respect Conference Report*. Dublin: Pavee Point.

Crowley, N. (2006). *Traveller Ethnicity: an Equality Authority report*. Dublin: Equality Authority.

Crowley, N. (2006). *An Ambition for Equality*. Dublin: Irish Academic Press.

Department of Justice, Equality and Law Reform (1995). *Report of the Task Force on the Travelling Community*. Dublin: The Stationery Office.

Gaine, C. (2005). *We're All White Thanks: The persisting myth about 'white' schools*. Staffordshire: Trentham Books Ltd.

Immigrant Council of Ireland (2005). *Glossary of Migration Terms*. Dublin: Immigrant Council of Ireland.

Kenny, M. (2010). 'Sociology of inclusive education'. Module delivered as part of the BA Hons programme, St Nicholas Montessori College. Unpublished.

Lane, J. (2008). *Young Children and Racial Justice*. London: National Children's Bureau.

Mac Gréil, M. (2011). *Pluralism and Diversity in Ireland*. Dublin: Columba Press.

Murray, C., Cooke, M. and O'Doherty, A. (2004/2011) *Ar an mBealach: Diversity and equality training of trainers manual*. Dublin: Pavee Point.

Quinn, J. (2009). *The Curious Mind*. Dublin: Veritas.

Watt, P. (2006). 'Worth making the effort to find the right words', *Irish Times*.

## CHAPTER FOUR

### References

Bronfenbrenner, U. (1979). *The Ecology of Human Development: Experiments by nature and design*. Cambridge, MA: Harvard University Press.

Centre for Early Childhood Development and Education (2006). *Síolta*. http://www.siolta.ie/ about.php, accessed 1 March 2008.

Department of Education and Science (1999). *Ready to Learn: White Paper on Early Childhood Education*. Dublin: The Stationery Office.

Department of Health and Children (2000). *The National Children's Strategy. Our Children – Their Lives*. Dublin: The Stationery Office.

Department of Justice Equality and Law Reform (1999). *National Childcare Strategy: Report of the Partnership 2000 Expert Working Group on Childcare*. Dublin: The Stationery Office.

European Commission (2011). *Early Childhood Education and Care: Providing all our children with the best start for the world of tomorrow*. Brussels: European Commission.

European Commission Network on Childcare and Other Measures to Reconcile Employment and Family Responsibilities (1996). *Quality Targets in Services for Young Children: Proposals for a ten-year Action Programme*. Brussels: European Commission.

National Council for Curriculum and Assessment (2009). *Aistear/Creatchuraclam na luath-óige: The early childhood curriculum framework principles and themes*. Dublin: National Council for Curriculum and Assessment.

Office of the Minister for Children (2006). *Child Care (Pre-School Services) (No 2) Regulations 2006*. Dublin: The Stationery Office.

Office of the Minister for Children (2006). *Diversity and Equality Guidelines for Childcare Providers*. Dublin: The Stationery Office.

Ward, H. (1995). *Looking After Children: Research into practice. The second report to the Department of Health on assessing outcomes in child care*. London: H.M. Stationery Office.

Wilkinson, R. G. and Pickett, K. (2009). *The Spirit Level: Why more equal societies almost always do better*. London: Allen Lane.

## CHAPTER FIVE
### Further reading

Bronfenbrenner, U. (1981). *The Ecology of Human Development: Experiments by nature and design*. Cambridge, MA: London: Harvard University Press.

Cannella, G. S. (1997). *Deconstructing Early Childhood Education: Social Justice and Revolution (Vol. 2)*. New York; Washington D.C./Baltimore; Boston; Bern; Frankfurt; Berlin; Vienna; Paris: Peter Lang.

Dalli, C. and Urban, M. (eds). (2010). *Professionalism in early childhood education and care: International perspectives*. London and New York: Routledge.

Freire, P. (2000). *Pedagogy of the Oppressed* (30th anniversary ed.). New York: Continuum.

Mac Naughton, G. (2003). *Shaping Early Childhood: Learners, curriculum and contexts*. Berkshire: Open University Press.

Penn, H. (2008). *Understanding Early Childhood: Issues and controversies* (2nd ed.). Maidenhead: McGraw-Hill/Open University Press.

Robinson, K. H. and Jones-Diaz, C. (2008). *Diversity and Difference in Early Childhood Education: Issues for theory and practice*. Maidenhead: Open University Press.

Urban, M. (2008). 'Dealing with Uncertainty. Challenges and Possibilities for the Early Childhood Profession', *European Early Childhood Education Research Journal*, 16(2), 135–152.

### References

Argyris, C. and Schön, D. A. (1996). *Organizational Learning II: Theory, method and practice*. Reading, MA and Wokingham: Addison-Wesley.

Bateson, G. (1973). *Steps to an Ecology of Mind: Collected essays in anthropology, psychiatry, evolution and epistemology*. St Albans: Paladin.

Bateson, G. (2000). *Steps to an Ecology of Mind*. Chicago and London: University of Chicago Press.

Boud, D. E., Keogh, R. E. and Walker, D. E. (1985). *Reflection: Turning experience into learning*. London: Kogan Page.

Freire, P. (2000). *Pedagogy of the Oppressed* (30th anniversary ed.). New York: Continuum.

Freire, P. (2007). *Daring to Dream: Toward a pedagogy of the unfinished*. Boulder, CO: Paradigm Publishers.

Habermas, J. (1990). *Moral Consciousness and Communicative Action*. Cambridge: Polity Press.

Lindon, J. (2010). *Reflective Practice and Early Years Professionalism: Linking theory and practice*. London: Hodder Education.

Mac Naughton, G. (2003). *Shaping Early Childhood: Learners, curriculum and contexts*. Berkshire: Open University Press.

Mezirow, J. (1990). *Fostering Critical Reflection in Adulthood: A Guide to transformative and emancipatory learning*. San Francisco: Jossey-Bass Publishers.

National Council for Curriculum and Assessment (2009). *Aistear/Creatchuraclam na luathóige: The early childhood curriculum framework principles and themes*. Dublin: National Council for Curriculum and Assessment.

Urban, M. (2010). 'Duurzame verandering: professioneel leren in een kritische leergemeenschap' in A. van Keulen and A. del Barrio Saiz (eds), *Permanent leren. Van zelfreflectie naar teamreflectie*. Amsterdam: SWP.

Urban, M., Vandenbroeck, M., Van Laere, K., Lazzari, A. and Peeters, J. (2011). *Competence Requirements in Early Childhood Education and Care. Final report*. London and Brussels: European Commission Directorate General for Education and Culture.

Van Keulen, A. and Del Barrio Saiz, A. (eds) (2010). *Permanent leren. Van zelfreflectie naar teamreflectie*. Amsterdam: SWP.

## CHAPTER SIX

### References

Biesta, G. and Osberg, D. (2007). 'Beyond re/presentation: A case for updating the epistemology of schooling'. *Interchange*, 38(1), 15–29.

Bronfenbrenner, U. (1981). *The Ecology of Human Development: Experiments by nature and design*. Cambridge, MA; London: Harvard University Press.

Burman, E. (2008). *Deconstructing developmental psychology* (2nd ed.). London: Routledge.

Cannella, G. S. and Viruru, R. (2004). *Childhood and postcolonization. Power, education and contemporary practice*. London; New York: Routledge Falmer.

Chung, S. and Walsh, D. J. (2000). 'Unpacking "child-centeredness": a history of meanings'. *Journal of Curriculum Studies*, 32, 215–234.

Freire, P. (1997). *Pedagogy of the heart*. New York: Continuum.

Freire, P. (2000). *Pedagogy of the Oppressed* (30th anniversary ed.). New York: Continuum.

Lerner, R. M. (1998). 'Theories of human development: contemporary perspectives', in W. Damon and R. M. Lerner (eds), *Handbook of Child Psychology. Vol.1, Theoretical models of human development*. New York; Chichester: Wiley, 1–24.

Mead, M. (1978). *Culture and Commitment: The new relationships between the generations in the 1970s*. New York: Columbia University Press.

National Association for the Education of Young Children (2009). 'Developmentally Appropriate Practice'. NAEYC http://www.naeyc.org/DAP, accessed 6 June 2011.

Pence, A. R. and Marfo, K. (2008). 'Early childhood development in Africa: Interrogating constraints of prevailing knowledge bases', *International Journal of Psychology*, 43(2), 78–87.

Steup, M. (2010). 'Epistemology'. *The Stanford Encyclopedia of Philosophy*. http://plato. stanford.edu/archives/spr2010/entries/epistemology/, accessed 10 October 2011.

Vygotsky, L. S. (1978). *Mind in Society: the development of higher psychological processes* (M. Cole, trans.). Cambridge, MA.; London: Harvard University Press.

Walsh, D. J. (2005). 'Developmental theory and early childhood education', in N. Yelland (ed.), *Critical Issues in Early Childhood Education*. Berkshire; New York: Open University Press.

## CHAPTER SEVEN

### Further reading

DECET (2011). Diversity and Social Inclusion. *Exploring competences for professional practice in early childhood education and care*. Brussels: DECET.

### References

Centre for Early Childhood Development and Education (2006). *Síolta*. http://www. siolta.ie/ about.php, accessed 3 March 2008.

Community Workers Union (2008). *Equality Proofing*. London: Community Workers Union.

Darder , A. (ed.) (2002). *Reinventing Paulo Freire: A pedagogy of love*. Boulder, CO: Westview Press.

Derman-Sparks, L. (1989). *Anti-Bias Curriculum: Tools for empowering young children*. Washington, D.C.: National Association for the Education of Young Children.

Freire, P. (1997). *Pedagogy of the Heart*. New York: Continuum.

Murray, C., Cooke, M. and O'Doherty, A. (2004/2011). *Ar an mBealach: Diversity and equality training of trainers manual*. Dublin: Pavee Point.

Murray, C. and O'Doherty, A. (2001). *'éist': Respecting diversity in early childhood care, education and training*. Dublin: Pavee Point.

National Council for Curriculum and Assessment (2009). *Aistear/Creatchuraclam na luath-óige: The early childhood curriculum framework principles and themes*. Dublin: National Council for Curriculum and Assessment.

National Economic and Social Forum (1996). *Equality Proofing Issues*. Dublin: National Economic and Social Forum.

NCCRI (2008). *Spectrum newsletter issue 16: Ireland's strategy for European year for intercultural dialogue*. Dublin: NCCRI.

Office of the Minister for Children (2006). *Diversity and Equality Guidelines for Childcare Providers*. Dublin: The Stationery Office.

Taylor, M. and MhicMhathúna, M. (2012) (eds). *Early Childhood Education and Care: An Introduction for Students in Ireland*. Dublin: Gill and Macmillan.

Urban, M. (2010a). 'Dealing with Uncertainty. Challenges and Possibilities for the Early Childhood Profession', in C. Dalli and M. Urban (eds), *Professionalism in Early Childhood Education and Care: International perspectives*. London and New York: Routledge.

Urban, M. (2010b). 'Zones of professional development: arguments for reclaiming practice-based evidence in early childhood practice and research', in J. Hayden and A. Tuna (eds), *Moving forward together: Early childhood programs as the doorway to social cohesion. An east-west perspective*. Newcastle upon Tyne: Cambridge Scholars.

## CHAPTER EIGHT

### Further reading

Derman-Sparks, L. (1989). *Anti-Bias Curriculum: Tools for empowering young children*. Washington, D.C.: National Association for the Education of Young Children.

Thomas, M. (1974). *Free to Be You and Me*. Philadelphia and London: Running Press.

Holland, P. (2003). *We Don't Play with Guns Here*. Philadelphia: Open University Press.

### References

Mac Naughton, G. (2000). *Rethinking Gender in Early Childhood Education*. London: Paul Chapman.

Honig, A. S. and Wittmer, D. S. (1983). 'Early signs of sex role stereotyping among day care toddlers'. Paper presented at the Biennial Southeastern Conference on Human Development on 7 April 1982. Baltimore, MD.

Derman-Sparks, L. (1989). *Anti-Bias Curriculum: Tools for empowering young children*. Washington, D.C.: National Association for the Education of Young Children.

Maccoby, E. and Jacklin, C. (1974). *The Psychology of Sex Differences*. Stanford, CA: University Press.

Bredekamp, S. and Copple, C. (eds) (1997). *Developmentally Appropriate Practice in Early Childhood Programs*. Washington, D.C.: NAEYC.

Jipson, J. (1998). 'Developmentally Appropriate Practice: Culture, curriculum, connections', in M. Huaser and J. Jipson, (eds). *Intersections: Feminism/Early Childhoods*. (New York: Peter Lang Publishing).

Mallory, B. and New, R. (1994). *Diversity and Developmentally Appropriate Practices*. New York: Teachers College Press.

Cahill, L. (2005). *His Brain Her Brain in Scientific America*. New York: Scientific American.

Murphy, C. and Caffrey, L. (2009). *Supporting Child Contact: The Need for child contact centres in Ireland. A research report by One Family*. Dublin: One Family.

Central Statistics Office (2010). *Women and Men in Ireland: Report*. Cork: Central Statistics Office.

Valiulis, M., O'Driscoll, A., Redmond, J. (2007). *An Introduction to the Gender Equality Issues in the Marketing and Design for Goods for Children: Report for the Equality Authority*. Dublin: Equality Authority.

Wayman, S. (2011). 'Daddy's got a new job', *Irish Times* (17 May 2011).

## CHAPTER NINE

### References

National Council for Curriculum and Assessment (2009). *Aistear/Creatchuraclam na luathóige: The early childhood curriculum framework principles and themes*. Dublin: National Council for Curriculum and Assessment.

Urban, M. (2010). 'Zones of professional development: arguments for reclaiming practice-based evidence in early childhood practice and research', in J. Hayden and A. Tuna (eds), *Moving forward together: Early childhood programs as the doorway to social cohesion. An east-west perspective*. Newcastle upon Tyne: Cambridge Scholars.

## CHAPTER TEN

### References

Derman-Sparks, L. and Olsen Edwards, J. (2010). *Anti-Bias Education for Young Children and Ourselves*. Washington, D.C.: NAEYC.

Mac Naughton, G. and Hughes, P. (2011). *Parents and Professionals in Early Childhood Settings*. Berkshire: Open University Press.

## CHAPTER ELEVEN

### Further reading

Brown, B. (2001). *Combatting Discrimination: Persona dolls in action*. UK: Trentham Books.

Brown, B. (1999). *Unlearning Discrimination in the Early Years*. UK: Trentham Books www.persona-doll-training.org.

### References

Centre for Early Childhood Development and Education (2006). *Síolta: National quality framework for early childhood education*. Dublin: Centre for Early Childhood Development and Education.

Derman-Sparks, L. (1989). *Anti-Bias Curriculum: Tools for empowering young children*. Washington, D.C.: National Association for the Education of Young Children.

Gartrell, D. and Epstien, A. S. (2003). *Me, You, Us: Social-emotional learning in pre-school*. Michigan: High/scope Press.

Murray, C., Cooke, M. and O'Doherty, A. (2004/2011). *Ar an mBealach: Diversity and equality training of trainers manual*. Dublin: Pavee Point.

National Council for Curriculum and Assessment (2009). *Aistear/Creatchuraclam na luath-óige: The early childhood curriculum framework principles and themes*. Dublin: National Council for Curriculum and Assessment.

Wagner, P. (2008). *Categorisations and Young Children's Social Construction of Belonging in Early Childhood Matters: Enhancing a sense of belonging in the early years*. The Hague: Bernard van Leer Foundation.

## CHAPTER TWELVE
### References

Baissangourov, P. (2008). 'English as an Additional Language: A Study of the supports available in local preschool services in the Donegal area', BA Hons dissertation, Belfast: Queens University.

Baker, C. (2007). *A Parents' and Teachers' Guide to Bilingualism* (3rd edition). England: Clevedon England.

Centre for Early Childhood Development and Education (2006). *Síolta: National quality framework for early childhood education*. Dublin: Centre for Early Childhood Development and Education.

Centre for Early Childhood Development and Education (2007). *Síolta: National quality framework for early childhood education research digests*. Dublin: Centre for Early Childhood Development and Education.

Crutchley, A. (2000). 'Bilingual Children in Language Units: Does having "well-informed" parents make a difference?', *International Journal of Language and Communication Disorders*, 35(1), 65–81.

Department of Health and Children (2000). *National Childcare Strategy: Report of the Partnership 2000 Expert Working Group on Childcare*. Dublin: The Stationery Office.

Department of Health and Children (2006). Childcare (Preschool Services) Regulations http://www.hse.ie/en/publications/preschoolinspectionreports, accessed 15 August 2007.

Flood, E. (2010). *Child Development for Students in Ireland*. Dublin: Gill & Macmillan.

Goldschmied, E. and Jackson, S. (2004). *People Under Three* (2nd edition). London: Routledge Multilingual Matters.

Health Service Executive (2009). *Caring for Your Child, Six Months to Two Years*. Dublin: Health Service Executive.

Mc Govern, M. (2008). 'Parental Involvement and Bilingual Support by Early Years Professionals for Non-Irish National Children', BA Hons dissertation, Belfast: Queens University.

National Council for Curriculum and Assessment (2009). *Aistear/Creatchuraclam na luath-óige: The early childhood curriculum framework principles and themes*. Dublin: National Council for Curriculum and Assessment.

Office of the Minister for Children (2006). *Diversity and Equality Guidelines for Childcare Providers*. Dublin: The Stationery Office.

Siraj-Blatchford, I. and Clarke, P. (2000). *Supporting Identity, Diversity and Language in the Early Years*. Buckingham: Open University Press.

Tabors, P. (1997). *One Child, Two Languages: A Guide for preschool educators of children learning English as a second language*. Baltimore, MD: Brookes.

Tabors, P. and Snow, C. (1994). 'English as a Second Language in Preschool Programs', in F. Genesse (ed.), *Educating Second Language Children: The Whole child, the whole curriculum, the whole community*. New York: Cambridge University Press.

# CHAPTER FOURTEEN
## Further Reading

Brooker, L., Woodhead, M. (eds) (2008). *Developing Positive Identities: Diversity and Young Children. Early Childhood in Focus 3*. Milton Keynes: Open University.

Derman-Sparks, L., Ramsey, P. G. and Edwards, J. O. (2006). *What If All the Kids Are White?: Anti-Bias multicultural education with young children and families*. New York; London: Teachers College Press.

Mac Naughton, G. and Williams, G. (2009). *Teaching Young Children: Choices in theory and practice (2nd edition)*. New York: Open University Press.

York, S. (1991). *Roots and Wings: Affirming culture in early childhood programs*. Minnesota: Redleaf Press.

## References

Derman-Sparks, L. and Olsen Edwards, J. (2010). *Anti-Bias Education for Young Children and Ourselves*. Washington, D.C.: NAEYC.

Murray, C., Cooke, M. and O'Doherty, A. (2004/2011). *Ar an mBealach: Diversity and equality training of trainers manual*. Dublin: Pavee Point.

Woodhead, M. (2008). 'A Sense of Belonging', in Bernard van Leer (eds), *Enhancing a Sense of Belonging in the Early Years*. Netherlands: Bernard van Leer.

# CHAPTER FIFTEEN
## Further Reading

Lesovitch, L. (2005). *Report: Roma Educational Needs in Ireland Context and Challenges*. Dublin: City of Dublin VEC.

## References

Council of Europe (2007). *Report by the Commissioner for Human Rights, Mr Thomas Hammarberg on his Visit to Ireland, November 2007*, Department of Foreign Affairs.

http://www.dfa.ie/uploads/documents/Political%20Division/final%20report%20ireland.pdf, accessed 10 October 2011.

Department of Social Protection (2010). *Habitual Residence Condition Guidelines for Deciding Officers on the Determination of Habitual Residence.* Dublin: Stationery Office.

DECET (2011). Diversity and Social Inclusion. *Exploring competences for professional practice in early childhood education and care.* Brussels: DECET.

DTEDG and Speirs, D. (1991). *Pavee Pictures.* Dublin: Traveller Education and Development Group.

European Commission (2011). *Communication from the Commission to the European Parliament, the Council, the European Economic and Social Committee and the Committee of the Regions 173/4: an EU framework for national Roma integration strategies up to 2020.* Brussels: European Commission.

European Union Agency for Fundamental Rights (2010). 'The Fundamental Rights Position of Roma and Travellers in the European Union'. European Union Agency for Fundamental Rights, http://fra.europa.eu/fraWebsite/roma/roma-travellers-factsheet_en.htm, accessed 10 October 2011.

Habitual Residency Condition Act (2009). http://www.dsfa.ie/EN/OperationalGuidelines/Pages/habres.aspx, accessed 10 October 2011.

Kenny, M., Binchy, A. and Mac Donagh, M. (2009). 'Irish Traveller identity and the education System', in Danaher, P. A., Kenny, M. and Remy Leader, J. (2009). *Traveller, Nomadic and Migrant Education.* London: Routledge.

Mac Gréil, M. (2011). *Pluralism and Diversity in Ireland.* Dublin: Columba Press.

Mac Naughton, G. (2003). *Shaping Early Childhood: Learners, curriculum and contexts.* Berkshire: Open University Press.

Murray, C. (2002). 'The Traveller Child: A Holistic perspective', in Barnardos (ed.), *Diversity in Early Childhood: A Collection of essays.* Dublin: Barnardos.

Pavee Point (2008). Interview with Traveller children on their educational experience. Unpublished. Dublin: Pavee Point.

Pavee Point (2009). *Barriers to Roma Accessing Health Services.* Dublin: Pavee Point.

Pavee Point (2010). *Providing Quality Education to the Roma Community: An Introductory guide.* Dublin: Pavee Point.

Pavee Point (2011). *Shadow Report Irish Traveller and Roma: A Response to Ireland's third and fourth report on the international convention on the elimination of all forms of racial discrimination (CERD).* Dublin: Pavee Point.

University College Dublin (2010). *All-Ireland Traveller Health Study: Our Geels.* Dublin: University College Dublin.

UN Committee on the Rights of the Child (2006). *Concluding Observations of Ireland's Second Report under the UN Convention on the Rights of the Child,* CRC/C/IRL/CO/2, (para 79(a)).

# CHAPTER SIXTEEN
## Further reading
Crowley, N. (2010). *A Roadmap to a Strengthened Equality and Human Rights Infrastructure in Ireland*. Dublin: Equality and Rights Alliance.

## References

Centre for Early Childhood Development and Education (2006). *Síolta*. http://www.siolta.ie/ about.php, accessed 1 March 2008.

Children in Europe (2008). 'Young Children and their Services: Developing a European approach', *Children in Europe*, www.childrenineurope.org, accessed 10 October 2011.

Coolahan, J. (ed.) (1998). *Report on the National Forum for Early Childhood Education*. Dublin: The Stationery Office.

DECET (2011). Diversity and Social Inclusion. *Exploring competences for professional practice in early childhood education and care*. Brussels: DECET.

Department of Education and Science (1999). *Ready to Learn: White Paper on Early Childhood Education*. Dublin: The Stationery Office.

Department of Health and Children (2000). *The National Children's Strategy. Our Children – Their Lives*. Dublin: The Stationery Office.

Department of Justice Equality and Law Reform (1999). *National Childcare Strategy: Report of the Partnership 2000 Expert Working Group on Childcare*. Dublin: The Stationery Office.

Department of Justice Equality and Law Reform (2002). *Quality Childcare and Lifelong Learning: Model framework for education, training and professional development in the early childhood care and education sector*. Dublin: The Stationery Office.

European Commission (2011). *Early Childhood Education and Care: Providing all our children with the best start for the world of tomorrow*. Brussels: European Commission.

European Commission network on childcare and other measures to reconcile employment and family responsibilities (1996). *Quality Targets in Services for Young Children: Proposals for a ten year action programme*. Brussels: European Commission.

Eurydice (2009). *Early Childhood Education and Care in Europe: Tackling social and cultural inequalities*. Brussels: European Commission.

Murray, C. (2006). 'The conceptualisation of diversity and equality in early childhood care and education'. Unpublished MSc thesis, University College Dublin, Dublin.

Murray, C. and O'Doherty, A. (2001). *'éist': Respecting diversity in early childhood care, education and training*. Dublin: Pavee Point.

National Economic and Social Forum (2005). *Early Childhood Care and Education Report*. Dublin: National Economic and Social Forum.

OECD (2001). *Starting Strong: Early childhood education and care*. Paris: OECD.

OECD (2006). *Starting Strong II: Early childhood education and care*. Paris: OECD.

Penn, H. (2009). *Early Childhood Education and Care: Key lessons from research for policy makers. An independent report submitted to the European Commission by the NESSE network of experts.* Brussels: European Commission.

Sylva, K., Melhuish, E., Sammons, P., Siraj-Blatchford, I. and Taggart, B. (2004). *The Effective Provision of Preschool Education (EPPE) Project: Final report.* University of London: EPPE Project.

UNICEF Innocenti Research Centre (2008). *Report Card 8: The child care transition. A league table of early childhood education and care in economically advanced countries.* Florence: UNICEF Innocenti Research Centre.

Urban, M., Vandenbroeck, M., Van Laere, K., Lazzari, A. and Peeters, J. (2011). *Competence Requirements in Early Childhood Education and Care. Final report.* London and Brussels: European Commission Directorate General for Education and Culture.

# Index